Ancient Peoples and Places

THE BALEARIC ISLANDS

General Editor

DR GLYN DANIEL

To the memory of María Luisa Serra Belabre, who devoted the best part of her life to researching the remote past of Minorca

ABOUT THE AUTHOR

In 1914 Luis Pericot García entered the University of Barcelona, to become the first pupil of Professor Bosch Gimpera. In due course he joined the staff, serving as Assistant Professor from 1923 to 1925, when he was appointed to the Chair of Ancient History in the University of Santiago de Compostela. In 1927 he moved to the University of Valencia, which enabled him to engage in extensive field-work in the area, returning in 1933 to the University of Barcelona. There he has been, successively, Dean of the Faculty and Director of the Institute of Prehistory (Research Council), and has concentrated specifically on the archaeology of the Balearic Islands since 1956. He retired from teaching in 1969. Professor Pericot is an Honorary Fellow of the Society of Antiquaries and of the Royal Anthropological Society, a Corresponding Fellow of the British Academy, and an Honorary Corresponding Fellow of the Prehistoric Society.

THE BALEARIC ISLANDS

L. Pericot-García

Translated by Margaret Brown, FSA

73 PHOTOGRAPHS
39 LINE DRAWINGS
7 MAPS

THIS IS VOLUME EIGHTY-ONE IN THE SERIES
Ancient Peoples and Places
GENERAL EDITOR: DR GLYN DANIEL

First published 1972

Filmset by Keyspools Ltd, Golborne, Lancs and
printed in Great Britain by Camelot Press Ltd, Southampton.
Not to be imported for sale into the U.S.A.
ISBN 0 500 02079 5

CONTENTS

LIST OF ILLUSTRATIONS 6

PREFACE 8

I INTRODUCTION 11

The Geographical Background 11

The History of Research 16

The Cultural Sequence 20

II THE PRE-TALAYOT PERIOD 23

The Earliest Settlements 23

The Balearic Cave Culture 27

III THE CYCLOPEAN OR TALAYOT PERIOD 45

The Talayot Culture in Majorca 46

The Talayot Culture in Minorca 67

First Connections with the Classical World 92

Life in the Talayot Period 97

Anthropology 109

Origin and Connections of the Talayot Culture 110

IV THE PUNIC ISLANDS: IBIZA AND FORMENTERA 114

Ibiza 114

Formentera 124

V THE CLOSE OF ANCIENT TIMES 126

After the Roman Conquest 126

Underwater Archaeology 130

Conclusion 132

BIBLIOGRAPHY 135

NOTES ON THE PLATES 177

INDEX 180

List of Illustrations

PLATES

1 Flint knife
2 Bronze knife
3 Beaker
4 Greek jug
5 Sant Vicens cave
6 Son Boscana cave
7 Son Hereu cave
8 Enclosure at Sant Vicens
9 Son Oms talayot
10, 11 Sanctuary enclosures, Almallutx
12 Sa Canova talayot
13 Entrance, Ses Paisses, Artá
14, 15 Hypostyle courts, Ses Paisses
16 Son Real cemetery
17 Son Noguera del Recó talayot
18 Capocorp Vell
19 Sa Canova square talayot
20–22 Tombs in the Son Real cemetery
23 Bronze bull's head
24 Bronze bull's horns
25 Bronze bull's head
26 Bronze warrior's head
27 Bronze bird on a rod
28 Bronze panther's head
29 Solid-hilted swords
30 Post-talayotic vase
31, 32 Antennae swords
33 Sandstone mould
34, 35 Bronze implements and weapons
36 Bronze pectoral
37 Bronze belt
38 Bronze warrior, Torelló
39 Warrior, Roca Rotja
40 Minorcan landscape
41 Trepucó taula
42 Torralba d'En Salort taula
43 Warrior, Roca Rotja
44 Entrance, Torellonet Vell
45 Pilaster, Cala Morell
46 Cemetery, Cales Coves
47 Trepucó talayot
48 Column, Binigaus nou
49 Els Tudons, façade
50 Els Tudons, apsidal end
51 Rafal Rubi Nou, chamber
52 Rafal Rubi Nou, façade
53, 57 Bronze warriors, Son Favar
54 Warrior, Can Carrió
55 Bronze bull's head
56 Warrior, Son Favar
58 Warrior, Son Taxaquet
59–62 Clay figurines, Ibiza
63 Burial, Illa dels Porros
64 Punic clay figurine
65 Tombs, Illa dels Porros
66 Roman Pollentia
67 Christian mosaics
68 Roman bronze handle
69 Hellenistic gold figure
70 Roman bronze figurine

FIGURES

1 Map: The Balearics, p. 13
2 *Myotragus balearicus*, p. 24
3 Map: cave sites in Majorca, p. 29

4 Cave, Sant Vicens, p. 33
5 Cave, Son Antem, p. 35
6 Cave, Son Suñer, p. 35
7 Cave, Son Oms, p. 36
8 Pre-talayotic incised pottery, p. 37
9 V-perforated buttons, p. 38
10 Pre-talayotic pottery, p. 39
11 Map: cave sites in Minorca, p. 43
12 Map: talayots in Majorca, p. 47
13 Plan of S'Illot, p. 49
14 Plan of Ses Paisses, p. 51
15 Square talayots, Cala Pi, p. 56
16 Son Lluch talayot, p. 57
17 Sa Plana D'Albarca talayot, p. 57
18 Boat-shaped houses, Sa Vall, p. 60
19 Son Real cemetery, p. 63
20 Tombs, Son Real cemetery, p. 65
21 San Agusti Vell talayot, p. 68
22 Map: talayots in Minorca, p. 69
23 Map: navetas in Minorca, p. 75
24 Naveta d'els Tudons, p. 76
25 Naveta Son Merce de Baix, p. 77
26 Naveta Llumena d'en Montañés, p. 77
27 Map: taulas in Minorca, p. 81
28 Trepucó taula, p. 83
29 Torralba d'En Salort taula, p. 83
30 Torre Trencada taula, p. 83
31 Talatí de Dalt taula, p. 83
32 Sanctuary, Almallutx, p. 87
33 Lead plaque, p. 99
34 Talayot pottery forms, p. 101
35 Bronze birds, p. 102
36 Bronze bird on a rod, p. 102
37 Bronze bull, p. 103
38 Bronze head of a bull, p. 103
39 Tintinabulo, p. 104
40, 41 Bronze discs, pp. 104, 105
42 Bronze axe, p. 106
43 Bronze helmet, p. 107
44 Section through Puig des Molins, p. 121
45 Roman Pollentia, p. 129
46 Post-talayotic pottery forms, p. 130

Preface

It has been an elating experience for me to write this book, since I had always intended to do more work on the Balearics. Circumstances of life, however, have cut across many of my youthful plans, though it would be pointless to lament that from some of my projects it is already too late for me to gather more than a scant harvest.

Spanish archaeologists, with few exceptions, have in fact held off from work on the islands, and events are to blame if a concerted and sustained attack on their problems has been wanting. In 1935 it did appear that a programme, based on Barcelona, would begin; but the time proved unpropitious. Only since 1952 have I personally been able to instigate archaeological research in the Balearics. My work was supported by an award in 1958 from the March Foundation. Eduardo Ripoll, Guillermo Rosselló Bordoy, María Luisa Serra and María Petrus became members of my team, and many others collaborated with us on occasion. This grant, however, lasted only for two years and, understandably, the team then dispersed to other work; nor was provision made for publishing our results. María Luisa Serra, who had been so active in her beloved Minorca, died prematurely in 1967. G. Rosselló Bordoy has proved the most constant in continuing our joint projects, and his publications form an increasingly vital and systematic study.

We have also collaborated with the William L. Bryant Foundation in excavations at Pollentia and in the Son Real cemetery in Majorca. The tenth National Congress of Archaeology held at Mahon in 1967 marked the culmination of our group's efforts and was a great moment for all the islands' archaeologists, whose cooperation I have constantly enjoyed. It marked, too, the start of a new era. A new, and well-equipped, generation has reached the helm. Let us not feel too regretful that their predecessors may not have achieved all they had hoped for. Nowadays all things are studied better, and the young have moreover been alerted to the shoals they must avoid in this perilous science of prehistory.

For my part, these are the last pages I shall write on Balearic archaeology. With this popular account, which my pupils and young colleagues will soon better, I shall retire. No one will deny that we have been without any book from which the uninitiated – for whom the beauties of the islands prove such an attraction today – can acquaint themselves with even an elementary knowledge of local antiquities. Perhaps I should have ceded the task of compilation to a younger man; but the temptation was too great. I have the impression that the next few years will see a break-through, even in chronological problems, which will set the islands in their true historical context. In some ways this volume is an account of the generation who lifted Balearic archaeology out of its initial phase of theorizing, to secure the permanent interest of Spanish scholarship.

It may possibly be said I have over-emphasized buildings and architecture at the expense of equipment and reconstruction of ancient ways of life. The fact remains that while material finds are sparse and the pottery, which usually enlivens prehistoric studies, rather unattractive, stone monuments in the Balearics are splendid and imposing in their abundance. The one project for which I feel some pride, and may perhaps claim to have initiated, is the restoration of the naveta of Els Tudons, which is the earliest building in Spain standing above ground in a good state of preservation.

The hours I have spent on the enchanting islands of Majorca and Minorca with my friends and fellow workers have been unforgettable. I found delight in the sheltered coves and distant landscapes viewed from the heights, against the dark blue of the sea, and in contending with the north wind or the invasive wild olive, and always in a nightmare setting of huge masses of stone. This the early inhabitants, in what seems an obsessive fever of titanic effort, have cut, transported and set up into the prodigious structures which still fascinate us, as though they had foreseen that after the lapse of generations people would come, intent on the old assertions and symbols embedded in the enduring stone.

It remains for me to express my sincere gratitude for the help of colleagues and friends too numerous to name in this brief preface, and to offer my best wishes for their future projects on the islands. I have been much moved by the cooperation of all concerned.

I should like especially to record my great indebtedness to María Luisa Serra Belabre, whose enthusiasm and vocation initiated a most fruitful phase of archaeological research in Minorca, which must eventually be resumed where she left off. Shortly after the public acknowledgement of her contribution, by the National Archaeological Congress at Mahon in 1967, we were to lament her death.

My thanks are due to a number of institutions and individuals who have given me constant assistance, and have now provided photographs and drawings for this book: the Barcelona Archaeological Museum (through its Director, Dr E. Ripoll), The Bryant Foundation (Professor D. Woods), the Mahon Museum, G. Florit Piedrabuena, J. Hernandez Mora, María Petrus, V. Tolós, D. Cerdá, J. Camps, Guillermo Rosselló Coll, Barbara Pell, W. Waldren, A. Arribas, Professor G. Lilliu and his colleagues Professors Atzeni and Biancofiore, Luis Amorós, B. Font Obrador, P. Christobal Veny, Professors M. Tarradell and P. de Palol; B. and C. Enseñat, with whom I have made many excursions to Majorcan sites. From these colleagues I have learnt all I know of the Balearics. I must make particular mention of the generosity of J. Mascaró Pasarius, an untiring researcher in Balearic prehistory. With immense labour he has compiled lists and maps of the monuments, which are practically unequalled in Spanish archaeology.

My colleague and former pupil, Professor G. Rosselló Bordoy, has been good enough to read my manuscript, and from his profound knowledge of the subject has made numerous suggestions. He has also afforded material for illustrations, both from the Majorcan Museum which he directs and from his own studies, which have provided a chronological framework for some of the views I express.

Finally, I am grateful to Glyn Daniel and to the publishers, Thames and Hudson, for their invitation to write this book and for assistance in its production; also to Margaret Brown for her careful translation.

My hope is that these pages may serve to inspire enthusiasm for the mysteries of the islands' past, both in the general reader and, by recalling the problems, among archaeologists.

L.P.G.

CHAPTER I
Introduction

THE GEOGRAPHICAL BACKGROUND

The Balearic Islands lie north-east by south-west midway along the western reaches of the Mediterranean. Closest to the mainland is Ibiza, 92 km. out from the coast of Alicante. The other islands stretch away, with Majorca 167 km and Minorca 200 km. from the nearest points on the Catalan coast. This leaves a narrow Balearic sea between the Spanish Levantine coast and the archipelago, exposed to the stormy Gulf of Lions to the north. Minorca, at the outer limit of the chain, faces the coast of Provence (370 km. from Toulon) and lies 340 km. from Sardinia, 320 km. from the Algerian coast of Africa.

These islands are the most important, but three others have also been settled: Cabrera and Conejera, close dependants of Majorca, and Formentera, barely separated from Ibiza. These last two were the Pityusae islands of antiquity, 90 km. distant from Majorca and divided by seas approaching 500 m. in depth. Majorca and Minorca, separated by a strait of only 48 km. and for the most part less than 100 m. deep, together with their minor islands, formed the ancient Gymnesiae, or Balearics proper.

Majorca is the largest of the islands, with 3,740 sq. km., far bigger than Minorca (702 sq. km.) and Ibiza (541 sq. km.), while Formentera measures only 82 sq. km. There is an obvious contrast in size with the big islands of the west Mediterranean; Corsica, Sardinia and Sicily, though the Balearics are larger than Malta and its tiny dependencies. The relative smallness of the islands helps to account for some aspects of their past history.

Two distinct geological systems are represented in the Balearics, with Formentera, Ibiza and Majorca linked in contrast to the quite distinct formations of Minorca. The first groups represent a continuation of the mountain ranges of the Peninsula and in them the Peni-Baetic folds terminate under the sea. On Majorca the central plain is a prominent feature, lying between two mountain systems of which the northern is the larger and higher. The mountain ranges of Ibiza correspond to the cordilleras of northern Majorca, while the limestone platform of Formentera is a continuation of the central Majorcan plain.

Minorca by contrast is linked with orogenic movements to the north and corresponds geologically with the mountains of Catalonia, in part with the Ampurdan massif and its extensions in southern Provence. The island presents marked contrasts, between these ancient, predominantly Devonian, formations in the north and the tertiary plain of Miocene (Burdigalian) limestone which to the south covers over half of its area, and is similar to other parts of the islands.

As a result of their position and morphological diversity the three large islands of the archipelago, although in part homogeneous or similar, do present highly distinctive features. It is this which lends them their beauty. It has also contributed to the diversity in their history to which we shall return in the course of this book.

The island with the most to offer in resources, variety and extent is obviously Majorca. It can be divided into four regions. In the north, running south-west to north-east along the coast, is a mountain range which falls precipitously to the sea in one of the world's most picturesque littorals, a veritable *Costa Brava*. There are sheltered harbours, like the enclosed bay of Soller. The highest peak is Puig Mayor (1,445 m.), and from here it is occasionally possible to see the main peaks of the Catalan coastal range. Huge gorges, such as the impressive Torrent de Pareys, and valleys with rich mountain vegetation, like the Escorca or that containing the Lluch sanctuary, add to the great charm of these folded mountains. In the western part, of which the islet of Dragonera forms an extension, the ranges intersect at Calviá and Galatzó, and there are waterfalls down to the sea round Banyalbufar, followed by the still pools of Valldemosa and the picturesque slopes of Miramar and Deyá. From Soller past the Pareys gorge and Sant Vicens cove the coast becomes even wilder, to terminate in a bold promontory and the headland of Formentor. Inland the steeply falling slopes of the cordillera provide the central plain with a protective wall against the fierce north winds blowing from the Gulf of Lions. It is easy to understand the role of this northern barrier as a refuge in times of trouble.

Almost parallel in the south-east of the island runs a second range of hills. In the main these rise above the limestone platform which forms the basis of the island, terraced above the sea and cut back into numerous

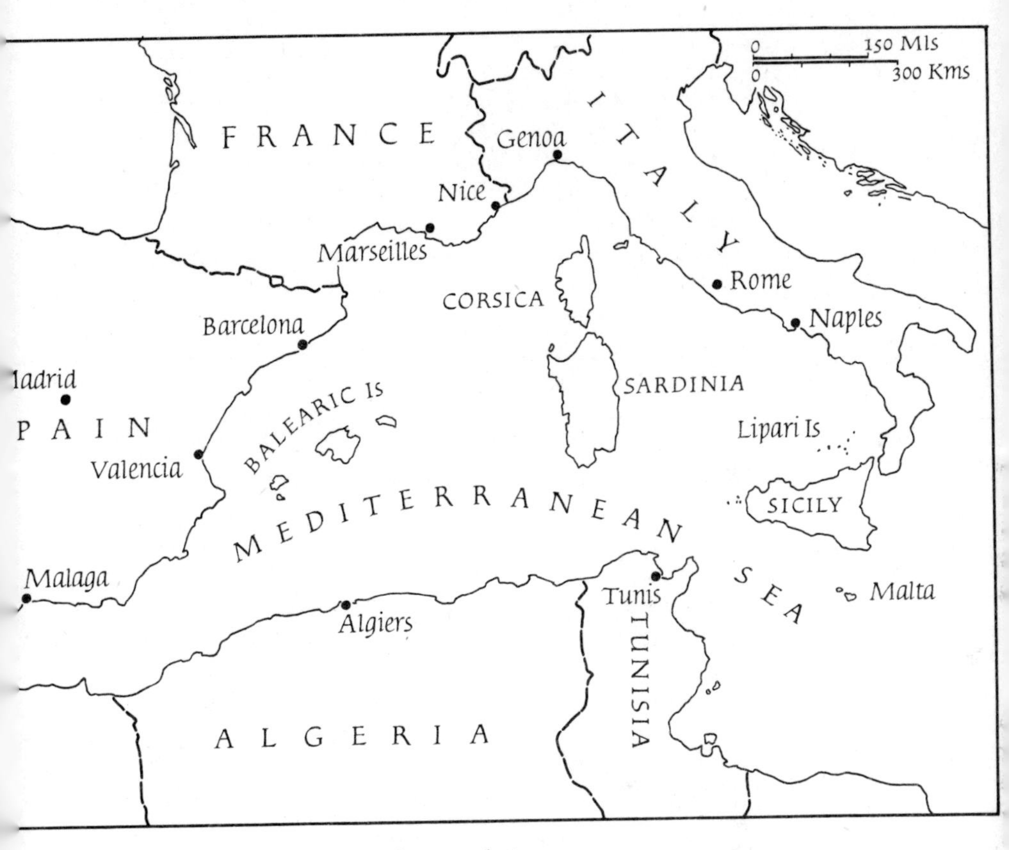

Fig. 1 The Balearics in the western Mediterranean basin

inlets. In the north-east, opposite neighbouring Minorca, the mountains of Artá and Capdepera reach 562 m. in Monte Morey and form steep cliffs. There are some imposing caves along the coast. Further south lies another line of heights, which include San Salvador de Felanitx and Randa, near Lluchmayor (549 m.), affording view-points across the plain. The small islands of Cabrera and Conejera are an extension of the same system.

Between the mountains, the intervening plain is broad and fertile, despite the restricted depth of the humus, below which the underlying limestone, the *marés*, is soon revealed. The ease with which this can be prised out and worked accounts for the development of an architecture in stone, and the numerous artificial caves. An easily tapped underground water supply, which nowadays contributes to the picturesque landscape of central Majorca with its many windmills, must have been an important factor in the enduring richness of the country.

Deep inlets, associated with marsh and lagoons (notably that of Alcudia) are a feature of the central coastline. To the west the wide bay of Palma was predestined to be the site of a sheltered port and commercial centre. On the east coast, by contrast, there are two deep inlets flanked by mountainous promontories (the peninsulas of El Farrutx and Formentor) and separated by the high, narrow peninsula of Alcudia.

Minorca is visible from Majorca's eastern coast. This island lacks the variety of the Majorcan landscape, the magnificence of its mountains and indented coasts, and the magnitude of its plains. The face of Minorca is more uniform and monotonous, despite the geological contrast between the ancient rocks of the north and the tertiary formations of the south. The highest point, Monte Toro, reaches only 358 m., but from its almost central position commands a view of the whole island. The rolling limestone tableland is intersected by deep ravines and hills, but there is a softness to the landscape which contrasts with the violence of the wind and the wildness of the broken northern coast. Here there is no shelter from the winds, especially from the north wind (*tramontana*) which blows from the Gulf of Lions and frequently cuts off this rocky coast for days at a time. One needs only to observe the inclination of the trees and bushes to realize what role the wind plays in the life of Minorca.

The coastline of Minorca is rather more indented than it appears. Dozens of small coves, many with sandy beaches or with cliffs which define the entrances to gorges (Cales Coves, for example) provide pleasantly vivid scenery, or open into deeper bays with shelter for fishermen. The port of Ciudadela stands in marked contrast. Its narrow, twisting channel, characteristic of marine erosion into the island's rocky platform, is more than a kilometre long and is unusable in a rough sea. Diametrically opposed to it in the south-western corner of the island lies another morphological fault, though an exceptionally large one, forming the port of Mahon, famed as the best natural harbour in the Mediterranean. Little more than 500 m. across the mouth, it opens out to a maximum length of about 6 km., with delightful inlets round its shores and several small islands inside its bay.

Thus Minorca, though much smaller and poorer than Majorca, possesses its own distinctive personality, with a wilder but no less imposing beauty.

The island of Ibiza is farther away from Majorca. It is far more mountainous than Minorca, the highest peak, Atalayas, reaching 475 m., and there is more vegetation. The coastline is broken by picturesque small bays, notably that of Santa Eulalia and the delightful San Antonio on the west coast, in addition to that which determined the siting of the town of Ibiza. Ibiza has also been fortunate in a good water supply, flowing from its numerous springs. The closely adjacent Formentera, by contrast, is flat, with low-lying, swampy coastlands and salt workings.

If we wish to picture the islands in pre-Roman times, we may suppose that the climate will not have changed greatly over the past four thousand years. It is possible that the earliest human settlement took place during the final phases of the climatic optimum. Later some climatic deterioration may have intensified the atmospheric changes which increased the severity of the north winds all round the shores of the Gulf of Lions. Today the average winter temperature on Palma is 12°C, with 25°C in the summer. Average rainfall is calculated at 477 mm. (18.8 ins).

The islands' spontaneous vegetation cover has changed and it is not easy to determine what was previously there. Prickly pear, a constant feature of the present-day landscape, must be excluded, since we know it was brought from America. Another dominant species, by contrast, must already have been well established in antiquity, namely the wild olive (Latin *oleaster, ullastre* in Catalan, pronounced *uastre* in Minorca). It has invaded the ancient sites and plagues the archaeologist, who constantly finds himself committed to the arduous labour of clearing it away. We should notice the abundance of holm and kermes oak, the evergreen mastic, and other typically Mediterranean species. Pine, too, is extremely characteristic, notably the Aleppo pine, though maritime pine is also represented. Today the twisted trunks of centuries-old olive trees are the essence of the classic landscape of Majorca, especially in upland regions. In earlier times, the Balearics must in general have been heavily wooded.

By contrast, there are few indigenous animals. Today the islands carry numerous cattle, sheep, goats and pigs; some of these animals seem to preserve old strains imported by the first settlers.

The Balearics are also poor in mineral resources. Anthracite is nowadays worked in Majorca, and a few small deposits of copper have been found on the same island. It would be interesting if we could determine that at least some of the archaeologist's copper and bronze finds had been worked from local metal. However, it appears that copper was never abundant and would have had to be imported in any period; which explains why the early inhabitants provide us with so little evidence of themselves from metal deposits in their tombs.

What abounds on all the islands is stone. Lavish use has been made of it for drystone work, using techniques we call cyclopean, or megalithic, and building continues today. On Minorca, for example, it is not always easy to distinguish ancient remains from the walls which divide modern properties and cover the whole island with, as it were, a mural network of stone. Building seemed predestined to take megalithic forms, although this is not to deny the influence of ethnic or cultural borrowings from other Mediterranean centres, where these techniques had developed early. The influence of geology is again evident in another type of archaeological site. Not only are there very many natural caves in the gorges of Majorca and Minorca, but the underlying rock of the islands can easily be excavated into artificial caves; hence the enormous number of cave sites we find, particularly for burials.

That geography did not entirely determine the course of the islands' early history, however, is evident from the fact that, despite the similarities between the ancient Gymnesiae and Pityusae, these last islands contain no prehistoric remains, and come into the picture only with Punic colonization.

THE HISTORY OF RESEARCH

From their nature, the prehistoric monuments of the Balearics attracted early attention, both among scholars and local antiquarians, and among foreign travellers. At the same time scholars were also turning to account the more or less clear references to the islands and their inhabitants in classical texts, dating from the fifth century BC onwards.

The monuments are first mentioned in general histories. Thus in 1593 Binimelis speaks with respect of the magnificent structures, which in his time must have been more impressively preserved than today; so amazed is he by them that he attributes them to giants or demons. He cites the most important groups of talayots (Chapter III) and supposes that the first inhabitants of the Balearics were Chaldeans, companions of Tubal. Dameto wrote an account in 1632 based on classical sources. Historical studies multiplied in the eighteenth century, and Vargas Ponce (1787) stands out among Spanish authors. During the English occupation of Minorca the engineer John Armstrong wrote *The History of the Island of Minorca* (London, 1752), with a chapter on the ancient monuments. He described them as funerary, religious or defensive, attributing them to the Celtic druids who were beginning to be fashionable among English antiquaries. Shortly afterwards J. Chr. Wernsdorff published *De Antiquitatibus Balearicis* (Brunswick, 1760), giving greater weight to classical sources.

1818 is the date of the first prehistoric study in Spanish, *Antigüedades célticas de la isla de Menorca desde los tiempos más remotos hasta el siglo IV de la Era cristiana*, published in Mahon by the great Minorcan scholar Juán Ramis y Ramis. As the title indicates, Ramis followed the eighteenth-century predilection for druids; but though his work is full of errors and questionable interpretation it merits to stand at the head of our bibliography. His drawing of the naveta Els Tudons is an invaluable record.

A slightly earlier travel book by the French consul, André de Grasset de Saint Sauveur, contains a chapter on the monuments, which he had visited. The first scientific study, in 1840, came from an Italian, Alberto della Marmora,who previously had studied Phoenician coins from the Balearics. He made the comparison between talayots he had visited and the nuraghi of Sardinia, noting structural differences, and made apposite observations on the navetas and taulas in Minorca. In the same year a classification of monuments by Bover designated those near Campos 'druidical pyramids'. Quadrado and Piferrer in the Minorcan volume of their *Recuerdos y bellezas de España* were more prudent, comparing the cyclopean techniques employed on Balearic monuments with those of Greece, Gozo, Malta and Sardinia. As proof of the growing interest in archaeology among Majorcan scholars we have the curious fact that an Archaeological Committee for the Balearics was set up in 1844, dedicated to studying and preserving monuments and artistic treasures.

The monuments were increasingly explored and described in the second half of the nineteenth century, and interest was stimulated by the start of a *Revista de Menorca* in 1888, following the establishments of the Luliana Archaeological Society in Palma in 1880. Important accounts of travels and discoveries were frequent. We may mention the works of Pagenstecher, Martorell y Penã, Pons y Soler, Seguí Rodriguez, Vuillier, Oleo y Quadrado, Riudavets and Sanpere y Miquel (with his fantastic theories of Egyptian contacts). J. Fergusson wrote a classic treatise on megalithic architecture in 1872, while the work of the well-known French prehistorian, Emile Cartailhac, *Monuments primitifs des Iles Baleares*, published in 1892, drew together all earlier studies on a scientific basis. There was an accompanying study of Minorcan cranial finds by Professor Verneau.

Work continued during the early decades of the present century, with contributions by L. C. Watelin, who proposed a relative chronology based on typology, A. Mayr, who attempted the first catalogue of known remains, Hernandez Mora and Vives Escudero, among others.

A decisive step towards systematic work was begun in 1920 by the Archaeological Excavations Service of the Institut d'Estudis Catalans of Barcelona, under the direction of Professor Bosch Gimpera. Excavations in the Balearics were conducted by José Colominas, and later by José Malverti, under the general guidance of Bosch Gimpera. In south-west Majorca the sites of Capocorp and Son Juliá at Lluchmayor, Es Mitjá Gran and Els Antigors at Ses Salines and the caves of Santueri at Felanitx were among those examined. The work continued for some years, and enabled Bosch Gimpera to define problems of chronology and relationships in the Mediterranean. It culminated in 1935, in a commission formed to study western Mediterranean prehistory, which met in the islands. Julio Martinez Santa-Olalla who, as a young scholar, worked principally on Minorcan antiquities, was a leading member. Simultaneously the city of Palma created an Excavation Service (unfortunately short-lived) and established local museums, notably for art, all of which stimulated local archaeologists.

The interest of foreign scholars continued, with the work of Kessler, Chamberlin and significant publications by W. Hemp. The largest foreign undertaking was the Cambridge mission of 1930, directed by the Egyptologist Margaret Murray, excavating at Trepucó and Sa Torreta, with publications in 1932 and 1934.

After some years of inactivity Balearic archaeology resumed its progress and in the last thirty years has shown remarkable advances and promise. The visit of the international IV Curso de Ampurias to the islands in 1950 provided a stimulus. The National Excavation Service has been active and the Bryant Foundation has supported important work at Pollentia (Alcudia) and Son Real. With help from the March Foundation it has been possible to undertake planning and excavation (Torelló, Alcaidus), and restoration of the Els Tudons naveta, on Minorca, with various other excavations, site-clearing for descriptive recording, etc. on Majorca. Recent excavation at Ses Paisses, Artá, by an Italian team has been especially important, enabling its director Professor G. Lilliu to propose a systematic chronology.

Among the numerous archaeologists and local workers who have been active in the islands, space allows us to single out only L. Amorós and B. Enseñat; P. C. Veny; Dr B. Font; D. Cerdá; J. Mascaró Pasarius, who has listed and mapped all the known sites on Majorca and Minorca, with many plans; G. Rosselló Bordoy, director of the Majorcan museum, and the late María Luisa Serra Belabre who worked with exemplary industry as director of the Mahon museum; Professors J. Maluquer, M. Tarradell, P. de Palol, A. G. Bellido.

The cooperation of foreign workers has also continued. There was English and American assistance (notably from Professor Daniel Woods) at Pollentia. The German archaeologists Dehn and Frey examined the talayot settlement of S'Illot. Finally, W. Waldren, as director of a museum organized in Deyá, has collaborated with Spanish workers to achieve remarkable results from cave excavations in the northern mountains of Majorca. Besides pottery, these produced Carbon 14 dates which seem to take occupation of the islands back two thousand years earlier than we had supposed, with interesting implications for the history of navigation in the west Mediterranean.

Archaeological research on Ibiza has followed a different path. The absence there of monumental remains will explain why we know of no significant studies before 1903. An Archaeological Society was then formed, a museum to house the island's many antiquities initiated, and excavations begun at Puig des Molins and other sites. The amateur archaeologist largely responsible, J. Román y Calvet, published his results in 1906. Excavations proceeded with official recognition, and Vives Escudero who directed them from 1910 published the findings in book form in 1917. The writings of Carlos Román, who excavated in the Ibiza necropolis from 1918 to 1924, and of Perez Cabrero brought Ibizan archaeology to popular attention, while works by Schulten, Macabich and Garcia Bellido have provided great stimulus. Excavations were resumed in 1942, conducted by museum directors Mañá de Angulo and, later, Josefa Almagro. The late Miriam Astruc from France set about evaluating earlier finds. Astruc's important assessment of the Punic period was among their contributions. Underwater exploration, and excavation by both German archaeologists and local amateurs on Formentera, as well as the important studies of Professor Tarradell on Punic archaeology, and those of Miss Aubet, Catalina Enseñat and E. de Fortuny, are the most recent development in the field.

The future for archaeology on the Balearics is therefore bright: the lasting interest of both Spanish and foreign scholars has been secured. There remains the enormous task of cleaning and restoration, so that the most impressive collection of monumental remains in Europe, especially on Minorca, may be exhibited. Systematic excavation, down to the first settlements, must continue on stratified sites to provide the needed chronology. Important Roman and Early Christian material also remains to be studied, especially the wealth of early basilicas. These are the many reasons why the Balearics will surely emerge in the next years as a magnet for European archaeology. Once connections with neighbouring lands are defined, the early history of the western Mediterranean will become clearer to us.

THE CULTURAL SEQUENCE

The difficulties and uncertainties involved in establishing a relative chronology for the island's successive cultures are manifest. The evidence is contained within the comparatively short period (thirty to fifty generations) available for construction of the immense number of known monuments, the work of some thirty thousand inhabitants at most, which alone afford slight indications of historical sequence. The whole record of the region lies contained in a few poor and thin strata, and there are no clear divisions.

Analysis of chronological schemes proposed by present-day authors, notably Rosselló Bordoy, Rosselló Coll, G. Lilliu, and P. Veny, shows that in outline they are basically similar. They diverge on minor points of evaluation, and the different dates they propose are in any case not usually verifiable. The scheme I shall put forward, based on my own interpretations but similar to that proposed by Professor Lilliu, should be regarded as a further hypothesis, offered as a guide to the uninitiated who wish to explore this enigmatic period of our past history.

The first dividing line is obvious. Everything prior to the adoption of cyclopean, or megalithic, building techniques must be considered together. The date of the first settlement has not yet been fixed, but I do not believe it could be earlier than that given by Carbon 14 analysis. It appears that Majorca was already inhabited before 4000 BC, and this little-known Neolithic phase could have lasted until the middle of the third millennium.

A second phase evidently covers the use of natural and artificial caves for burials and as living sites, and this is associated with incised pottery, including beakers, and frequent bronze finds. Here again there are Carbon 14 dates: 1800 and 1500 BC. A first wave of megalithic peoples (with dolmens) will have arrived during this phase.

The third phase is the cyclopean, the period of the *talayot* towers. Following an already established usage, it may be termed Talayot I. The naveta of Els Tudons marks its apogee. It would appear to have begun between 1400 and 1200 BC, ending in about the eighth century.

Talayot II is not easy to define. Phoenician and Greek colonial activity introduced many novelties, and both settlements and monuments on the islands multiplied. This stage could have lasted from the eighth to the fifth century BC.

With the development of navigation the islands increased in importance. Greek and Punic trade brought enrichment, off-setting the fact that many of the young men left in search of wealth and adventure, or were sought out from abroad for their mastery of the sling as a weapon.

A Talayot III period may be inferred, lasting from the fifth to the second century BC, and finds accord with this. It was a time of contact with neighbouring peoples of the Mediterranean. The Balearics found themselves involved in wars between Roman and Carthaginian for mastery of the seas and dominion over islands hitherto independent. The conquest of Majorca in 123 BC by Q. Caecilius Metellus terminated the independence of the native population. However, despite the recognized Roman capacity for colonization and Romanization of conquered peoples, native Balearic culture persisted quite a long time, especially in rural and mountain regions.

We may call the period beginning with the Roman conquest either Roman, or post-Talayot. Disturbed by invasion, the indigenous culture was gradually to die out, leaving few traces of the mentality and life of the islands' early inhabitants.

These dates, as I have said, represent my personal interpretation of the Balearic evidence, but I am also privileged to refer, in advance of his own publication, to an alternative scheme proposed by G. Rosselló-Bordoy. According to Professor Rosselló's hypothesis the first talayot phase would fall as early as 1500–1300 BC, the second between 1300 and 1000, and the third from 1000 to 750. True talayotic culture, he thinks, then gave way to the post-talayotic (or Talayot IV) phase, which lasted until the Roman conquest. Although there is a basis for this high chronology in C-14 dates, I feel that we need more information before we accept so long a post-talayotic stage. A change of the proposed terminal date from 750 BC to the fifth or fourth century would be more acceptable.

CHAPTER II

The pre-Talayot Period

THE EARLIEST SETTLEMENTS

Opinions differ widely as to when human occupation of the Balearics began. The problem must be considered in the general context of cultural developments round the western Mediterranean, but for the Balearics there is the additional question of how well primitive people could navigate.

Local scholars, naturally, have tended to regard the first settlements as very early, though there has never been any serious suggestion that the islands were populated during the Palaeolithic. Even those of us who accept that Palaeolithic man could overcome the difficulties of traversing a narrow sea, like the Straits of Gibraltar, do not believe that human beings could have established themselves on the Balearics in such remote times. In this sense the Balearics (like Sardinia or Corsica) were unfortunately placed, in comparison with Sicily, which is rich in Upper Palaeolithic remains. We cannot dismiss the possibility of an accidental landing by some craft from the Alicante coast on Ibiza; but I believe that so unimportant an incident would have left no material traces.

With the Neolithic, circumstances change. Rich cultures are known to have flourished round the Mediterranean coasts, and there is ample proof of sea travel and development of trade. It is now established that by about 6000 BC true cities were initiating an urban phase of civilization in Anatolia, Syria and Palestine. The Greek mainland and the Aegean were receiving influences from across the sea, which were promptly transmitted to Malta, Sicily, Sardinia and Corsica. We already know that by about 4000 BC Neolithic innovations must have reached Spain, and it would be reasonable to suppose these will have been carried at least partly by sea. Placed as they are, strategically in the centre of west Mediterranean routes, the Balearics might some day be expected to yield confirmation of this, in finds of pottery or stone tools.

Advocates of a high chronology for the Balearic Neolithic have argued principally from pottery and flint finds. It is relatively easy to establish that the latter, generally in the form of blades and often of

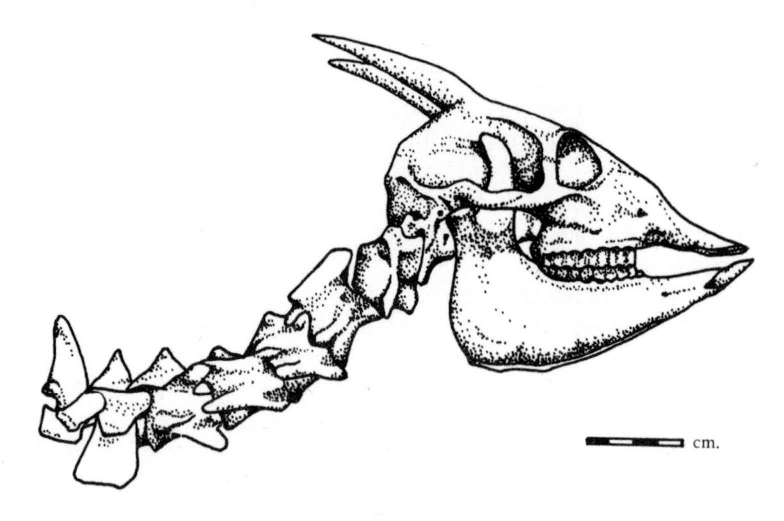

Fig. 2 Myotragus balearicus (after Waldren)

tabular flint, are hardly diagnostic, since the forms last through many periods. The pottery seems more convincing. There are numerous examples of incised ware, including one sherd of Beaker type from Majorca, and it is this ware that has always been held to be characteristically Eneolithic. At some sites, like the burial cave of Sa Canova at Ariany explored by P. Cañigueral, incised ware is abundant. When I examined this pottery, however, it seemed to me we should call it Epi-neolithic, the decoration being classifiable as already Early Bronze Age, possibly continuing even longer. There are parallels in Sardinia and in the rich Ligurian cave of Arene Candide. The sherd of beaker type from the Cueva dels Bous, Felanitx, could be assigned to a parallel group. From such evidence as this, therefore, it seemed difficult to date what were apparently the earliest finds from Majorca to before 2000 BC. There was no reason to suppose that finds from Minorca were any older, despite the convictions of local enthusiasts.

A fragment of painted ware found by B. Enseñat in a small cave near Soller, recalling finds from Sicily, scarcely provides diagnostic evidence. However, a further argument repeatedly advanced in recent years, which has often seemed convincing, is based on the discovery of rock art, especially engravings, on the walls of certain caves in Majorca and Minorca. The style is always schematic, and though the quality is rather poor, the possibility of some symbolic import cannot be denied. The drawings are of crosses or crudely stylized human beings, where the signs are not obviously modern. There can, however, be little doubt that this type of cave art survived for a long time, since we now see very low dates accorded to schematic cave art, both in Spain and in other Mediterranean lands.

On Ibiza, the absence of any Neolithic material becomes increasingly evident, although pre-metal age finds are avidly sought there.

Since 1966, however, there has been a radical change in the evidence available, which must modify profoundly our views on cultural diffusion round the Mediterranean. The amount of incised ware from recent finds was already increasing to an extent which suggested that it could date back earlier than I had supposed. The decisive evidence, however, came from fruitful excavations in the northern mountain ranges of Majorca. The American archaeologist W. Waldren and his assistants began work in 1958 in the picturesque region of Deyá, organizing there a museum, and their results have been surprising. Several caves known to local archaeologists were examined; one, the Muleta cave, was found to contain an accumulation of some fifteen hundred specimens of the antelope *Myotragus balearicus*. Similar to the gazelle, this was the largest animal indigenous to the Balearics, where it was isolated and underwent a curious evolution. This was first described in 1909 by the English palaeontologist Miss Dorothea Bate. Its presence on Minorca as well, raises the question of whether evolutionary changes there correspond closely enough to suggest that man has been instrumental in transporting the animal between the islands.

Fig. 2

The greatest interest attaches to the Carbon 14 dates obtained from the bones: the readings seem to be entirely reliable, and among the various results is a date of 5184 ± 80 BC. While it is significant, this result would not interest us directly were it not for the fact that human remains, comprizing a mandible, eight molars and several extremity bones, were discovered in the same layers as the *Myotragus* finds. In 1966 a new find of human bones and, moreover, two flint blades and several bone points, produced a further reading: 3984 ± 109 BC. These two dates taken together show that the last of the Balearic antelopes were contemporary with the first human inhabitants of Majorca, who as hunters were perhaps responsible for their extinction.

Waldren's results go to confirm those obtained by G. Florit Piedrabuena in 1962 in Minorca (to which I confess I had not given due attention). Florit reported a find, from caves near Ciudadela, of *Myotragus* horns showing signs of trimming, associated with coarse, globular pottery. Evidence from the two islands is thus complementary; though despite present indications opinions differ as to whether a true Neolithic existed there or not.

There is no need to be alarmed by such high dates, since all round the eastern Mediterranean, in Greece and Crete as well as in Anatolia, Syria and Palestine, an early Neolithic is now known to have been established by 6000 BC. However, before we are obliged to accept a date of 4000 BC, or even earlier, for settlement in the Balearics we shall require a greater number of consistent datings, or sites with clear stratigraphy, since there is a gap of some two thousand years to be filled.

Should the new hypotheses be confirmed, it will be necessary to revise our notions about the western Mediterranean and peninsular Spain. With proof of navigation two thousand years earlier than we believed, cultural movements which have hitherto seemed impossible during the fourth and third millennia could become credible. New ideas on the spread of the Neolithic revolution to the west would follow from the possibility of direct transmission by sea, in place of overland movements through Europe.

I find it difficult to accept that the newly found settlement in Majorca was really at a pre-ceramic stage. I prefer to ascribe the apparent lack of pottery to the poverty of the site; and on no account would I allow the possibility of very much older, that is Mesolithic or Epi-palaeolithic, migration.

There is the similar problem of how and when Minorca was first settled. Here again there has been dispute between laymen, who want the first Neolithic to be early, and professional opinion, working from sound evidence and resisting attempts to date it before 2000 BC. There is no shortage of reports of incised ware, flints and rock art, which suffice for some as evidence of a Neolithic phase. Certain caves in the region of Ciudadela, still partly unpublished, and in particular the discoveries of Florit, have produced such material. Although all the types could be interpreted as survivals, into the Bronze Age, of forms which in peninsular Spain developed in the fourth and third millennia, I now incline to accept their antiquity. Account must be taken of the presence of the famous *Myotragus* horns in the caves (Cova Murada), with signs of having been worked. The case for the material being early has become stronger since the C-14 readings from Majorca, so that, although definite proof is still wanting, a settlement date contemporary with the Majorcan is, *a priori*, acceptable. It would seem probable that there were simultaneous landings on the two islands.

THE PRE-TALAYOTIC PERIOD: THE BALEARIC CAVE CULTURE

So imposing and numerous are the cyclopean structures of Majorca and Minorca, that it is difficult not to feel they must represent the work of several thousand years, thereby precluding the existence of earlier remains. Investigation soon showed, however, that certain archaeological material and, in addition, the use of artificial and some natural caves, falls outside the context of this grandiose Talayot culture. These were recognized as features of a pre-talayotic period, which could alternatively be called 'The Balearic Cave Culture' (this is quite distinct from what has sometimes been termed the *cultura de las cuevas* which begins with the Neolithic on the Spanish mainland).

Fig. 3

It proves difficult, however, to subdivide this pre-talayotic period. As we have seen, we may allow a remote Neolithic (possibly even pre-ceramic) phase, and this is followed by the Eneolithic, which could have begun during the third millennium. While natural caves continued to be used as living sites and for burials during this phase, it also saw the development of the artificial, rock-cut cave. At this point, however, we must tread warily. While we are still unable to determine exactly when the following cyclopean period began, we are obliged to classify a quantity of artificial caves as pre-cyclopean/pre-talayotic simply from their form, whenever there are no finds to indicate the true chronology. This is unfortunately an inevitable state of affairs at the present stage of Balearic research.

A further complication has arisen from a comparison by Bosch Gimpera and Colominas of material from the caves, which they termed Bronze II or advanced Bronze, with the El Argar culture in Spain. Apart from general features, like the use of simple bronzes, it was the carinated pottery which was held to be characterisitically El Argar. But it is now realized that carinated ware occurs fairly early, in the Eneolithic of many western lands, and moreover that the Argaric culture is confined to a limited area of south-eastern Spain. While not denying the possibility of some contacts, I feel that Balearic chronology should be freed from the notion of close connections with El Argar.

As we have already indicated, incised ware and flint tools are the principal features of this early period. Until a few years ago there was some doubt about the reality and composition of the phase, since there was only the one sherd from the Bous cave at Felanitx in Majorca to indicate a connection with beaker ware. Since then, our knowledge has greatly increased, with the rich series discovered by P. Cañigueral in the natural cave of Sa Canova near Ariany on the central Majorcan plain, complemented by numerous other finds in the same region by B. Enseñat, and a number of recent discoveries in the caves of Soller and the slopes of the northern mountains. Analysis of this pottery with its elaborate decoration, recalling Sardinian and Ligurian ware (notably Arene Candide), allows us to ascribe it to an advanced Eneolithic. In due course the predominance of incised ware gave way to plain or simply decorated pottery, generally globular, or of truncated-conical or carinated form. At the same time the use of bronze was spreading. The difficult task of subdividing this great mass of material and assigning each of the dwelling or burial caves to an appropriate stage is made easier by postulating an Eneolithic phase, with greater settlement densities in the northern mountains of Majorca, followed by another phase, embracing the Early Bronze Age and chiefly characterized by artificial caves in the regions of the plain. We are fortunate in possessing evidence that is sufficiently extensive and homogeneous to throw light on the cultural unity which prevailed for rather more than a thousand years on Majorca and Minorca.

For a deeper knowledge of this period in Majorca we are especially indebted to two young archaeologists, and there is general agreement between their typological classification of the various caves. Professor G. Rosselló Bordoy, who has excavated in many of them, recognizes three phases. The first comprises natural caves, which are most frequent in mountain regions, with incised or plain ware predominantly of what Spanish archaeologists call 'truncated-conical' form (e.g. Vernissa and

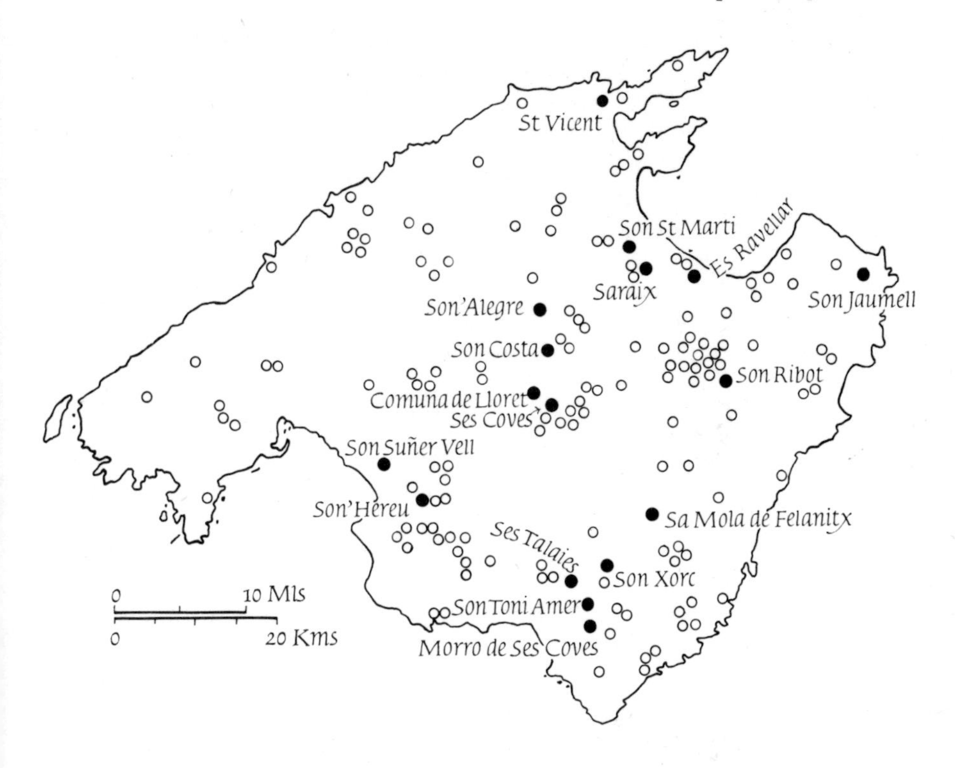

Fig. 3 The distribution of principal cave sites in Majorca (after Mascaró)

Sa Canova). In his second phase (Cas Hereu and Trispolet) the pottery is undecorated and the conical forms disappear. Some simple artificial caves are possibly contemporaneous. Rock-cut caves are the principal component of Rosselló's third phase during which they develop a great variety of ground plans. Most often, the rock-cut tombs occur in cemeteries, of the Son Toni Amer and Cala Sant Vicens type. Here, the grave material seems more evolved.

The second study, a valuable doctoral thesis by P. Cristobal Veny, goes into more detail, and is shown in the following table. It is summarized overleaf.

The chronology and features of Majorcan caves (after P. Cristobal Veny, 1968)

Approximate dates	Type	Phase	Artificial caves	Natural caves	Pottery	Flints	Bronzes	Features
2000–1800	I		Pont den Cabrera	Son Torrella, Cueva dels Bous	Incised A	Blades		Small circular chambers without corridor
1800–1600	II		Son Suñer IX	Sa Canova, Son Marroig	Incised B	Flakes (atypical)	Pentagonal daggers	Large circular chambers with simple corridor
1600–1200	III	a	Sa Tanca, Son Mulet	Els Rossells Cueva Lledoner	Plain ware predominently bowls and jars	?	Awls, tri-angular daggers, arrow-heads	Elongated chamb with no burial trench, short corridor or shaft.
		b	Cemeteries of Son Suñer, Son Toni Amer, Sa Mola	Cometa dels Morts, Sa Mata, Solleric	Plain ware, all forms	Unworked atypical flakes	Awls, daggers	Elongated chamb with central trencl and funerary bencl Long corridors w 'double vestibule'
			Necropolis of Cala Sant Vicens		Plain ware	?	?	Exterior vestibule Long corridor wi 'double vestibule' Elongated chamb with high ledge inside

Natural caves with burials. Veny lists twenty-seven of these, a number which will doubtless increase. Of particular interest is the Vernissa cave, Santa Margarita, excavated and published by Colominas. Plain pottery, one incised sherd and a triangular bronze dagger were found. The burials were laid in rows, separated by stone slabs, under a rough paving, with the pottery close to the heads. The dagger came from the lowest layer in the cave. There is a noticeable absence of the globular pots with suspension handles which characterize more evolved forms of rock-cut tomb. Instead, a hemispherical bowl predominates. Generally represented too are conical and biconical pots, types which occur only sporadically in artificial caves. Another important site is the Sa Canova cave, explored by Cañigueral and Enseñat. Here there was a rich variety of incised ware, and nine daggers and fourteen awls of bronze. Other sites with significant material include Cas Hereu, Lluchmayor, studied by Colominas; Trispolet, Artá; Es Rossells, Felanitx; Sa Cometa dels

Morts, Lluch, where there were quantities of bone buttons; Tossals Verts, Escorca; Son Torrella, Escorca, which like several other caves in the Soller region was excavated by Enseñat; Ariant, Pollensa; Solleric, Lluchmayor, and more besides. Naturally, these caves continued in use during the following Talayot period, as can be seen by the occasional finds of late pottery.

Especial importance attaches to three caves in the Deyá region of Majorca's northern mountains, which have provided C-14 readings. The Cueva de la Muertos-Gallard contained burials from various periods, ending with what the excavators (W. Waldren and his team) term 'cremation in lime'. The lowest layer produced as many as fifteen sherds in Beaker style, together with a markedly brachycephalic skull, and sufficient carbon and bones for a C-14 sample. Human remains from the near-by Marroig cave occurred as secondary burials. The pottery here was the simple type of the local Bronze Age, with only a single truncated-conical vessel of black burnished ware, with incisions at the rim. The third cave, Son Matge, contained Beaker ware. The C-14 date from the first cave was 1840 ± 80 BC, with 1870 ± 120 BC from Son Matge and 1520 ± 80 BC from Son Marroig, where the material looks more recent. Thus we have satisfactory datings for the Eneolithic – Early Bronze period in Majorca, which preceded the great wave of cyclopean building.

Plate 3

Inhabited caves. These are not nearly so numerous as burial caves. We may cite Cova Calenta, Coll de Sa Batalla, Son Torrella (Escorca), yielding numerous bone tools and flint finds, the caves of the Confessionari dels Moros and Els Bous, both in Felanitx. The first find of incised ware in Majorca, now lost, came from Els Bous; because it remained unique for many years its authenticity was questioned. Artificial inhabited caves are quite unusual. Veny lists in fact only nine, of irregular shape, in the Cala Sant Vicens group.

Artificial, or rock-cut, tombs on Majorca. We may lay claim to a good knowledge of the burials we assign to this period, though always with the proviso that some – since we are not equally well informed about corresponding settlement sites – may in fact belong to builders of the talayots, or at least to their earlier representatives. Excavation of rock-cut tombs for collective burial is, however, a practice widely known in the Mediterranean area, and as such would have arrived in the Balearics at an early date. The islands' geology favoured a remarkable development and density of tombs. The current evidence has been fully presented in P. Veny's study (which utilizes reports by Rosselló and Mascaró) of the hundred odd examples known. Unfortunately, most of the tombs have been broken open, or re-used, at all periods, up to the present day. The only remaining basis for a relative chronology, therefore, is the assumption of development from older, simple and circular plans to the more complex and elaborate.

Rosselló Bordoy, who has studied and excavated many sites, has made the following classification. He first distinguishes the simple from complex caves, which may be circular, oval or elongated in plan. The initial type is a simple, circular chamber, entered directly. The commonest form is an oval chamber, and some of these have an entrance corridor. In other examples the chamber is extended, and becomes more or less rectangular in outline (Ses Talaies at Campos, Es Rafalet at Manacor, and others). More evolved forms include those entered through a pit or shaft, with vestibule or inner court, and corridor (leaving aside those connected with talayot enclosures or pre-Roman sanctuary caves).

Most frequent among the complex forms is an elongated chamber, with or without side chambers. Generally the main chamber is large, with either an entrance opening directly from the outside, a short entrance corridor, or a small opening in the roof (Son Toni Amer). Another variant is entered through an oval shaft, with a squared or rounded doorway blocked by a stone slab to conceal the entrance, and a few rough steps for descent into the main chamber. Sa Tanca, Alcudia, is a splendid example of this type. I was able to visit this cave immediately it was discovered, and experienced the thrill of opening the slab, to be the first for some 4000 years to penetrate the tomb. What I found did not match my hopes. Once the impenetrable mesh of roots was cleared, a mass of poorly preserved bones, half hidden by the infiltrating soil, was revealed, with a series of inverted pots, undecorated but of early forms, placed in an orderly fashion along the chamber walls. A number of similar tombs have been found in various districts. Their entrance shaft ends as an approach corridor (as at Sa Mola den Bordoy, Felanitx), leading to a long chamber with lateral benches and side

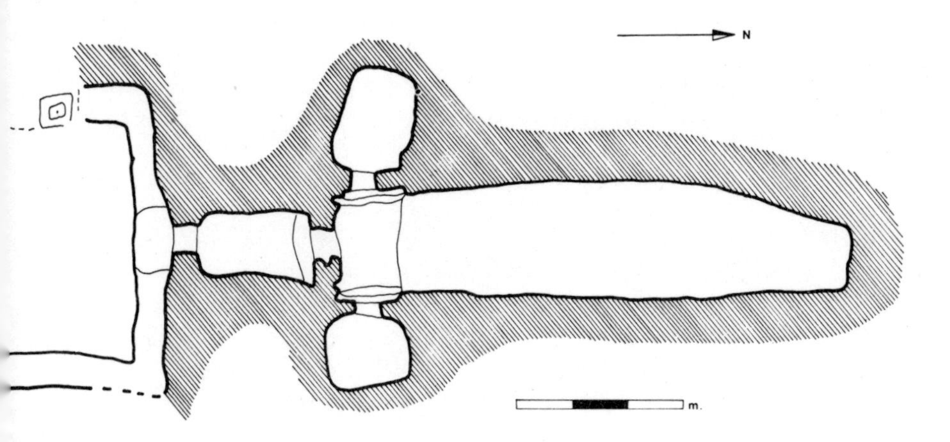

Fig. 4 Plan of artificial cave no. 7, Cala Sant Vicens, Majorca, considered the best preserved of known caves (after Rosselló Bordoy)

chambers. There are also many tombs with an antechamber, ante-chamber and corridor, or with a corridor only which may be either simple or complex. At site E at Son Toni Amer we find a variant with a stepped corridor, which is remarkable for parallels among the tombs of Provence. There is a different type still where the corridor is widened to form an antechamber composed of successive compartments. The rock-cut tombs found in cemetery groups are especially interesting: Sant Vicens, Son Sureda, Son Suñer, Son Antem, Son Jaumell.

The various tombs in the cemetery near the bay of Sant Vicens (which have already been published by Cartailhac in his classic study) demonstrate the development of the entrance corridor. Tomb 7 here may rank as the finest example known in Majorca. A very short corridor leads down to a small vestibule ('double vestibule'); a further short passage connects with a rectangular antechamber flanked by side chambers, which gives on to the long main chamber. A narrow ledge projecting just below the 'barrel-vault' roof runs almost the length of the side walls. Tomb 9 has a bench along the chamber wall divided by transverse ribs into compartments, and there are four apsidal chambers.

Plate 5
Fig. 4

The Son Jaumell cave, near Capdepera, published by Crespi and Hemp, also has a very short entrance passage combined with a vestibule, and an approach ramp with four steps near the entrance. Three steps immediately inside give access to the floor of the chamber, which is elliptical in plan, with two small side chambers. A more archaic, or at least cruder, type is the Son Antem cave, with a corridor divided into two vestibules, a circular chamber, irregular side-chambers and a rudimentary bench. One of the best studied groups is that in and about Son Suñer, near Palma, where Rosselló has found ten tombs. Son Suñer II is notable for its six metre long stepped approach ramp, which leads into a sort of tunnel for reaching the chamber entrance.

Fig. 5

Fig. 6

Son Suñer V and VII deserve special mention. The former has a long chamber, 7.25 × 3.10 m., and 2 m. high, with side-chambers. A trench, 5.30 × 1.30 m. and stepped at the ends, had been dug 1.10 m. deep in the main chamber. In it the excavator, Rosselló Bordoy, distinguished eight layers, the top four ending with material from the sixteenth century, when the cave was pillaged. Layer 5 produced abundant local globular pottery, with human remains and a perforated and serrated bone disc. Layer 7 contained globular pots with everted rims, either handleless or with small lug-handles horizontally or vertically perforated, pots with flattened globular outline, bowls, flat-based conical pots with triangular lugs projecting upwards, combined with incised decoration encircling their junction with the vase body. The bronze finds comprised seven awls of circular cross-section, some flattened at the point, two of rectangular section, a tanged arrow-head 2 cm. long, and a fragment of a small triangular dagger. There were also miscellaneous bone objects: a small disc (less than 2 cm. in diameter), serrated and perforated, eleven triangular discs with V-perforation, a truncated cone, one domed and one flat piece. Finally, there were human remains.

Son Suñer VII is simple in form, an irregularly circular chamber with two side chambers and a domed roof; the maximum diameter is only 2.35 m. and the height at the centre 1.20 m. A step in the rock separates the chamber from a trapezoidal corridor 2.60 m. long. It appeared that they had also been separated by several stone slabs. Local ware was found in the lowest layer in the chamber, and what may be a fragment of a flint arrow-head, with human remains, including eight skulls. The corpses had apparently been laid radially, possibly in a flexed position, with the heads outwards and supported on a slight ledge running round the chamber walls. The same phenomenon was reported by Amoros in 1957 at the cave of Sa Tanca, Alcudia. The hand-made pottery from Son Suñer VII includes globular pots and bowls, one with

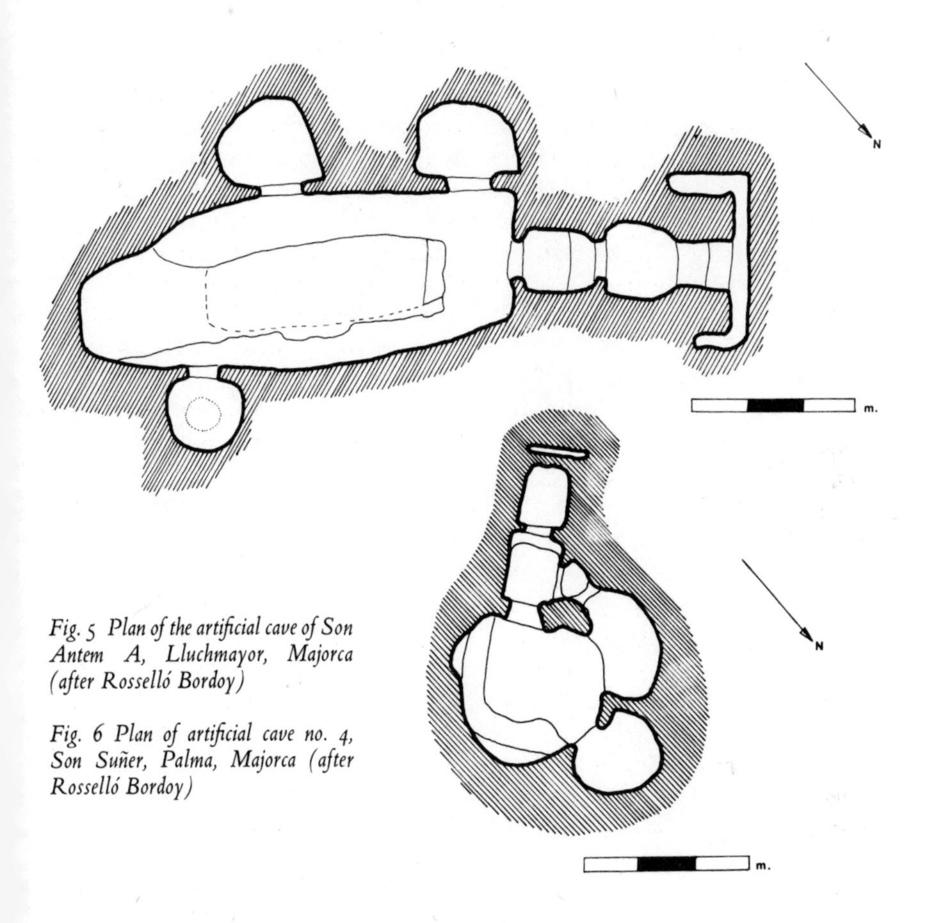

Fig. 5 Plan of the artificial cave of Son Antem A, Lluchmayor, Majorca (after Rosselló Bordoy)

Fig. 6 Plan of artificial cave no. 4, Son Suñer, Palma, Majorca (after Rosselló Bordoy)

a zigzag line; the upper trench layers contained Campanian, Roman and grey ware indicative of an advanced date, which contrasts with some unclassifiable, though trimmed or notched, flints and a possible tanged arrow-head. I take this as evidence of an old site re-used in later times. The same thing is reported in Son Suñer VIII, which is entered through an elongated shaft. The drop of more than two metres, via several steps, to the floor of the ovoid, domed chamber makes the cave ostensibly one of the most archaic on the island, and nearest to original prototypes.

Rock-cut tombs which appear in conjunction with, or beneath, structures of cyclopean type (especially the boat-shaped structures or

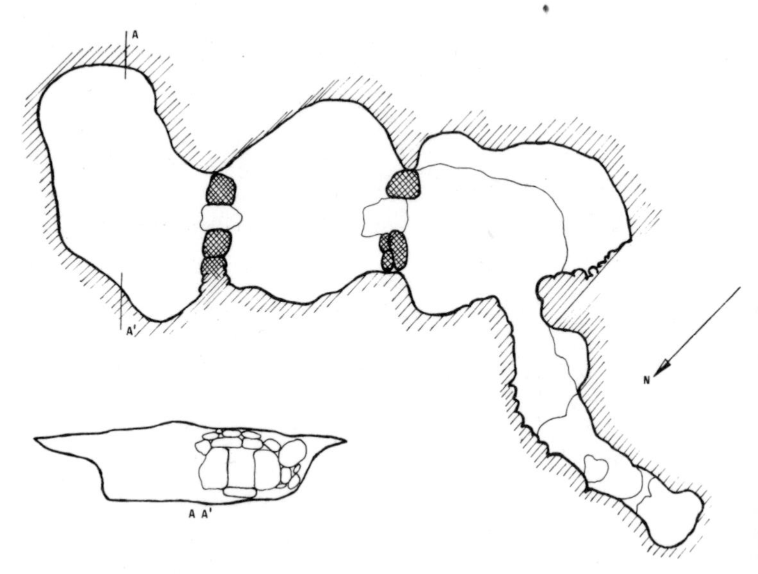

Fig. 7 Plan of the multiple cave in the Son Oms complex, Palma, Majorca (after Rosselló Bordoy). 1:100

navetiformes) present a particular problem. There are instances at San Jordi and Es Rafal, Palma, and in the Son Oms enclosure etc. Clearly, these are explicable as survivals of the rock-cut form until the transition to the following cultural phase. Similarly, study of a classic cyclopean *naveta*, like Els Tudons, also suggests transition: its form is simply a rendering of the elongated rock-cut tombs, using different techniques of construction.

Fig. 7

The material culture of the cave-users. Although certain finds have already been mentioned, we may conclude with a general summary of the material, which shows an apparent uniformity.

As might be expected, the principal finds are of pottery. Incised ware was becoming an increasingly important element, and there is no doubt that the Beaker ware was contemporary with it. Veny distinguishes an older, Type A, incised ware (including beakers), found in the Coveta dels Pous, in Son Torrella and in the Coveta dels Morts at Deyá, from a Type B, for example from Sa Canova, Son Marroig and Son Bauçá.

Fig. 8

Among the undecorated ware Veny recognizes nine forms: bowls, more or less hemispherical; simple oval jars; oval jars with rudimentary

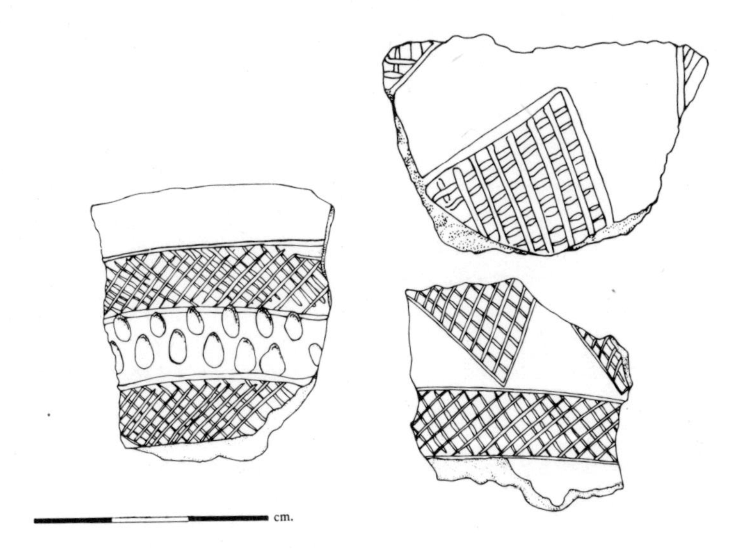

Fig. 8 Fragments of pre-talayotic incised pottery, from the Son Gallard cave, Deyá, Majorca. Deyá Archaeological Museum

neck; carinated forms; jars with everted neck and perforated handles; truncated-cone shapes, sometimes with handles, or carinated forms narrowing to the neck; sub-cylindrical; carinated with a high flaring neck; ovoid top and bottom, sometimes with everted rim.

Fig. 10

The pots are hand-made from fairly crude clay, more or less dark greyish in colour, or reddened in some instances, with the surface irregularly burnished. It is possible that leaves may have been used for moulding pots, to judge from the calcined imprints of palmetta on the inside of some from Es Trispolet, and from other sites in Artá. We have already stressed the predominance of globular forms, often squat, and the numerous hemispherical bowls. A globular form, with small handles vertically perforated for suspension, is highly typical. Biconical and carinated forms are also fairly common. A fragment reported from Son Jaumell could belong to a large funerery vessel like those of the El Argar culture. The almost cylindrical footed jars from Sa Vall and Cas Hereu (Lluchmayor) are exceptional.

Plate 6, 7

Stone finds include some axes, reminiscent of Neolithic times, and examples of perforated rectangular plaques for use as archers' wrist-guards (e.g. at Sa Vall). This might suggest that the bow, and not the

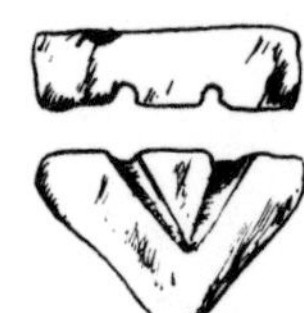
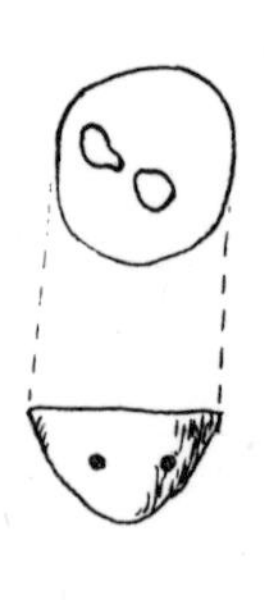

Fig. 9 Conical bone buttons decorated with a v-shaped triangular perforation. Majorca, pre-talayotic period

sling, was the principal weapon. Among the flint finds, apart from numerous trimming flakes, there are crude scrapers and arrow-heads, although I know of no really typical, complete example of an arrow-head. Flint blades are the most frequent type, sometimes quite long and with two cutting-edges (an example from the Tossals Verts cave measures 22.5 cm. in length and is 5 cm. wide). Generally they are made from the tabular flint which seems to have been available in the islands.

Other materials have managed to survive on some sites. These include perforated shells and tusks, bone beads and discs, and in particular the v-perforated bone buttons, of uncertain purpose, which are most useful for comparatiá studies. Other buttons have ordinary perforations, and there are triangular and discoid ones with side perforations. The v-perforated buttons, however, which are common in Catalan megaliths, as on Sardinia and in other coastal regions of the western Mediterranean, are the most typical form. They may be prismatic, pyramidal, conical, hemispherical or discoid. The first two forms predominate in the natural cave sites of the northern mountains, and should be the oldest. Conical and hemispherical buttons are found above all in rock-cut caves on the plain. The most prolific sites are Sa Vall, Son Mulet, Sant Vicens and Son Jaumell. Quantities of bone points are also found, especially in the mountain caves.

The transitional Bronze Age date we ascribe to much of this material accounts for the relative abundance of metal finds in the Majorcan caves. The most common type is the awl, generally of circular section, though there are also some with square, rectangular or rhomboidal section, which are later in date. The Fonda cave at Felanitx alone produced about a hundred examples, and there were twenty-one from Sa Canova. There were bracelets in the Coveta dels Morts cave, and from Solleric came several wafers of metal and a small tube. Bronze arrow-heads and narrow-tanged knives are known from this phase at some sites, but the most characteristic finds are small daggers, which are a link between the Balearics and other zones of Europe. These take various forms: broad-tanged, pentagonal (as at Sa Canova), or of more or less elongated-triangular outline. There are numerous examples of this last form, for example at Sa Canova, Son Mari, Es Cabás, Son Toni Amer, Na Fonda, Cala Sa Nau, Sa Mata, Vernissa, Montblanc, Son Suñer, Son Puig, Ariant, as well as unlocalized finds.

Plate 2

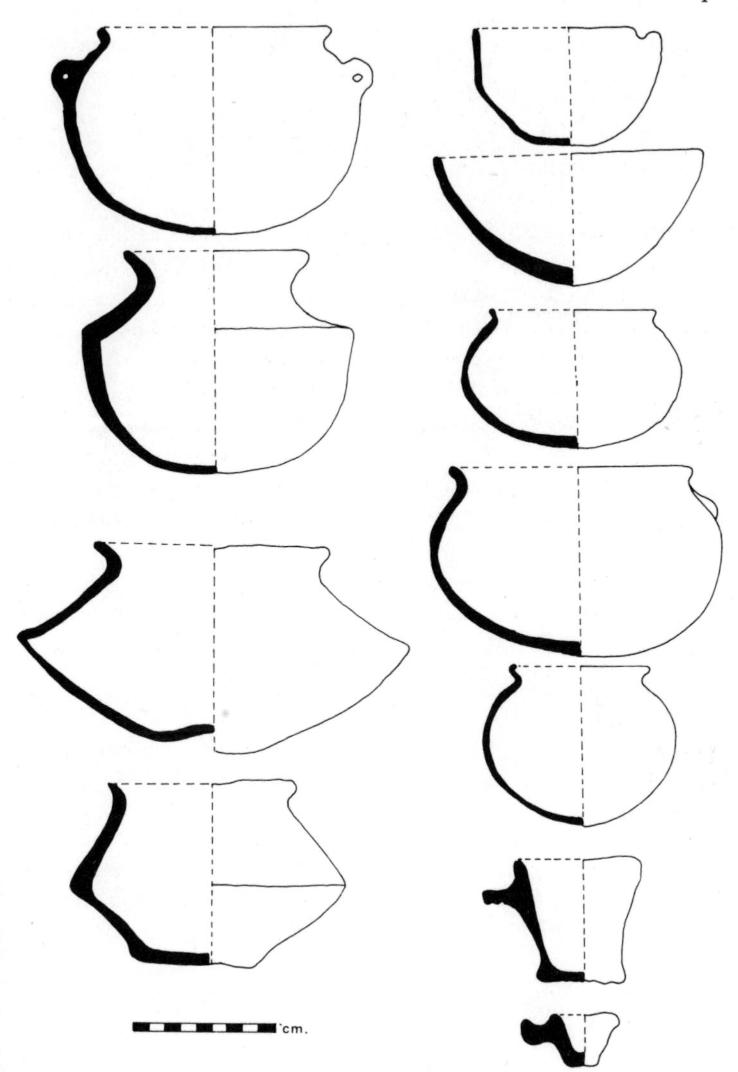

Fig. 10 Pre-talayotic pottery forms (after Rosselló Bordoy)

Analyses have shown a proportion of 7.7% – 9.7% of tin, with other impurities not exceeding 1%. The metal is thus a true bronze. A few discs and a button of lead may belong to this phase.

There are reports of very rich finds (for example at the Llucamet cave) which unfortunately cannot now be traced.

Chronology and phases. P. Veny's suggested chronology for the Balearic cave culture in Majorca is of great interest. His estimate that it lasted about eight centuries, from 2000 to 1200 BC seems reasonable, though this span is possibly a little short. For the intermediate dates of his successive phases, necessarily hypothetical in the absence of decisive data, Veny proposes 1800 BC and 1600 BC. I myself believe that the cave-culture could have begun a few centuries earlier, but also that it could have ended sooner. Possibly it is best to think of a slow succession of phases, for which rigid dates are not appropriate. Thus we might leave the years between 1400 and 1200 BC as transitional to the full establishment of Cyclopean culture.

We must also take account of the forthcoming chronology of Rosselló-Bordoy, whose chart, showing C-14 dates, follows.

A tentative systematic chronology of the prehistoric cultures of Majorca (after Rosselló-Bordoy)

PHASE	PRINCIPAL FEATURES		CHRONOLOGY	IMPORTANT SITES	CARBON 14 DA
	Types of site	*Material*			
Initial Settlement	Natural caves	Crude flints	4000–3800 BC	Cueva de Muleta, level 150 cm.	3984± 109 BC
	Rock shelters in northern zone	Fine bone points		Son Matge level 240 cm.	3800± 115 BC
Pre-talayotic	Natural caves Hut sites	Incised ware and plain truncated-cone shape v-perforated bone buttons, copper awls	2000 BC	Muleta (Soller) level 75 cm.	1960± 120
				Son Matge (Valldemosa) level 180 cm.	1870± 120
				Muertos-Gallard (Deyá) level 90 cm.	1840± 80
				Ca Na Cotxera (Muro) middle layer	1800± 100
	Simple artificial caves Complex artificial caves	Plain ware Bowls Globular and cylindrical forms		Ca Na Vidriera (Palma) Es Rafolet (Manacor) Son Toni Amer (Campos) Cala S. Vicens (Pollensa) Son Suñer (Palma)	

ayot I	Navetas *Navetiformes*	Decadent decorated ware Bone points	1500 BC	Pula: upper chamber abandonned Son Matge level 60cm.	1310 ± 59 1250 ± 100
	Multiple chamber caves	Plain ware, v-perforated bone buttons Triangular bone pendants (simple perforation) Copper awls Triangular bronze dagger Moulds Bracelets & Bronze swords	1300 BC	Son Oms (multiple cave) Son Oms: navetas under the stepped barrow	
ayot II	Free talayots: round & square Stepped barrows	Talayot ware Varied bronzes: axes, chisels, awls, ornaments	1300 BC	Son Real Escombrera: upper chamber S'Illot, central talayot lower level	1050 ± 120 1050 ± 80
		Bone points Querns	1000 BC	Son Real: upper chamber abandonned Capocorp: start (Lluchmayor) Son Serralta (Puigpuñent) Sa Canova (Artá)	1010 ± 80
yot III	Walled settlements, Houses accreted to talayots, Square houses Hypostyle courts	Analogous to II	1000 BC 750 BC	Ses Paisses (Artá) Capocorp, middle phase Rossells	
yot IV	Talayot settlements continue	Iron, Bronze and lead ornaments	750 BC	Cueva de Son Maimó (Petra) Lloseta? Son Bauçá (Palma) Son Cresta (Lluchmayor) S'Illot, house Son Oms, hearth	 680 ± 80 580 ± 100
	Rock-cut hypostyle rooms Cave (natural) burials: inhumation & incineration Sanctuaries (horseshoe plan) Burials in lime	Vitreous paste beads Native ware *Halskragen* Jingles Votive idols: doves & bulls	500 BC	Son Real cemetery Son Mari Antigors Illa dels Porros Muertos-Gallard 30 cm. level Son Matge 40 cm. level Son Matge 20 cm. level Son Puig, burials	 480 ± 200 280 ± 100 280 ± 100 250 ± 100 230 ± 80
an	Conquest by Q. Caecilius Metellus Breakdown and gradual abandonment of talayot settlements	Native copies of classical ware Imported ware: Campanian fine ware Native pots with toothed edge	123 BC	Sanctuary of Son Oms	
	Final abandonment of talayot settlements		AD 50	Final abandonment of Son Oms. Disappearance of the *Oppidum Bocchoritanum*	

Veny's first phase is illustrated by the rock-cut cave of Pont den Cabrera and the natural caves of Els Bous and Torrella. It is characterized by flint blade knives and the older type of incised ware (the Beaker group). Artificial caves are small and circular in plan, and have no corridor. This corresponds with Rosselló's first group.

Sites characteristic of phase 2 (lasting 200 years) are the rock-cut tomb of Son Suñer IX and the natural caves of Sa Canova and Son Marroig. The flint finds here are irregular flakes, and the pottery is the decorated ware of type B. Bronze appears with the pentagonal awl. Rock-cut caves have a circular chamber and a simple approach corridor.

Veny's third phase subdivides into three. IIIa (e.g. the Sa Tanca and Son Mulet rock-cut caves and Els Rossells and Lledoner among natural caves) includes awls, arrow-heads and triangular bronze daggers, with undecorated pottery, predominantly of simpler forms, hemispherical or jars with rudimentary neck. Rock chambers are elongated and have a short corridor or pit entrance. In phase IIIb, represented in the rock-cut cemeteries of Son Suñer, Son Toni Amer and Sa Mola and in the Cometa dels Morts, Sa Mata and Solleric natural caves, there are bronze awls and daggers, irregular, untrimmed flint flakes, and plain ware of all forms. The rock-cut chambers are elongated, with a central trench and funerary benches. The approach corridors are long, with 'double vestibules', and there is sometimes a narrow trench near the entrance cut at right angles to the tomb axis. Veny assigns the Cala Sant Vicens cemetery to an advanced phase, represented by an outer court, long approach corridors with 'double vestibule', and a high ledge inside the elongated chamber. Pottery is undecorated.

Natural and artificial caves in Minorca. We have very little information about the pre-Talayot culture of Minorca. Although cave sites and rock-cut tombs are known, they are far less numerous than in Majorca and lack the variety encountered on that island. Generally the tombs, which are cut in the soft rock, include a sloping approach ramp, at times stepped, leading to a type of antechamber and a large chamber, which may reach 10 m. in length, with small chambers of recesses in the sides. On occasion, central pillars of rock were left standing when the cave was dug. Classic examples are known at the S'Hostal site at Ciudadela and at Benimaymut. Ten of this type were explored at S'Hostal. The French

Fig. 11

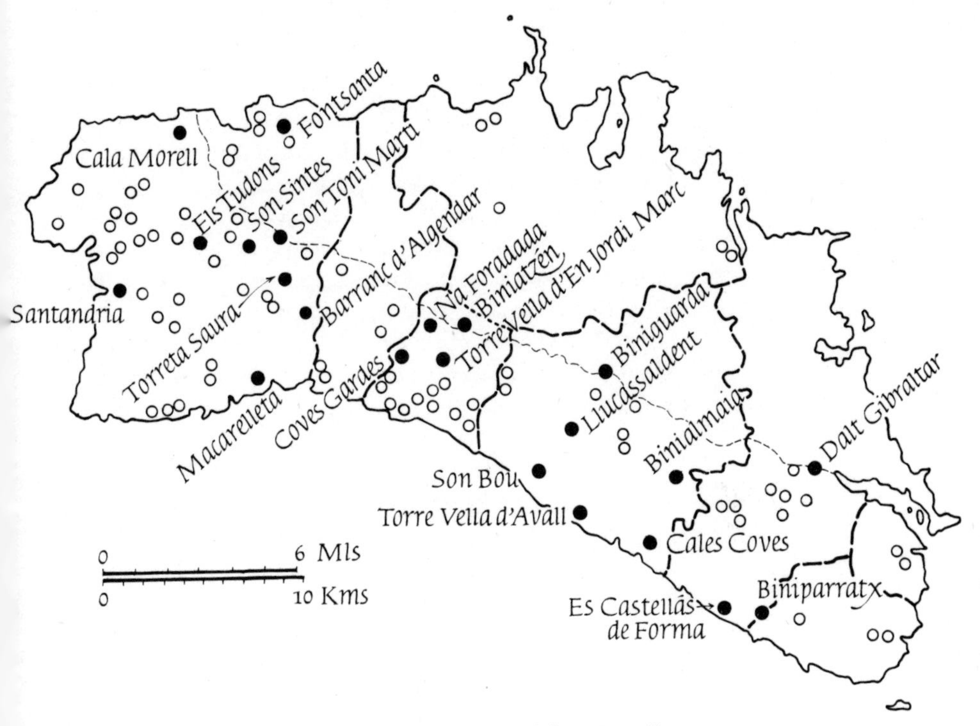

Fig. 11 Distribution of the principal cave sites in Minorca (after Mascaró)

anthropologist Verneau, who examined the bones found in one, reported features comparable with the brachycephalic French Neolithic race called Grenelle.

The large caves cut in the cliff face round certain coves and adjacent ravines I prefer to think were connected with the burial of already talayotic people; though it may be prudent to regard such burial sites as belonging to various periods, lasting into full talayotic times.

One highly characteristic group of natural caves is that in the district of Ciudadela; these have recently been explored by local amateurs, notably by G. Florit Piedrabuena, with interesting results. The caves were the Cova Murada, which contained stratified deposits, Sa Font de Sa Teula (Algayarens, La Vall) and Bellaventura. In the first cave *Myotragus* remains were found associated with human bones, bone tools, slipped ware and globular pottery decorated with bosses. The slip used is pale red or orange, recalling that in the final stage of the Sicilian

Stentinello culture. There were also v-perforated bone buttons. A fragment of an idol in hard stone has, in the opinion of the excavator, affinities with the 'ocular' idol from Tell Brak. In the Sa Font de Sa Teula cave, which has now been disturbed, Florit was able to establish a clear sequence. The lowest occupation layer produced red-painted pebbles, polished stone axes, fragments of copper ore from a nearby source, as well as bone points and spatulas, shell beads, v-perforated buttons, a perforated triangular piece of bone, and copper awls. A straight-sided jar, incised on its broad rim with a blunt point, was found in the ground beneath.

Pottery of late Neolithic aspect was found in the Bellaventura cave and in the Ses Arenes de dalt sand-pit in this same locality. In the Binimel-lá cave, Mercadal, a spiral bronze bracelet was found together with a trepanned skull.

CHAPTER III

The Cyclopean or Talayot Period

It is difficult to specify exactly when or in what form the techniques of cyclopean or megalithic construction were introduced into the Balearics, presumably by new and immigrant peoples. The surprising profusion and the massiveness of the building which ensued in the islands has set a stamp on the landscape which neither the passage of time nor depredation by later inhabitants has managed to efface.

The people of the islands have never ceased to be conscious of the grandiose ruins which they encounter at every turn, and which present such obstacles to farming. The most outstanding and considerable of the monuments are those called *talaia*, or *talayot*, the local word for 'watch-tower'. These, with other remains which are impressive for the amount of stone they contain, are also called *clapers* (or *clapers de gegants*), while *antigors* is also used as a general term for all types of ruin. When, on occasion, these assume particular shapes, they are called by special names, like the boat-shaped *navetas* or the strange megalithic *taulas* of Minorca. Ever since the eighteenth century the different types and their significance have been the subject of innumerable studies, by amateurs and scholars, and these are summarized in the second subsection of the Introduction. Only when J. Colominas began to excavate scientifically in 1916 did the role of the larger monuments which were still standing become clear: they were integral features in settlements which had been walled urban groupings, with talayots either around or inside the enclosure.

The culture which utilized these cyclopean techniques continued without a break from its beginnings until the imposed changes of Roman times. We are justified in giving it a single name, the Talayot culture, from its most obvious and best known feature.

There is an unmistakable uniformity of cultural and chronological development between Majorca and Minorca in the Talayot period, notwithstanding marked differences between the islands with regard to preservation of their antiquities and, more significantly, in the special monuments which are confined to the smaller of the two. I propose, therefore, to discuss the evidence from the two islands in successive sections, leaving until last any attempt at a historical conspectus, consistent with the chronology which Carbon 14 now seems to make possible. We have to concede that the culture's span of one thousand to fifteen hundred years, even when conditions were changing, is too short to leave much stratigraphy on which chronology could be based. This greatly handicaps any subdivision of the period, and the recognition of survivals or influences.

THE TALAYOT CULTURE IN MAJORCA

It was Emille Cartailhac who began the scientific study of Majorcan talayots, and his work was developed by Colominas. Recently my own research, with the assistance of young collaborators, together with the work of G. Lilliu and his assistants at the important site of Ses Paisses, Artá, has clarified certain problems and laid foundations for the growing body of knowledge of the culture which increasing numbers of younger archaeologists are now providing.

Fig. 12

The sites to be studied on Majorca comprise, among others, the walled settlements with their talayots, the navetas or boat-shaped structures, and enclosures in the mountain zones.

The settlements. Colominas deserves credit for recognising that the typical site on Majorca is basically a settlement, although he had often to excavate in unfavourable conditions where destruction had left only piles of stones round the talayots, which alone remained standing, either flanking the sites or inside the enclosed area. His initial excavation was in the ruined settlement of Son Juliá, Lluchmayor, where he uncovered a fifty-metre length of the surrounding wall. The outer face was formed of courses of rectangular blocks, up to 2 m. long, while the inner face, which completed the houses built against it, was of smaller stones. The intervening wall core, from 1 to 2 m. thick, consisted of stones and rubble. The houses had been added to, with proof of occupation up to Roman times. Beside the wall there were paired (or 'twin') houses of apsidal plan, 13 m. long. Their median wall was 2 m. thick. A wooden pillar would have supported the roof, which was some 3 m. high. Talayot pottery was found inside these paired houses, with bone points, querns, and a bronze 'mirror'.

Another important site was that of El Pedregar, Lluchmayor, which

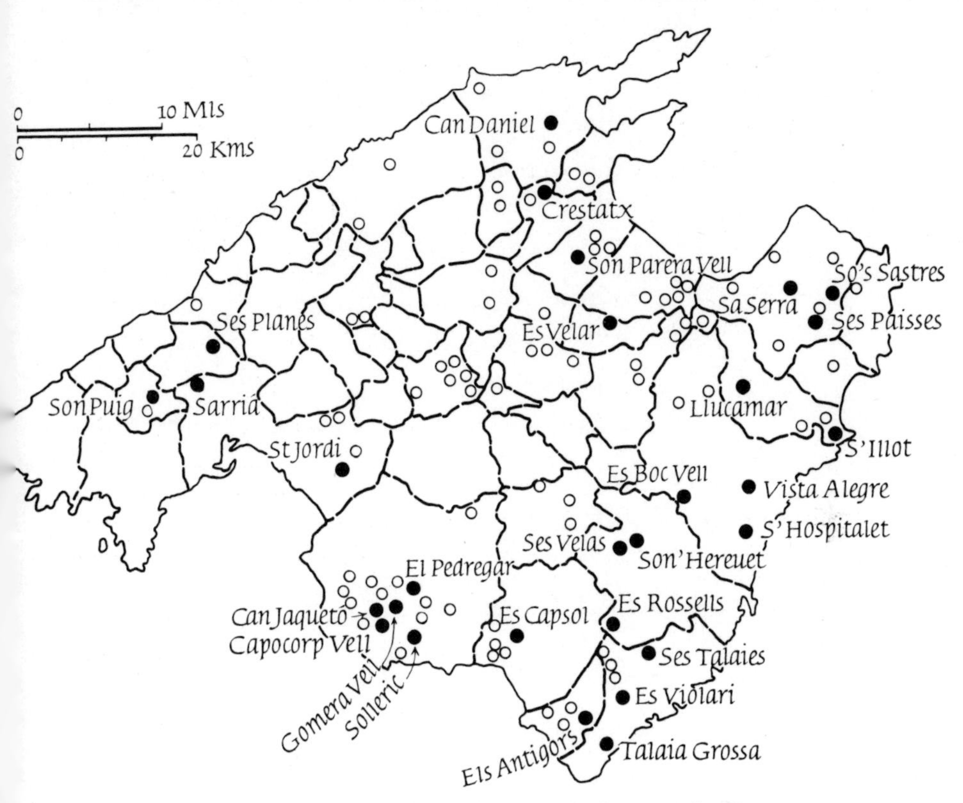

Fig. 12 Distribution of the principal walled settlements and talayot complexes in Majorca (after Mascaró)

is now destroyed. Part of the wall and a gate were preserved, the wall composed of alternating uprights and parallel courses of well-dressed squared stones. Several talayots were built against it and there were others inside the enclosure. Up to thirty houses could be traced and the walls between them were of horizontal slabs, with an earth and rubble core. Two or three pillars in each house must have supported the roof. Finds of talayot pottery and a small bronze head of a warrior, together with Roman ware, suggest there was a stratigraphy, which unfortunately was not properly examined.

Colominas obtained fuller results at the Capocorp site, inside the township of Lluchmayor, and recently the excavation has been resumed by Rosselló and Font Obrador. A length of coursed wall facing is clearly visible here, with a tower of truncated-pyramidal outline at

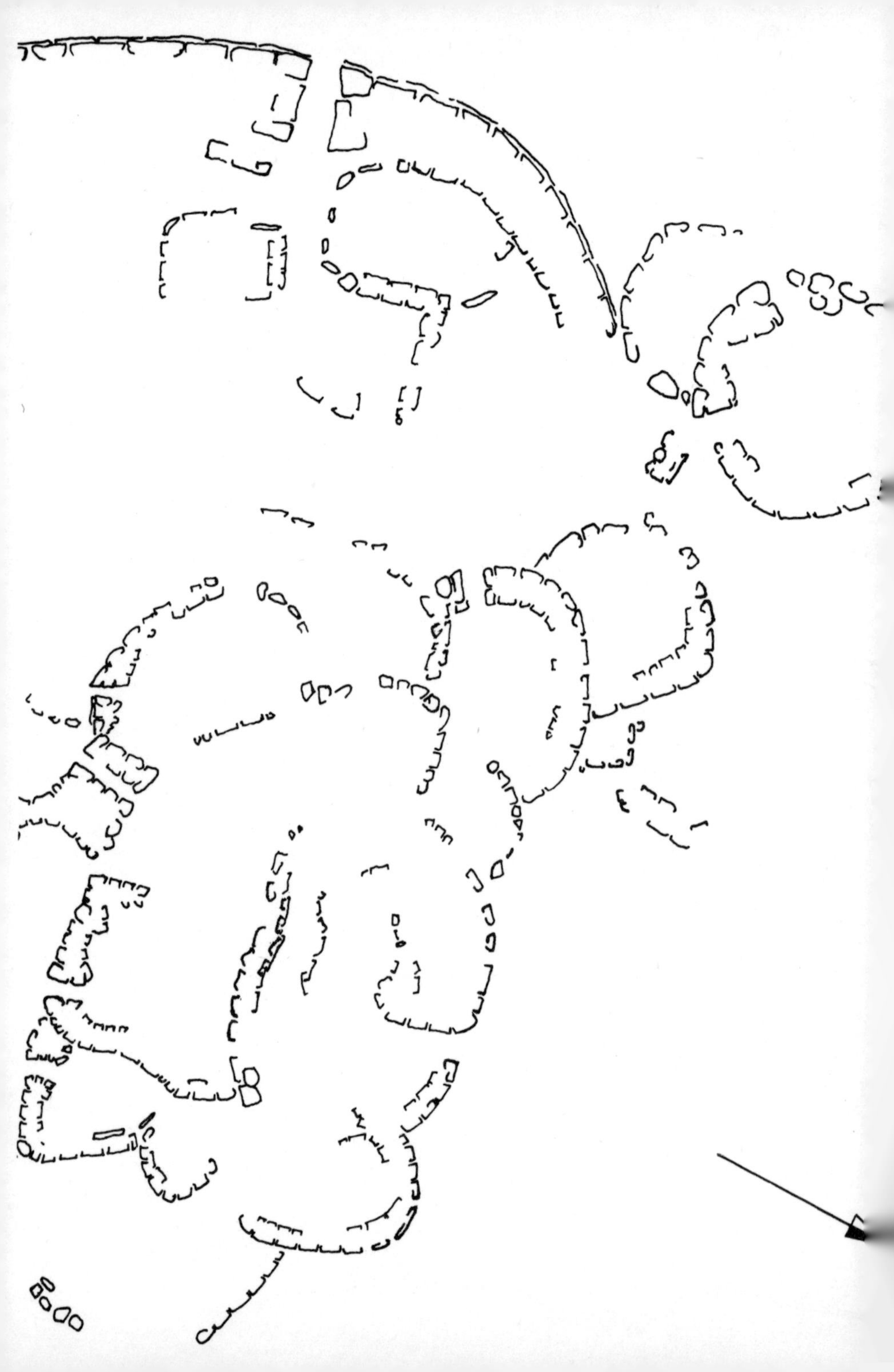

20m.

Fig. 13 The walled settlement of S'Illot, Sant Llorenç, Majorca (after Dehn and Frey)

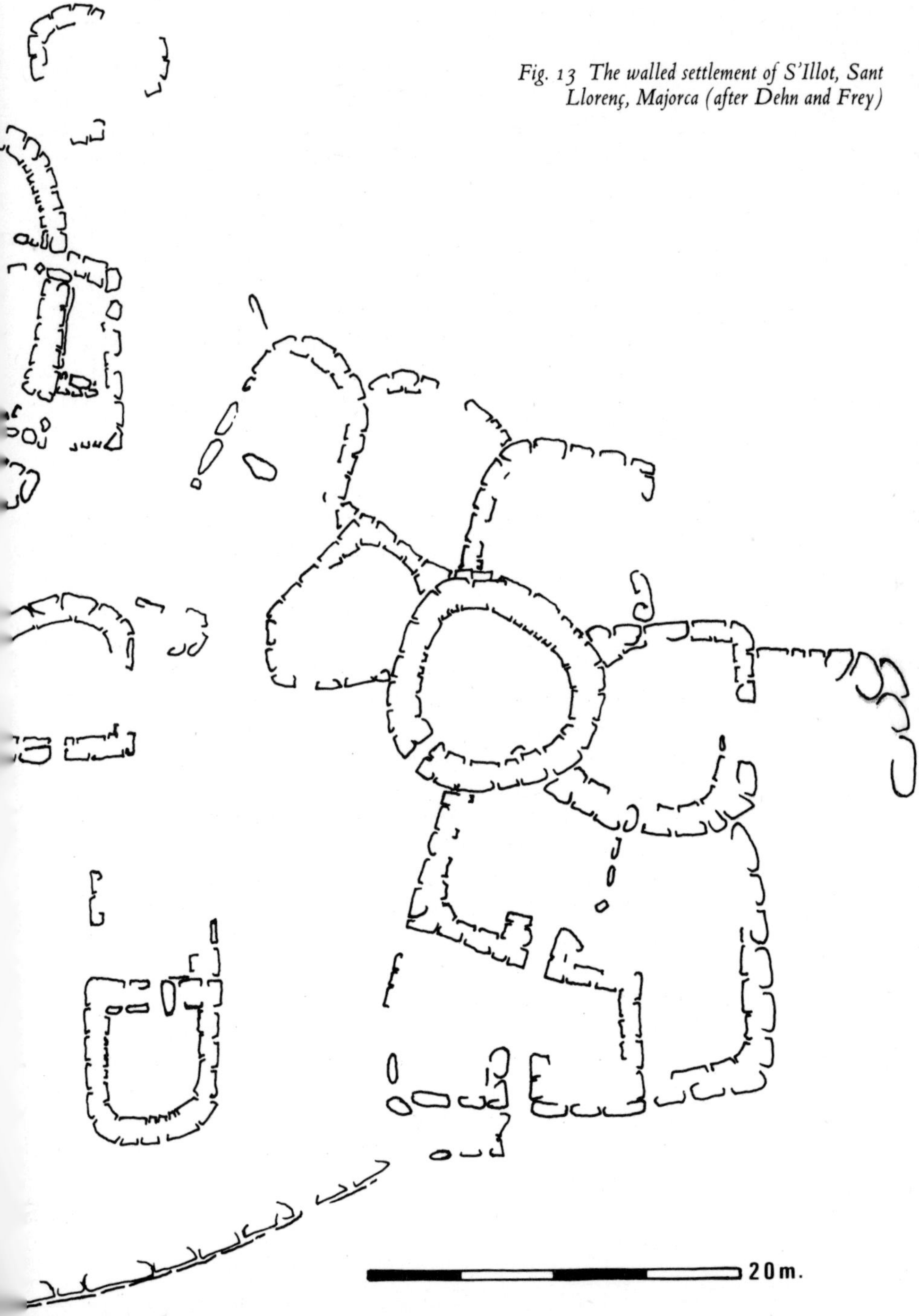

either end. The houses, of various forms but mostly rectangular, are built against the wall. Twelve of them were excavated and contained central columns to support the roof, with some remains of stairways which would have led to an upper storey. There were abundant pottery finds, bone points, querns and bronze bracelets. One of the talayots contained a two-storey chamber. There was a quantity of ashes on the upper floor, though the lower was almost empty. The spiral gallery running between the two contained a burial, no doubt a later intrusion.

Plate 18

Two important settlements have been examined in the Ses Salines district, that of Els Antigors and Mitjá Gran. The first site is extensive, with a wall flanked by talayots, of which three were excavated. These were circular, and two had a central pillar. One contained hand-made pottery, bone points and burnt bones. In the so-called Talaia Joana, which occupied the centre of the settlement, it is possible to see how the central chamber was roofed by means of flat stone slabs, supported by a pillar. The chamber measures 6.5 m. in diameter and the walls are 4 m. thick, with a maximum height of 5.5 m. The central column measures 1.5 m., and there are obvious traces of fire action. The finds from the excavation include abundant coarse, hand-made pottery, two bronze spear-heads of tubular form and the blade of an iron dagger with a central rib. A greater number of bronzes came from the excavation of some houses at Mitjá Gran (axes, daggers and gouges).

Fig. 13

An impressive wall, roughly oval in plan, surrounds the small settlement of Es Rossells, Felanitx. The wall at S'Illot, Sant Llorenç des Cardassar, where a German mission has recently excavated under the leadership of Professors Dehn and Frey, is less well preserved, though still imposing where it is visible.

Fig. 14

Much attention has been paid to the Ses Paisses settlement, less than 1 km. south-east of Artá, on account of certain features visible in its walls. Finally, the site was proposed for a joint Spanish-Italian project, and excavation began in 1959 under the direction of G. Lilliu, assisted by Biancofiore and Atzeni. The results have enabled Lilliu to propose a hypothesis of chronological stages within the Talayot culture.

The settlement lies on a hill and is near a spring. It is encircled by a great wall composed of small stones, faced externally by large stone slabs. Four gateways can be distinguished, the most monumental being the south-eastern one, which is preserved in all its glory. The second is a

Plate 13

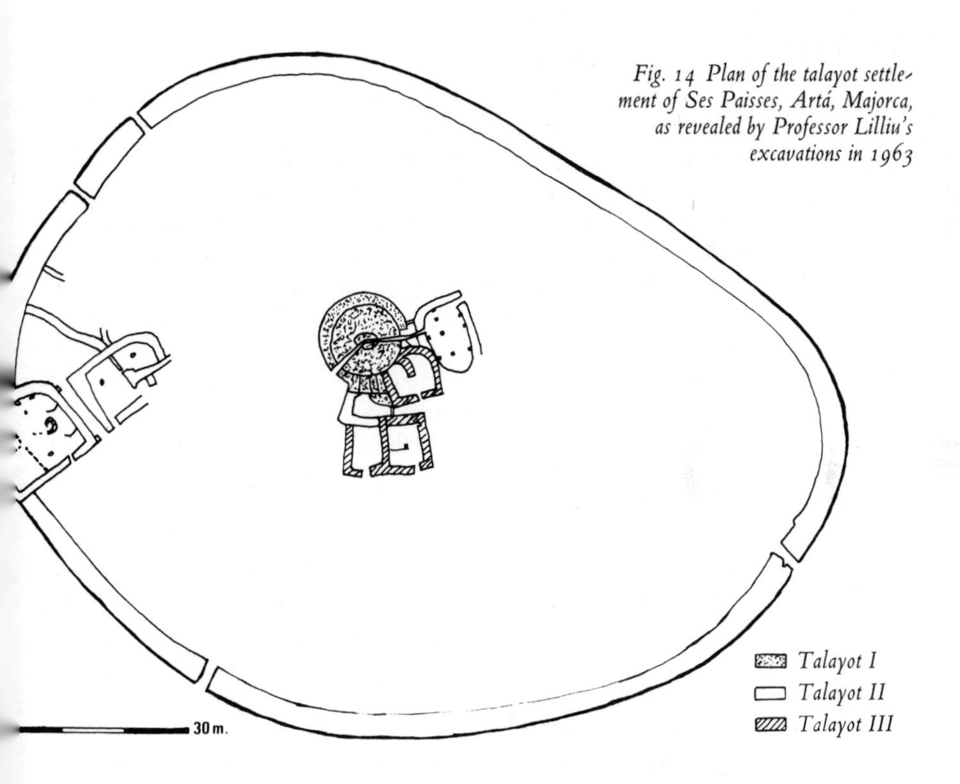

Fig. 14 Plan of the talayot settlement of Ses Paisses, Artá, Majorca, as revealed by Professor Lilliu's excavations in 1963

little lower down, facing north-west, while remains of the other two lie to the south-west and north-east respectively. The total length of the perimeter measures 374 m., and the site measures 94 × 106 m. at its widest points. One of the wall slabs weighs about eight tons, and there are doubtless others larger still.

Lilliu began excavating in the talayot which occupies a somewhat eccentric position in the middle of the settlement, forming the dominant feature around which the houses are grouped. It is a solid tower of truncated-conical outline, about 4.5 m. high and with a total volume of over 400 cubic m. A narrow passage, through which it is difficult to pass, since it is little more than 80 cm. wide, runs across the base of the talayot, branching at the centre into two arms, one 4.55 and the other 2.20 m. long. Lilliu surmised that a buttress built against the walls might have served as a ramp leading to a hypothetical chamber higher up in the tower.

Surrounding the two are various houses. Perhaps the best example which has been excavated in this context is House No. 3; it is rectangular (7.60× 3.70 m.) and fairly crudely built, with a sloping roof. In this it contrasts with other houses nearby, which appear to have had ridged roofs and are therefore probably of later date. The excavation revealed three occupation layers, and on these Lilliu has based a three-fold division of the Majorcan Talayot period. Although three such stages, with some variation in the limits, had already been recognized by other archaeologists, I feel it is Lilliu's evidence which affords the best support.

The upper layer, Talayot III, may be termed Hellenistic-Roman, and contains Roman pottery (amphoras) and Campanian ware of the third and second centuries BC. The local pottery is fairly coarse and includes globular, cylindrical and conical forms, with flat bases or a crude foot. There are handles or lugs (in one instance in the form of a stylized ox head) near the rim. One type found with late material, both in the talayots and in sepulchral caves, is a small conical vase with slightly concave walls. The finds continue into the second century AD, showing how long occupation lasted in the settlements. There are abundant animal bones.

The second layer in the Ses Paisses house corresponds to the middle Talayot, or Talayot II, phase. It reaches 2.50 m. in depth, and contains a quantity of ashes and bone indicative of prolonged or intensive occupation. Included in it at one level was an irregularly paved floor. Finds comprise the inevitable bone points, mortars and querns. As always, the pottery is crude, generally dark in colour with either a porous or smoothed surface. There were very rare examples of what Lilliu terms *para-bucchero*, on account of its polished black surface. The pottery in general is rather more carefully made than in the later layers. The pots have a conical or hemispherical outline and the large usually ovoid, vessels have everted rims with lugs in place of handles. Occasionally these have projecting extensions. The Talayot II phase is thought to run from the eighth to the fifth century BC.

It seems established that during Talayot II standards of wall construction, with less regularly coursed blocks, were inferior to those of period III. The strange passage in the central talayot at Ses Paisses should perhaps be attributed to the earlier period. Its purpose remains a mystery, but we cannot avoid recalling the passages in classical texts which tell of hiding-places where the population concealed themselves when the

Romans overran the country. The finds of bone and stone in the passage are reminiscent of an older phase, but the pottery is well made (superior to period III ware), without handles, and has already lost any carination in the profile.

In Lilliu's opinion period II represents the zenith of talayot culture, a view we may perhaps accept. A number of factors could be responsible. The period was one of intense naval activity in the Mediterranean and marked the start of true colonization in the West; a Punic colony was established on Ibiza. From the sixth century onwards we know that mercenaries from the Balearics began to be engaged in various areas round the Mediterranean, making themselves a reputation so that their services were sought after. Those who returned home would bring booty, or new skills, as well as a taste for novel ways of life and art. The period from the ninth to the sixth centuries BC also marked the zenith of the distinctive nuraghic culture of Sardinia. There were undeniably connections between the islands, and perhaps the influences were mutual.

The layer below, resting on the natural rock, represents Talayot I, and here are found archaic elements which followed the pre-Talayot phase, without any of the novel features directly indicative of colonial activity. It must, then, date from before the eighth century BC, but its initial date is not so easily defined. The central talayot at Ses Paisses is assumed to date from this first period, though the curious passage which runs through it might be the work of period II. One large rectangular house (with rounded corners) produced finds from all three periods, but its principal interest lies in the presence of several central pillars, which look as though the whole might form a hypostyle court.

Plates 14, 15

As is always the danger on composite sites, it is possible that the upper layers may incorporate material displaced from lower down. Much confusion of evidence has been experienced in Balearic archaeology, as for instance when it was argued that much of the talayot material was of Roman date, because Roman remains are found with it.

During the final phase of talayot occupation there may have been, with the *pax romana*, something of a revival, which is reflected in the finds. There is an increase in wheel-turned ware, and quantities of modelled bronzes, lead and silver finds, glass, polychrome vitreous pastes, fired clay figurines, bells, silver bracelets etc. Iberian pottery also came in from the peninsula.

In this way we may deduce a terminal date for the first phase of the Talayot culture; but we are left with the puzzle of its beginning. Bosch Gimpera and his followers favoured a date around 1200 BC for the influx of cyclopean techniques. This seemed consistent with the end of the El Argar culture – an argument which today is no longer permissible – and with what we know of disturbances connected with the Sea Peoples and consequent ethnic distruption. Later, it became fashionable to shorten the chronologies of the Mediterranean and Europe in general, and a much later initial date was proposed. Carbon 14 readings have now restored the higher dates, so that a beginning even as early as 1400 BC would not seem excessive. Talayot culture does include some archaic elements (dolmens, for example, and possible connections between the naveta and forms of Early Bronze Age tomb on the mainland). The Ses Paisses settlement proves that the first Talayot period cannot have been short. Its roughly constructed central talayot could belong to this initial phase, a conclusion apparently supported by various tower-like structures which have recently been studied in Corsica.

The Majorcan talayot and its forms. Present-day research into Balearic prehistory attempts to study settlements in conjunction with their cemeteries, but for a long time the talayot was the basic object of the island's archaeology. Colominas recognized it as only one element in an 'urban' complex, either strengthening the external defensive wall (Capocorp) or as the initial or nuclear structure in the settlement – or, maybe, having some other, less definable, function while still part of the complex. In many instances the towers alone have been left standing as a landmark, because of the difficulty of removing them, while the surrounding buildings, especially on the cultivated plain, have either been destroyed or rendered unrecognizable without being investigated first.

We should like eventually to complete an inventory of the talayots on Majorca and Minorca and group them in some way to reveal the settlements to which they belong, these being the true units which interest us. But it is still not possible to classify all the talayots into categories and give dates. There is so undeniable a contrast between circular examples containing a chamber with corbelled roof (false cupola) and central pillar on the one hand, and the simple solid ones on the other, that one is tempted to separate the first type under a special name. At the same time, there is nothing to establish the priority of any particular type. Did the more elaborate examples reach us from the East, and subsequently degenerate in isolation, or was it no more than a transmitted idea which developed locally? I confess I am undecided between these possibilities.

Fig. 15

There is an obvious distinction between talayots having a rectangular ground-plan and the circular ones; also between pyramidal talayots and those having a truncated cone-shaped outline, the latter being by far the more frequent. The variants occur together.

Among the talayots of truncated cone-shaped outline, some are built as solid towers, although they do include some narrow passages, ramps, and interior chambers. Others, by contrast, enclose a considerable space, having a central chamber with false cupola, on occasion with a central pillar and a well-built entrance.

The outer facing of the talayots varies from perfect courses of ashlar blocks to irregularly set stones in the cruder examples. But the absence of mortar is general; the blocks are fitted together in drystone masonry. Where there was a central chamber, roofing took the form of large stone slabs supported on the walls with each successive layer overlapping until the space was covered over; the central pillar, where present, served as an additional support. Frequently the trunks of the islands' abundant wild olive were used as beams. We find them in the Capocorp settlement and in the Minorcan talayot of Sant Agustí Vell.

It is impossible to make a representative selection from among the hundreds of talayots known, a task which must await a monographic study of the monuments. J. Mascaró has devoted many years of patient labour to the preparation of such a compilation, and we are indebted to him for many plans. Among the rectangular talayots we may cite that of Vilarets (Llenaire, Pollensa) as an example of solid construction, the largely destroyed Es Figueral (Son Real, Santa Margarita), with its small entrance passage and tiny side chamber, Son Siurana de dalt at Alcudia, with an incipient entrance corridor, Es Torrent at Ses Salinas, with an extensive central chamber which is also rectangular, and several at Sa Canova de Morell (Artá).

Plate 19

The circular talayots sometimes contain large chambers, with one or two entrances. The Son Lluch talayot at Puig de Son Corb, Son Servera, for example, has two. There are many examples with a short entrance corridor, roofed with flat slabs. Son Coll Nou at Algaida has

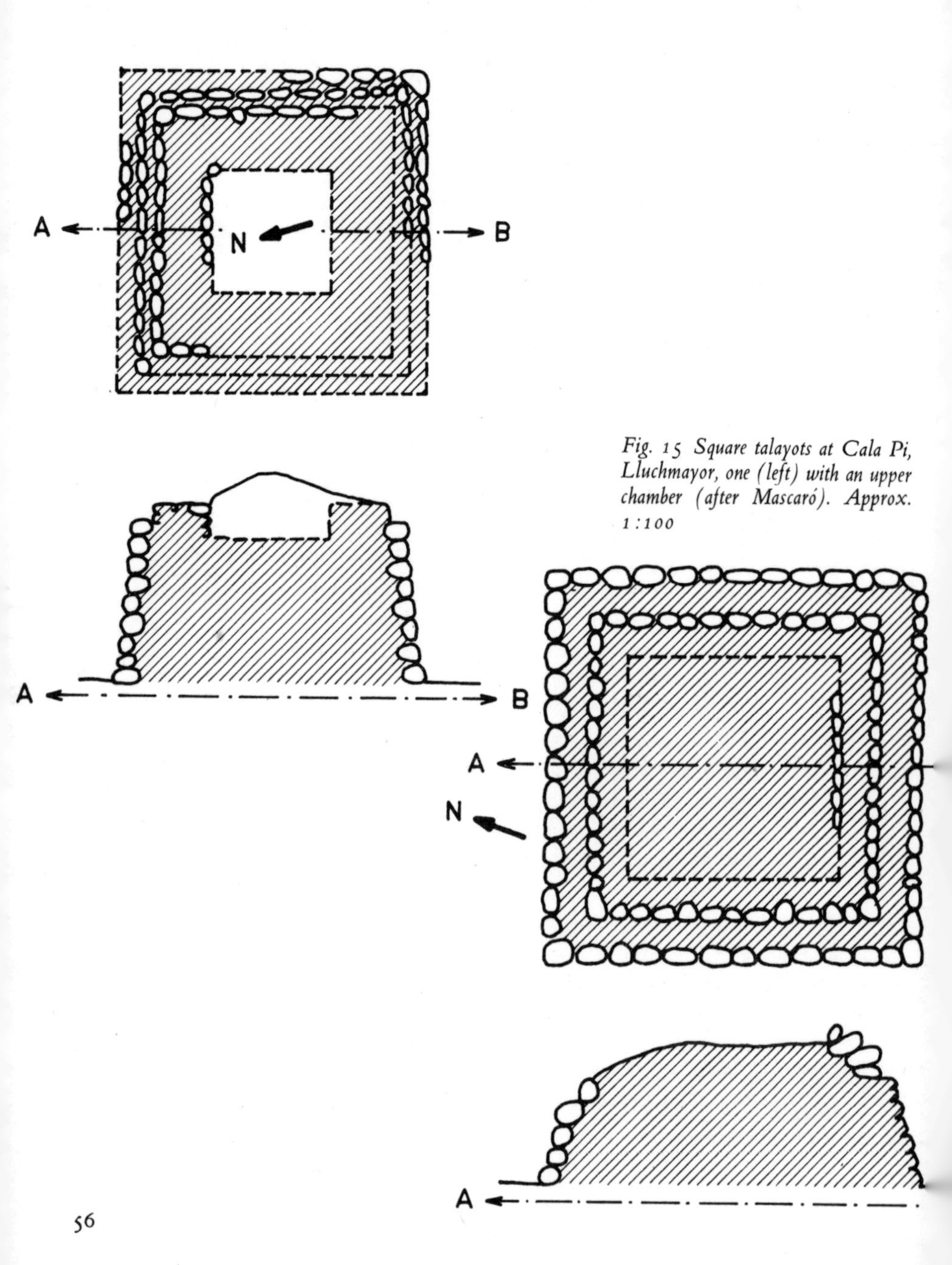

Fig. 15 Square talayots at Cala Pi, Lluchmayor, one (left) with an upper chamber (after Mascaró). Approx. 1:100

Fig. 16 Plan and section of the circular talayot of Son Lluch, Son Servera, Majorca (after Mascaró). 1 : 100

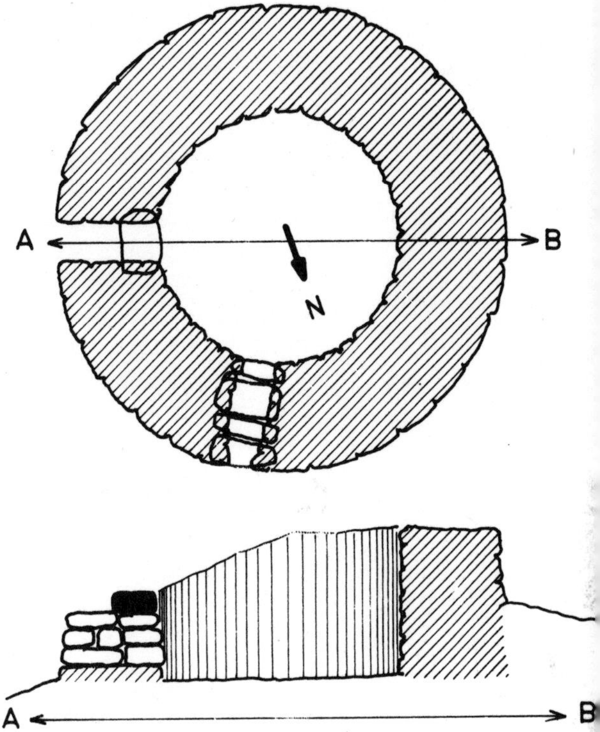

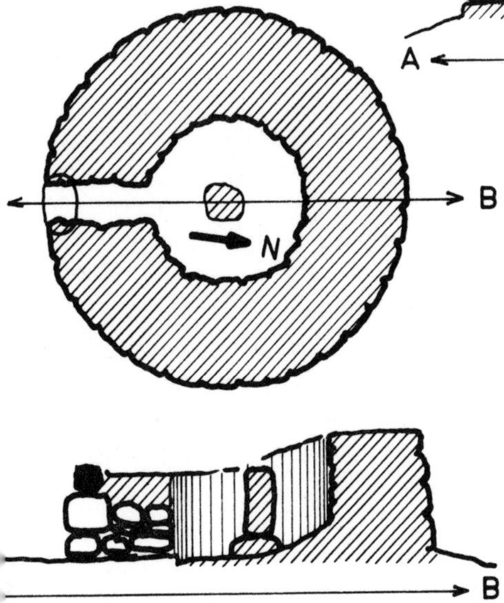

Fig. 17 Plan and section of the circular talayot with central pillar, Sa Plana d'Albarca, Escorca (after Mascaró). Approx. 1 : 100

two such entrances, a standard corridor and a longer, narrow one. In some of the circular talayots the entrance corridor is extended by a setting of slabs, forming a sort of interior corridor, as at Son Sastre at Inca, and S'Heretat at Capdepera, where the outer corridor is angled.

A typical feature is a central pillar composed of only lightly dressed blocks, which narrows towards the base, forming what has been called a 'Mediterranean column'. Bellver Ric at Manacor, Sa Plana D'Albarca at Escorca, Marola at Lluchmayor, Sa Casa Nova de Pina at Algaida offer examples. At Sa Plana D'Albarca the pillar is monolithic. Talayot B at Capocorp has a pillar of megalithic stones which leans against one of the chamber walls. The finest talayot of this class is Clova des Xot (Sa Canova de Morell), near Artá. This is a masterpiece, built from large, well-dressed blocks laid in almost perfect courses. We can only regret our inability to decide whether such a monument resulted from an impulse freshly arrived from what we are wont to term East Mediterranean centres, or represents the climax of evolution from the solid-built talayots with corridors and small chambers.

Fig. 16

In some instances, only the central pillar has survived, while all other remains of what was probably a talayot have disappeared. This is the likely explanation of the fine El Rafal pillar at Montuiri, known as the Campanari des Moros, and of the magnificent example which was adjacent to the San Juan airfield near Palma, before being sacrificed to that modern ogre, the aeroplane. There are also solid-built talayots which are penetrated by a short corridor, like those of Garonda and Sa Talaya, both at Lluchmayor. In the latter, the little corridor is irregular and zigzag in form.

Plate 17

Turning to rarer variants, there are first those which have two chambers, at different levels; a ramp, generally spiral, leads from one to the other. Another type includes a gallery which penetrates into the body of the tower, or which may cross it completely, for a reason we cannot explain. The Son Oms talayot and the talayot in the Artá settlement are examples.

Some of the talayots are stepped, and these include Son Oms. There must have been external stairways, for reaching the upper platform or galleries high in the tower.

Plate 9

The form and construction of doorways and corridors is also interesting. Mascaró has distinguished two kinds of entrances: those with three monolithic blocks, forming jambs and lintel, and those with a monolithic lintel supported by two or more stones on either side. Certain talayots have more than one entrance, as at Son Lluch, where the second is in the form of a roughly set arch. Entrances are sometimes to be found some distance above the level of the surrounding ground.

Fig. 17

The talayot corridors are roofed with flat slabs, the inner surface of which has been dressed. The majority of the corridors are straight, and fairly long. Sometimes such a corridor begins in the houses built against the side of the talayot, rather than in its external wall. This applies to the talayot we have mentioned in the Artá settlement. Not only may corridors run completely across the talayot, but occasionally they link its chamber with buildings outside. This happens in the S'Illot settlement (Sant Llorenç des Cardassar), and at Es Mitjá Gran (Ses Salinas).

All this points to the talayots having been intended for defence. In most instances people could not possibly have lived in them. Although they were not infrequently used for burial, I do not believe they were constructed for this purpose: the usual form of burial among the people of the settlements was in cemeteries of artificial caves. We shall see, however, that the large collective tombs, or navetas, which are found in Minorca were apparently not usual on Majorca, where Son Real is so far the only example known.

Boat-shaped structures (navetiformes). I have already commented on the enormous variety of cyclopean structures found in the Balearics, and pointed out how impossible it is to draw up a classification, of form and purpose, applicable to them all. There has been some terminological confusion with regard to buildings of more or less horseshoe-shaped plan, which abound in Majorca and Minorca. It has long been the practice to call them 'navetas,' although they lack the features of the true navetas of Minorca. It is now agreed they should be called 'boat-shaped houses' (*naviformes* or *navetiformes*).

Fig. 18

The irregularly built walls of these elongated horseshoe-shaped houses may be either parallel or divergent, and they are sometimes thicker round the apsidal end. The houses are frequently found two or more together, and at times there are larger groups, forming a whole settlement, as at Bóquer on Majorca, where the houses are surrounded by a wall of talayot type. There are several similar groups in the neighbourhood of the Sant Vicens bay on the same island. Altogether Mascaró has

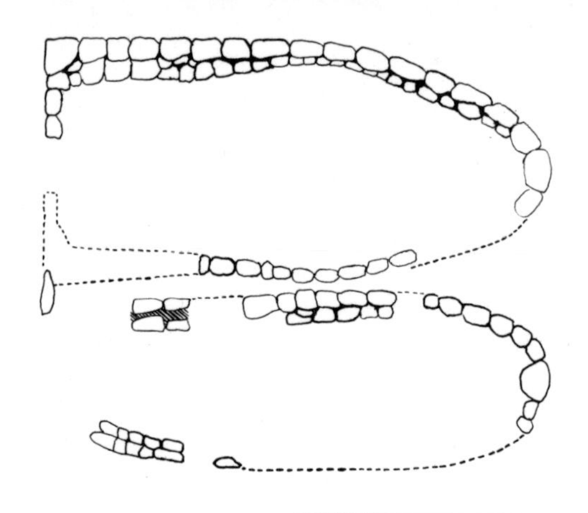

Fig. 18 Twin boat-shaped houses at Sa Vall, Son Maciá, Manacor, Majorca (after Rosselló Bordoy)

reported twenty-five single houses and a further twenty-five groups or settlements. Roselló Bordoy has studied and classified more than forty such houses on Majorca. Similar examples are found on Minorca.

Excavation has shown that these structures are usually true houses. There is some variation in plan: most examples have the extended horse-shoe-shaped outline, and there may be a bulge about the centre of the long walls; otherwise the external walls are almost parallel, with a more or less markedly semi-circular or ogival end. In another variant the house widens out away from the apse. In some instances the external plan can be apsidal while the inner room is rectangular in outline. Sometimes a pit at the rounded end of the house leads into a small subterranean chamber (Es Rafal, Palma).

Excavation of a boat-shaped house in the Sa Punta settlement at Son Carrió, Felanitx, in 1946, produced pottery, querns, bone points, wheat and carbonized barley, and six bronze spear-heads. As many as five houses of apsidal plan were studied at Son Mayor, Felanitx, one of which contained a necklace of polished stone. At Can Roig nou in the same district, Rosselló excavated a triple boat-shaped structure, in which the houses retained a somewhat horseshoe-shaped form. Excavation revealed a central chamber, measuring 16× 4.9 m. on the outside and 11.75× 2.6 m. inside. Its height was less than 2.5 m. The excavation of this significant site (in which Rosselló was assisted by Miss Pell, E. Ripoll and M. Oliva, among others) was one of the most careful to be conducted on Majorca. Rosselló inferred from it three successive stages, the first of which would have preserved the tradition of the naveta. This is evident in the underlying pebble layer, the apse buttressing, and in details of construction, such as the perfectly fitting large rectangular or polygonal blocks in the apse, as well as in the find of a triangular bone button with v-perforation. We should almost feel inclined to believe the structure was initially intended for burials, were it not for the absence of human remains, and likewise of the standard entrance features of the funerary navetas, known from the neighbouring island. At some undefined point in the Talayot period, the buildings were occupied as dwellings, as is shown by finds of bone points and more particularly by the pottery. Pre-Talayot or early Talayot forms are absent, while lug handles predominate. There were quantities of wheel-turned pottery in the eastern chamber. Although there is no *terra sigillata*, there is a little fine grey ware, including Campanian. The site was disturbed in medieval times, when the central chamber was subdivided to make several rooms, and still later it was again utilized. Very impressive is the boat-shaped room at Magalluf (Calviá) studied by C. Enseñat.

Other interesting excavations include those by Colominas at Son Juliá, where a bronze mirror similar to that from Lloseta was found. In a double house at Es Coll, Manacor, Alcover discovered two burials under slabs, with a bracelet, a copper knife, vitreous beads, bone points and goat horns. Excavations at Can Roig produced the two valves of a mould for a triangular dagger and a bracelet. Finally, there have been exciting discoveries recently at Son Oms (which has also fallen victim to the demands of an airport). Underneath the stepped talayot were found splendid navetiform rooms, with cyclopean walls.

The cemetery of Son Real. One of the most important developments in Majorcan archaeology in recent years has been the excavation of the cemetery of Son Real. Apart from its intrinsic interest, it has demonstrated how great the gaps in our knowledge still are, and what surprises yet await us, hidden beneath the soil of the islands.

Fig. 19

The site, lying on the Son Real estate in the Can Picafort suburb of Santa Margarita, centrally on the large bay of Alcudia, is so close to the sea that a part has been destroyed by its action. The cemetery extends onto the nearby islet, Illa dels Porros. Since people have long been aware of what is locally known as the 'Phoenician cemetery', several of its tombs have been pillaged. The priest of Can Picafort was able to recover some

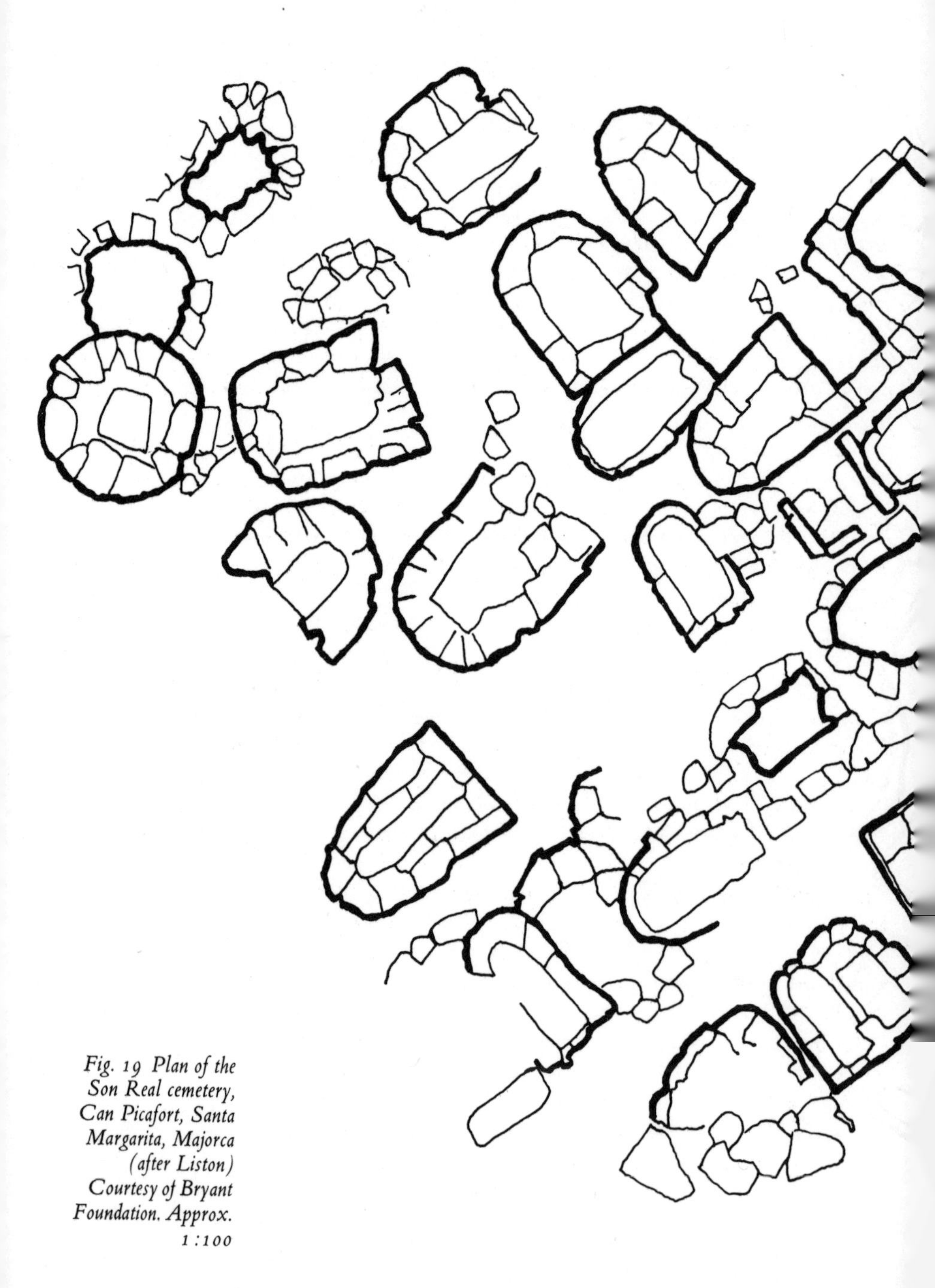

Fig. 19 Plan of the Son Real cemetery, Can Picafort, Santa Margarita, Majorca (after Liston) Courtesy of Bryant Foundation. Approx. 1:100

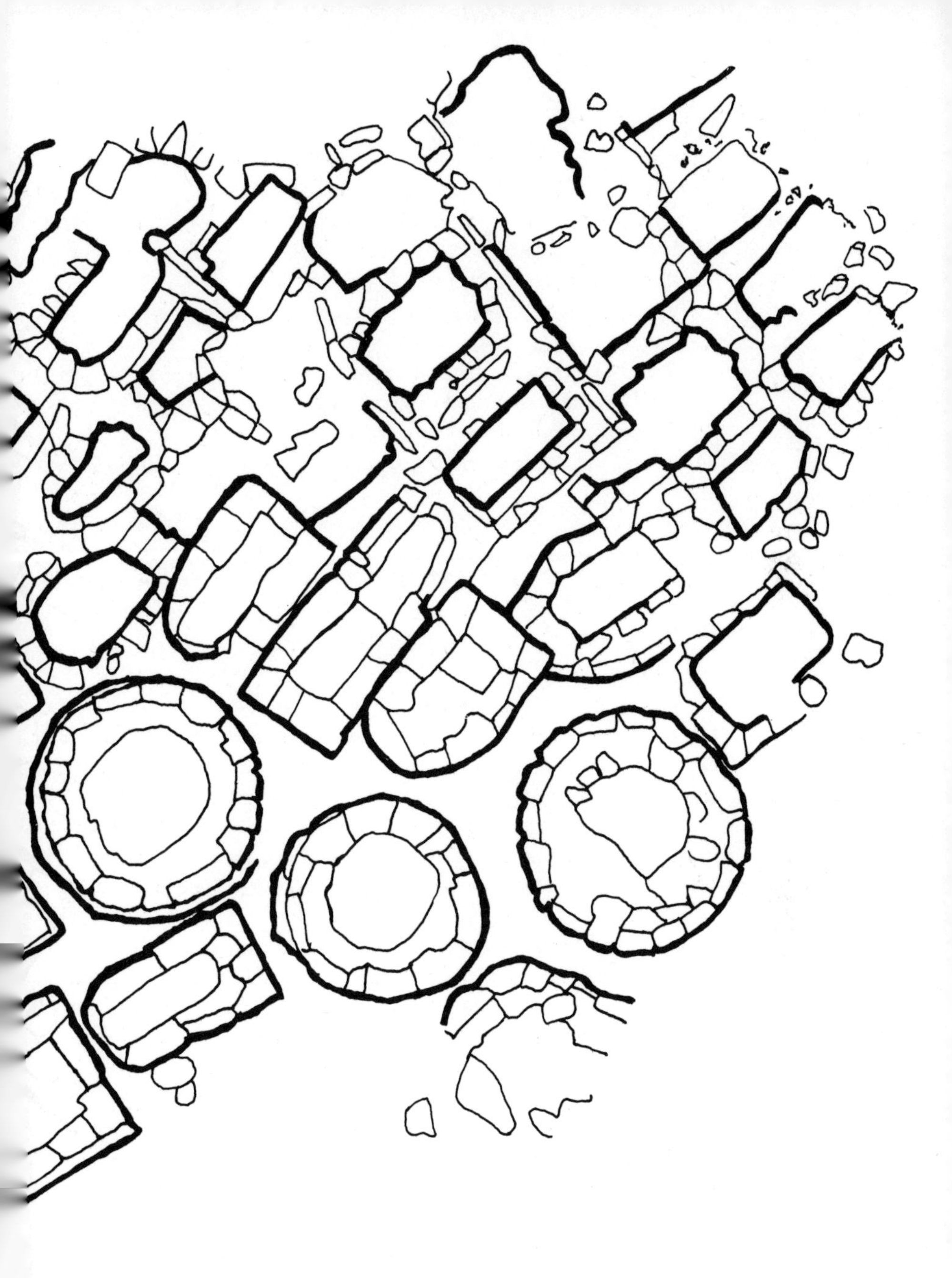

human bones salvaged from the site, and B. Enseñat managed to acquire bones and skulls, one of which had been trepanned. It is not surprising, therefore, that when the Bryant Foundation began excavating at nearby Pollentia, the cemetery came to be adopted as an additional project, because of the interest it immediately aroused.

The excavations, begun in 1957, have continued until recently, under the direction of Professor M. Tarradell (assisted by, among others, Arribas, Amorós, Pla, Woods, as well as several American architects working on the plans). It was soon realized that the site was of greater significance than had been supposed. Initial excavation revealed a quantity of tombs of various forms – round, rectangular and boat-shaped – set close together with hardly any space between. The quality of their construction and the fact that many were intact led us to cherish the hope that this site would be exceptional, in richness and preservation. As so often happens in Balearic archaeology, however, we were disappointed when the tombs came to be opened; for once again finds were generally too sparse to support any definitive dating of the various cultural phases represented.

Plate 16

Fig. 20

By the end of the excavation it had been possible to examine about a hundred tombs, closely packed together, sometimes with the walls of one tomb used in the construction of its neighbours. A form which from the start attracted our attention was the boat-shaped tomb, which we called a '*micro-naveta*' – a term suggested by its plan, though not by the elevation. They could also be called apsidal tombs. Variable in orientation, they are built, at least in the upper sections, of well-dressed blocks of stone, with a roofing of broad slabs. The average size is 3 × 2 m., with a height of 1 m. The tombs stand on the natural rock, and most exhibit the curious feature of a rough trench at either end of the chamber, reminiscent of the less pronounced cavities we shall find in stone sarcophagi from the Punic cemetery of Puig des Molins on Ibiza. Another odd detail found in a fair number of these tombs is the presence in the façade of two or three more or less rectangular apertures with a maximum size of 17 × 12 cm. Although most of these tombs, which account for one third of the total number discovered, contain only one or two skeletons, on occasion there are up to six, making them family vaults. The skeletons lie between the trenches in the chamber, with the head opposite the apsidal end, facing east, with the body in a contracted position.

Plate 20

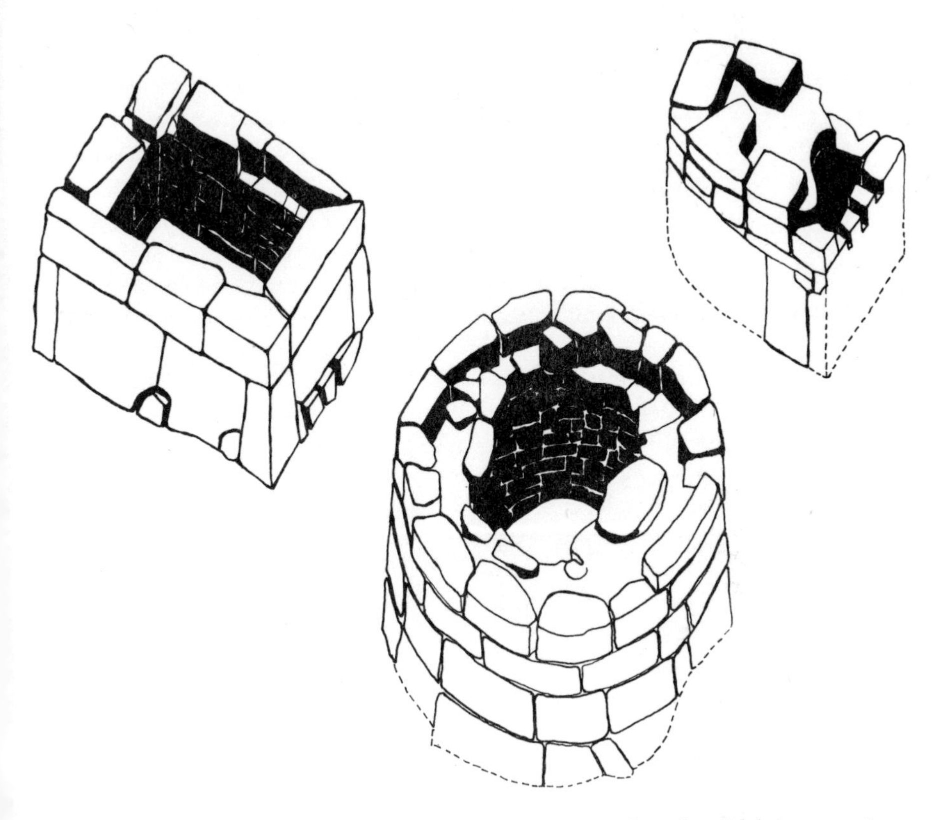

Fig. 20 Isometric drawings of the three types of tomb – rectangular, circular and apsidal (micro-naveta) – in the Son Real cemetery, Can Picafort, Santa Margarita, Majorca (after Liston). Excavations, directed by M. Tarradell, were financed by the Bryant Foundation

Another form of tomb, liberally represented, is rectangular. These are usually smaller than those just described, having no apse, and they are built in various ways. Some examples employ large and well dressed slabs. Another sort, less carefully constructed, has faced rubble walls, and in some instances includes the trenches and apertures of the apsidal tomb, which from certain structural details we may suppose was older. An obviously later form is seen in various tombs with rough walling, built on the sand, used for cremation burial. Two other variants are of circular or oval plan, either with the normal construction, or built low and tending to a corbelled roof. These were used for collective burial, remains of fifteen flexed skeletons being found in one.

Plates 21, 22

As already mentioned, grave goods were disappointingly poor, considering the large number of tombs discovered. The poverty of the offerings suggests an economy obliged to be sparing, especially with metal goods which were difficult to replace from the precarious commerce of the island's Bronze Age. An enigmatic object which appears, either singly or in several examples, in almost all the tombs of this sort is a kind of button, or plug, fashioned from the condyle of a femur. It has also been found at other sites of the Talayot culture. We have sometimes been led to wonder whether this object might not be meant to symbolize grave offerings which the islanders were prevented, by poverty, from depositing in their tombs.

Even pottery, which is usually abundant with other forms of island burial, is scarce at Son Real. The site produced only a limited number of whole pots, among the quantity of sherds. The forms reproduce Talayot types, the hand-made pottery being of more or less ovoid form, with everted neck and a slight vertical extension to the handle. The smaller pots are conical in outline, some with one, others with two handles.

The most important finds are of metal. In bronze there are various spear-heads, decorated discs, chisels, fibulae and a rectangular-handled razor with a rounded cutting-edge and semicircular blade opening. There was one side-looped socketed axe.

Iron objects appear in tombs of all types. Generally in a poor state of preservation, they include fragments of knives, daggers or spear-heads, rings and spiral bracelets. The two most interesting finds are the handle of an antennae sword and a curved sword blade; both came from rectangular tombs.

In the rectangular tombs, which we imagine were the latest, there were numerous finds of vitreous beads. Very rarely these also appear in apsidal or circular tombs. They obviously derive from Punic trade.

The chronology of the cemetery can be inferred from the dates usually ascribed to the finds. Its beginnings cannot be earlier than the eighth century BC and should more probably be put in the seventh, with the boat-shaped tombs. These would be followed by those of circular plan, in the fifth and fourth centuries. The more crudely constructed tombs, with traces of cremation, show either that the cemetery continued in use until later times or that, after a break, it may have been re-utilized during Roman times.

An important aspect of the evidence from Son Real is the physical anthropology, since it was possible to recover over a hundred skulls, a number of which had been trepanned. This represents a considerable and homogeneous series, and was consigned to the Anthropological Laboratory of Barcelona University, under Dr S. Alcobé. The study is not yet completed, but it is possible to say that a gracile Mediterranean type population is represented, with additional Armenoid features.

Part of the Son Real cemetery has been destroyed by the sea, which indicates a slight change in sea level. A number of tombs were found on the tiny islet of Els Porros (measuring 70× 45 m.) less than a hundred yards out from the present-day coast. Two of these tombs must have been monumental, partly excavated in the rock, with access steps and the remnants of columns. Above the level with round inhumation graves are found large cremation tombs, which apparently belong to Roman times. Among the usual finds there was a votive bronze double-axe.

Plates 63, 65

In all, Son Real has been one of the most remarkable discoveries of recent years. Even though it did not provide a key to dating the Talayot culture, as we had initially hoped, or prove to be the vestiges of some exotic culture from the eastern Mediterranean, what we have learned from the site is nevertheless encouraging. We now realize that the Talayot culture was more complex than we had thought. Possibly we should see Son Real as influenced by building techniques from Minorca, or as evidence of contact between the two islands. It is my belief that more such cemeteries will emerge, and we should not forget that Mascaró has reported other 'micro-navetas' similar to Son Real as, for example, Sa Begura at Sant Llorenç, Son Danús at Santanyí, Sa Mola at Felanitx, Puig den Nofre at Capdepera, and elsewhere. It remains to discover and excavate the corresponding settlement – and there are already some indications of it – in order to relate Son Real to the talayot sites of the region.

THE TALAYOT CULTURE IN MINORCA

Settlements and talayots. Complementary to the study of Majorca's wealth of monuments are the equally remarkable remains found in Minorca. But while on the larger island the over-all impression is somewhat blurred, since the monuments have deteriorated even where they are still majestic, on the smaller island they stand less affected by time. Possibly

Figs 21, 22

Fig. 21 Plan and section of the San Agusti Vell talayot, Migjorn Gran, Minorca (after Mascaró). 1 :100

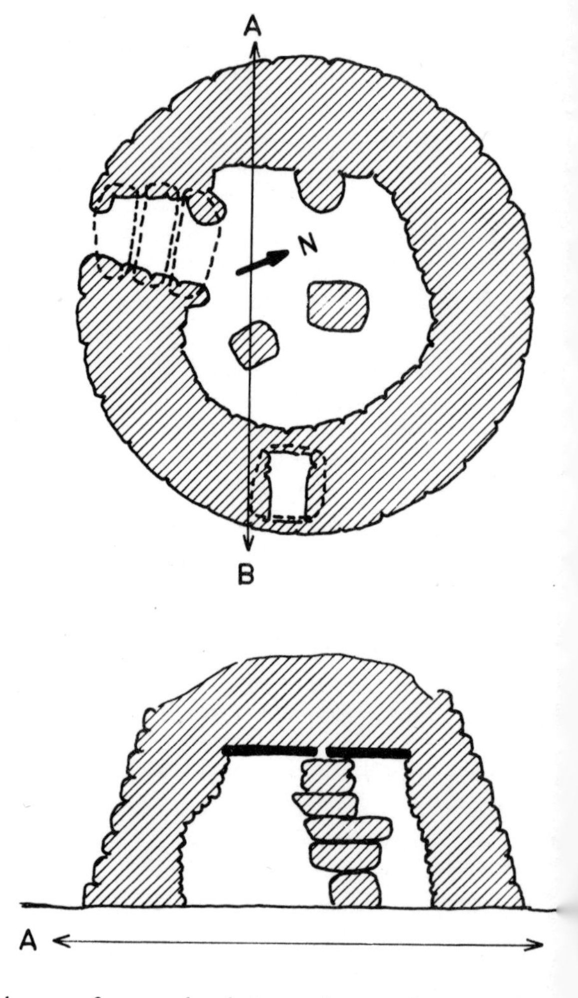

what we discern here are forms and techniques closer to the originals, and thus more striking; or it may be that the position of Minorca has laid it open to stronger influence from other Mediterranean lands.

Surveying the Minorcan landscape (and Monte Toro provides an excellent vantage point) the duality of the country suggested by a study of its geology is quickly confirmed. Approximately half the island, to the north, is clad in dark vegetation, thinly settled and supporting a rather precarious agriculture. It terminates in steep cliffs and inlets, including

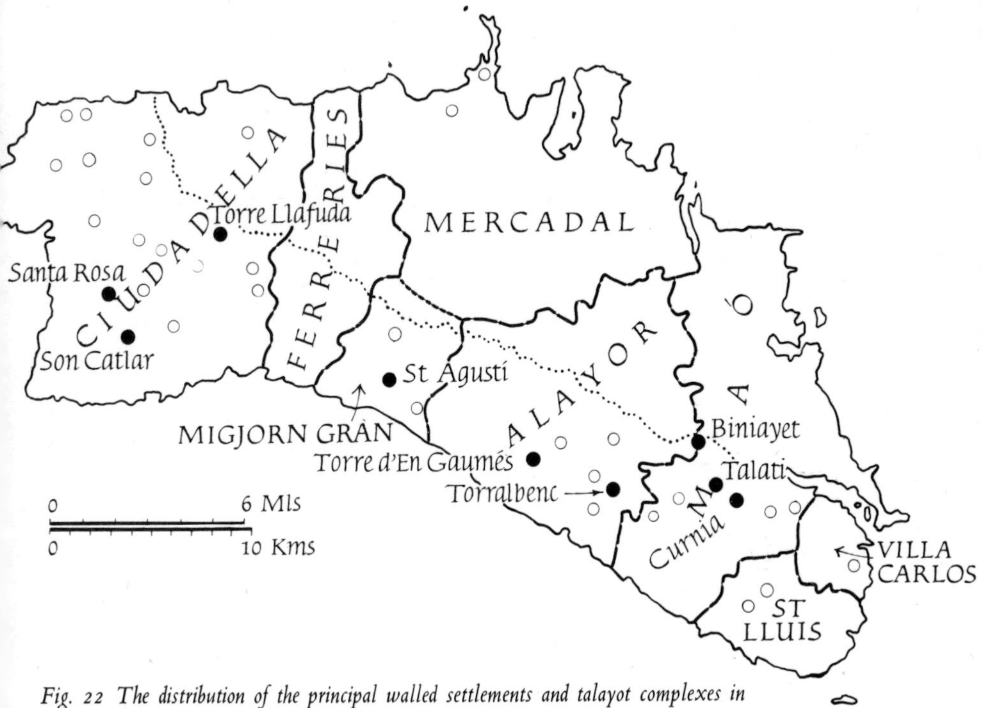

Fig. 22 The distribution of the principal walled settlements and talayot complexes in Minorca (after Mascaró)

the vast bay of Fornells. By contrast, the southern half of the island (which is also visible from the lower range of the Torre d'En Gaumés, or the hills above the old megalithic village of Talatí) reveals a prosperous countryside of villages and white-painted farmhouses, together with a multitude of walls separating the properties, which turn any walk into a laborious exercise. In a word, the density of archaeological remains is far higher than on Majorca, although this may arise from the fact that less intensive agriculture has preserved a greater proportion of the monuments.

When we wish to review the question of relations between the two islands during the span of more than a thousand years which can be ascribed to the period of cyclopean building in the Balearics, we are faced by some unanswerable questions. We must allow a common background and chronology for events in each. Their proximity would impose some community in building practice and in the way of life in general. None the less their mutual insularity did create barriers, allowing influences to reach one which are scarcely perceptible in the other. This, we must assume, accounts for the fact that their settlements do not always seem to follow the same pattern, and that in Majorca we find neither the typical naveta, nor the enigmatic taula, nor Minorca's huge cemeteries in coastal ravines, nor hypostyle courts or covered enclosures (at least, not in the grandiose Minorcan form).

As for relations between the peoples of the two islands, we may hazard the guess that these were not always peaceable. Who knows what legends and events have vanished with the passage of the centuries, for want of written texts, and after the devastating effect of successive conquests on the oral tradition of subjugated peoples.

We assume that the majority of Minorca's known remains, whatever their condition, belong to 'urban' groupings or dwelling sites. These would consist of walled enclosures, houses of different forms, talayots, houses or courts with pillared and beamed roofs (the so-called hypostyle courts), and the taula enclosures. The navetas are the exception: since we believe that their purpose was strictly funerary, they could have stood outside the walled limits of the settlements.

Sites of large towns are known on the island. There can be little doubt that the Torre d'En Gaumés is one such, and that it covered an extensive enclosed area, since its large buildings are dispersed round a central hill, on which stand three talayots, very close together. Seen from a distance they resemble, in a crude version, the classical outline of the three pyramids of Giza. By contrast, no section of the surrounding wall is obviously visible, and doubtless a good part of it will have been robbed, or lies hidden in the undergrowth. Another interesting site is that of Alcaidús, also in the district of Alayor. It was excavated by M.-L. Serra, who reported a most unusual plan of close-set houses. A settlement at Biniayet was partially excavated about 1916 by Vives Escudero; unfortunately nothing was published and the site has since been largely destroyed. Other groups of remains which deserve to be studied are those at Torre Llafuda, Trepucó and Torelló (the last two not far from Mahon). These sites are, however, surpassed by Son Carlá (Son Catlar), Ciudadela, where the surrounding wall has survived all round the enclosure. Son Carlá is irregular in plan, and measures about 160 m. across at the widest point. One face of the wall runs straight for more than 200 m. Recently, V. Tolós has been able to plan the whole extent of this defensive wall, bringing out the cyclopean character of its facing which

Plates 44, 47

makes the site so impressive. Elsewhere the wall has been altered or added to in later periods, in or around Roman times. We have managed to identify several gateways, and one has been cleared. At either end of the settlement, though not touching the wall, stands a large talayot, while the central position within is occupied by the precincts of the taula.

Plans which have been published of Son Carlá are not entirely accurate, however. The figure of some 900 m. given by Flaquer for the length of the perimeter wall is correct. Built against the wall inside the rampart there is a hypostyle court. This is constructed from large (at times huge) natural slabs of approximately equal thickness and height, set vertically on a stone base. Above these was a setting of small stones, at times fitted perfectly together in places, though more often this standard is not attained. By contrast, the inner face of the wall is made from smaller stones, and the space between filled with gravel and earth. The wall of the court was 2 m. thick over-all. The western section of the building, in particular, looks gigantic; the northern face is remarkable for having several rooms, or casemates, within the thickness of its wall. There are four doorways, of which three remain blocked by small stones. In the case of the fourth, which faces east, we have managed to restore the fallen and broken lintel and clear the floor to its original level. This gives some idea of how effective a total restoration would be. At regular intervals along this eastern face four round towers of perfect ashlar blocks were erected in Roman times.

The south-eastern angle of the rampart wall is formed by a talayot, now in ruins. No further signs of talayots are visible outside the wall, but there are remains of stone circles and pilasters.

Inside Son Carlá the precincts of the taula are impressive, although the horizontal stone which capped the pillar of the monument itself is missing. There is also a talayot built against the eastern rampart wall, to the north of the reconstructed gateway, important as being the only example which preserves a cupola roof closed by a circular slab. Adjoining it, and also backing against the wall, is a partly destroyed hypostyle court, containing a number of Mediterranean-type columns and their capitals. Other large buildings, either of talayot or circular form, can be discerned in the undergrowth, which has resisted our attempts to clear it.

Inside all such settlements of this type as can be distinguished through the covering vegetation we find circular buildings, which seem to have been the principal component of dwelling sites in Minorca. We may assume that the majority, having hearths, were lived in – though they could have served other purposes – and there are some indications of rectangular houses. The circular buildings are grouped together in an odd fashion. At Alcaidús, where we first became aware of them, they were built so close as almost to be in each other's way. It is possible that the remains of circular buildings and a hypostyle court which are reported as found at Alcaidús (Sant Vicens) may in fact form part of the neighbouring settlement, or a larger town, at Biniaiet, which Vives excavated partially. What was novel and interesting here was the discovery of interconnecting hut-circles (that is to say the arcs of the incomplete circles terminate against the walls of their neighbour). Internally the structure can be apsidal and there are adjoining hypostyle courts.

Plate 8

Once the enclosure was cleared, it was a relatively easy task to lift the fallen stones and pilasters, thus rendering the site attractive and accessible from the island's main transverse road.

Exploration of the group of remains at Talatí de Dalt yielded equally interesting results, despite the present ruined condition of the site. There were no less than five talayots, one of which was very small, ten covered enclosures (which have also been termed 'megalithic caves'), numerous stone circles, and part of the wall which must have surrounded the site. Three of the talayots were built radially round the largest – one of the island's principal monuments, and magnificently constructed. Although it now appears solid, it once contained a chamber, since filled in. Here also it appears that the large houses, or circular enclosures, had a hypostyle court built against them. The covered enclosures have been an object of curiosity since ancient times; Miss Serra's research has increased the number known, and revealed further details. One example, of excellent workmanship, was entered down a stairway.

We have already mentioned Torre d'En Gaumés, which has large, beamed buildings, interconnecting hut-circles, and fragments of a rampart. The talayot village of Sant Vicens de Cala en Porter is also interesting. It contains circles built from flat stone slabs, with pilasters inside. A notable feature, found also at Binicalaf, is a series of small houses of rectangular plan built against the foot of its single large talayot. The contrast with what we presume are the houses in other settlements leads us to suppose these date from a later period.

Fig. 23

Another group examined by Miss Serra was Torralba d'En Salort, in the archaeologically rich neighbourhood of Alayor. Near its talayot is the taula and a hypostyle court with pillars and capitals carefully worked and constructed, one of the island's finest examples. A single pillar, such as we also find on other similar sites, seems to mark the position of a court or a covered enclosure. The famous well of Na Patarrá is near by.

Let us now examine in more detail some monuments which occur in these extensive and very numerous groups of remains we suppose to represent the Island's ancient towns. As on Majorca, talayots are often the sole element that remains to be seen, and there are hundreds of them. Practically the only type in Minorca is that with a truncated-conical outline. A single example of the pyramidal form with a squared base is reported, at Binicalsitx, Ferrerías. Its present height is about 10 m. and it measures some 20 m. across the base. Minorcan talayots are rather crudely built, with large, unworked blocks in their lower courses, though sometimes the upper parts employ better dressed, almost squared stone (Binicodrell, Sona Casana, etc.).

As in Majorca, there is no doubt that some talayots were solid and could have been used only as watch-towers or for defence. The majority, however, contain a corridor, however short, or a more or less simple chamber. In all cases the core of the tower is composed of rough stones and earth. A further type has a narrow passage, which does not lead to any sort of chamber, but which may run as far as the centre of the tower (as at Biniatzem, for example). This corridor is faced, and roofed with flat slabs. In the Curnia talayot the short corridor turns into a stair half-way up, while in the second talayot at Biniatzem a short corridor leads up to a curved stairway. Another class of talayot contains a small chamber with a false cupola roof, closed by a large slab. Access to the central chamber is via a short corridor from the base of the talayot (for example at Binicodrell nou), or in rare instances (Llumassanet) the corridor opens half-way up the tower's side. At Binicodrell de Dalt there is one, angled, corridor leading to a small lateral chamber, while another, with no visible entrance, runs through the body of the tower on the other side. There are examples having a more complicated plan: a chamber of several compartments with a semicircular stairway at the end, entered from half-way up the tower (Fontsrodones de Baix); or a large corridor

Fig. 25

Fig. 26

at this height, which leads to a small circular passage, running round a great central support. Still more interesting is the plan of the Rafal Roig talayot, where the central chamber is trapezoidal in form and has flat slabs set like shelves in the walls; in addition to a normal entrance at floor level there is an extremely narrow passage between the chamber and the outside. Next we come to the classical type of talayot, with a large, circular central chamber, and the usual entrance, as for example at Es Mestay. This central chamber may have several side cells (Torre Nova), reminiscent of the plan of many of the island's rock-cut caves. The Torre d'en Lozano has, in addition to a somewhat oval chamber, a curved stairway leading to an upper storey, all within the body of the tower. Lastly, there are those talayots in which the central chamber contains a Mediterranean-type column; they have the finest plan. The famous Son Agusti Vell talayot at San Cristobal is one example, and here there is a second pillar at the side and a third up against the inner wall. It also contains a roof support beam made from a tree trunk (possibly of wild olive). Also found are further, very rare, types, such as the Santa Mónica talayot at Mercadal, where we find a second, irregular, tower built against a normal circular one; there is a corridor with a projection in the two sides, leading into the middle.

In all, more than two hundred talayots (their popular local name is *talaias*) have been reported. There is reason to believe that very many more will have been destroyed – as some have been even recently – for their supply of dressed stone. It is not possible to say how the talayots were finished off at the top, where they have all suffered damage from the elements. Neither are we able to determine whether there was any preference for siting them on level, or on higher, ground. It is evident they were components in what we have termed urban groupings, and within these they are often quite numerous. The entrances, Hernández Mora has reported, with rare exceptions face south, or very nearly south.

On the questions of whether the talayots were ever connected with burials, the complete dismantling of the much ruined one at Tornaltí, under the supervision of Miss Serra, was most instructive. The material was removed down to the natural rock and trenches were then cut to check for burials in the ground beneath. No material or bones of any kind were found, and there were similar results when several talayots were destroyed at Beniparrell, to allow for an extension of the airfield.

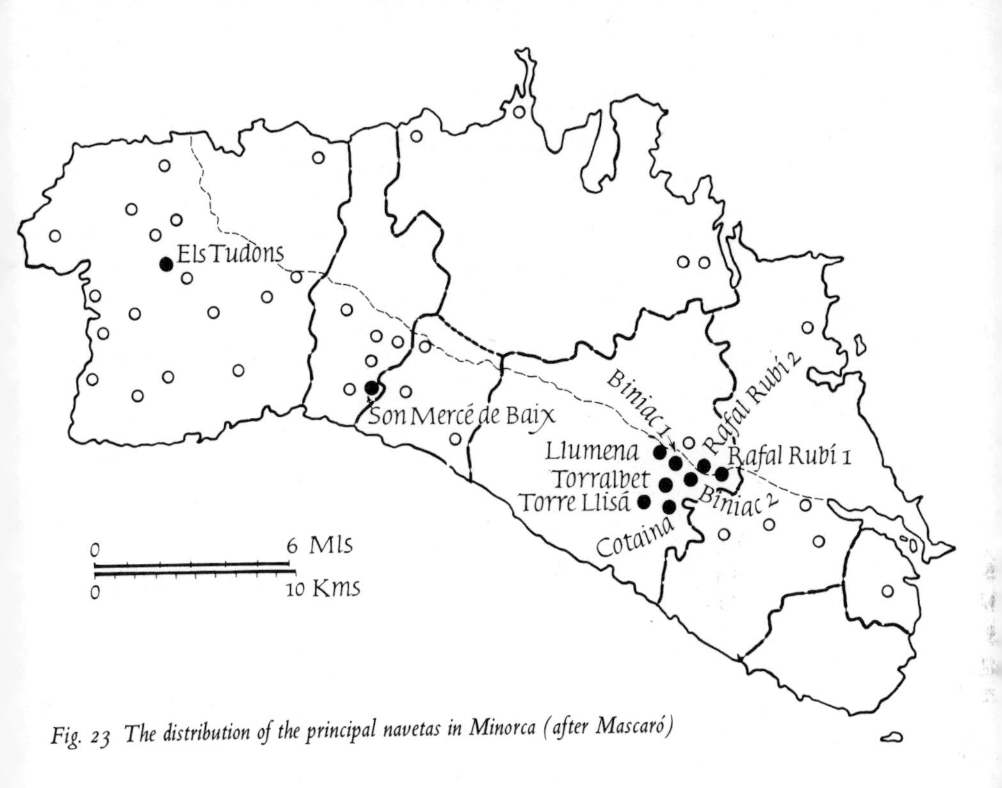

Fig. 23 The distribution of the principal navetas in Minorca (after Mascaró)

The Navetas of Minorca. With the navetas (or *nauetas*) we come to a more clearly defined group of monuments. Although in the field, when they have fallen into decay, they may be mistaken for talayots (and on the island they are called *talayetas*) there is a wide difference between the two types. Mascaró reported sixty-four examples in 1957, though it is doubtful whether some should have been classified as such. In 1968 he listed forty-five of what he termed the principal navetas in Minorca, and named ten as outstanding examples: those of Els Tudons at Ciudadela, Son Mercé de Baix at Ferrerias, Rafal Rubí 1 and 2, Biniac 1 and 2, Llumena, Torralbet, Torre Llisá and Cotaina, forming a group concentrated in Alayor. The name 'naveta' was coined by Ramis in 1818 to describe the sole example then known, the Naveta of Els Tudons, which he interpreted as a temple of Isis. It is still the finest and best preserved of the navetas, the most outstanding monument of the Balearic Bronze Age, and without doubt the oldest architectural structure still standing above ground on Spanish soil.

Fig. 23

Fig. 24
Plate 49

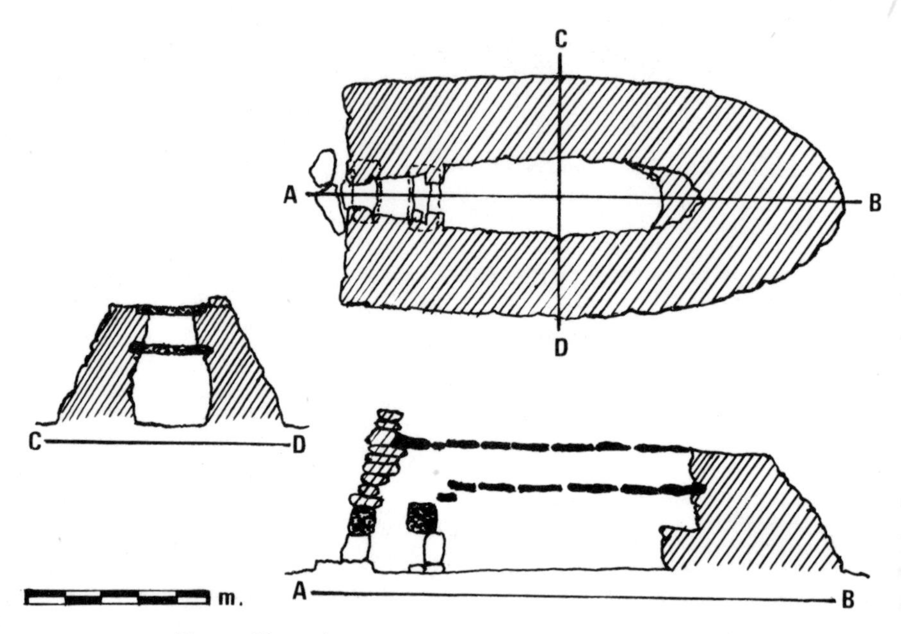

Fig. 24 Plan and sections of the Naveta d'els Tudons, Ciudadela, Minorca (after Mascaró)

The naveta is a funerary structure in which the usual talayot building techniques were employed with varying degrees of skill. In plan it is horseshoe-shaped, oval or sub-circular. Inside there is generally a chamber of elongated oval shape, entered through a small rectangular outer doorway and a corridor or vestibule, which opens into the main burial chamber by way of a second, narrow, door. These doorways are usually rabbetted to receive a blocking stone. The inside of the chamber is faced with stones of fairly regular shape and usually of medium size. Progressively projecting courses bring the walls together, until the space between can be capped by large roofing slabs. The vestibule is usually open at the top, which allows access to the second chamber which has been observed in several of the navetas, notably those of Els Tudons and Rafal Rubí. The funerary purpose of the navetas cannot be doubted, especially since Miss Serra's excavations at Els Tudons, where remains of at least a hundred individuals were found in the chambers.

Plate 50

Ramis' choice of the name 'naveta' for Els Tudons is derived from that monument's resemblance to an upturned boat. We do not know

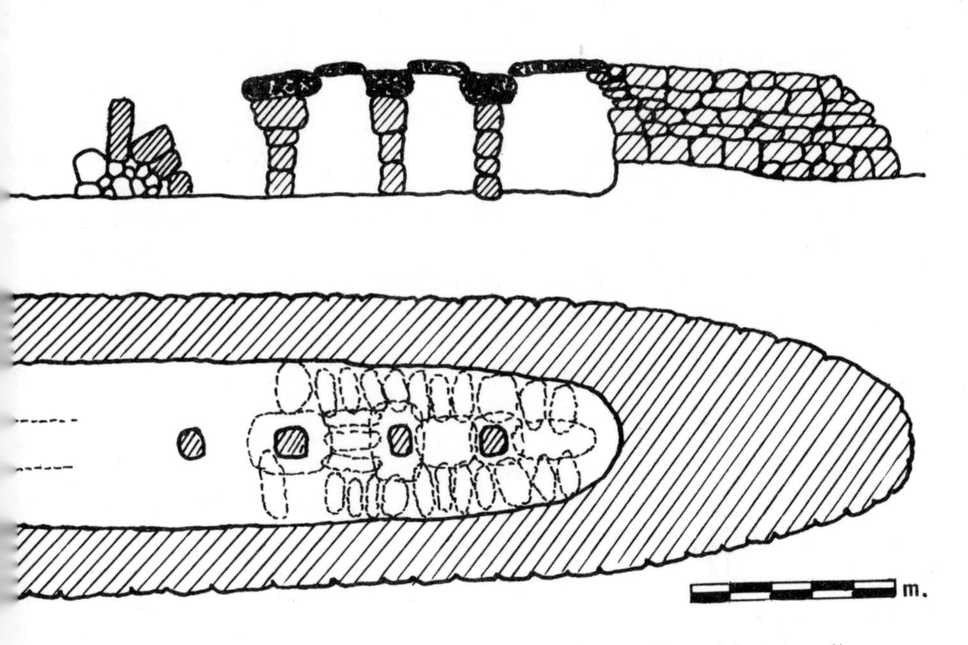

Fig. 25 Plan and section of the Naveta Son Mercé de Baix, Ferrerias, Minorca (after Mascaró)

Fig. 26 Plan and section of the naveta of Llumena d'en Montañé, Alayor, Minorca

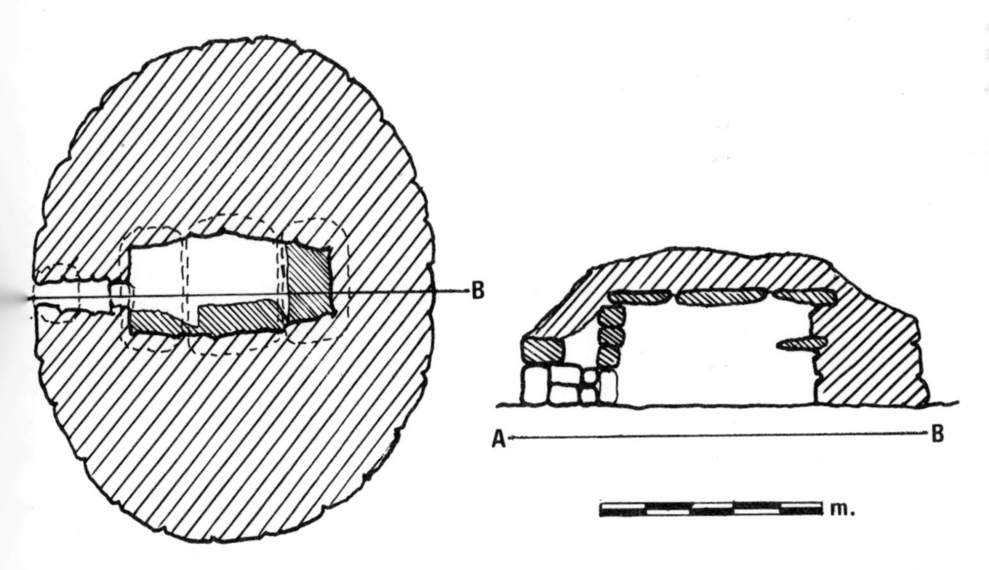

how the roof was finished off, but it may have carried this similarity further by being keeled, and is in fact represented like this in an old drawing in Ramis' volume. To judge from plans and elevations, however, none of the other navetas known reproduces this form in all details. Els Tudons is not the only example with a curved façade. Son Mercé de Baix and the two navetas of Rafal Rubí show this detail, together with a horseshoe-shaped plan and an upper storey; so they may be taken to belong to the same group. However, Son Mercé de Baix is unique in that its chamber contains three support pillars like those in the settlements, and thus combines the building techniques of the hypostyle courts with those of the simpler chambers. While other navetas are oval in plan, their chamber does not differ greatly from that of Els Tudons. In this type the burial chamber is sometimes entered from the long instead of from the short side of the monument, for example at Llumena and Torralbet. At Biniac and Torre Llisá the entrance is in the normal position, but a corridor takes the place of the antechamber. Other features of Els Tudons are a slight projection of the stone slab over the small outer doorway, and a platform formed by a large flat block of stone at the back of the chamber. At other sites (Llumena and Rafal Rubí) it seems that a ledge set against the wall replaces this platform. The Torralbet naveta stands on a natural rock platform, which forms a semi-circle in front of the entrance almost a metre high. The length of the most characteristic monument, Els Tudons, is 14 m., with a maximum width of 6.40 m. towards its centre.

Fig. 25
Plates 51, 52
Fig. 26

A few years ago the Els Tudons naveta was in a lamentable condition. It was overgrown, with roots of wild olive between the stones. This, and the additional depredations of the weather and of Man, had broken open the apse, threatening the monument's total ruin. Our plan for restoring it and excavating for possible archaeological remains could not be realized until the March Foundation had made a grant for archaeological research in the Balearics in 1958. Additional help then came from various public bodies, and the restoration was entrusted to the careful supervision of María Luisa Serra and the architect Victor Tolós. Fallen stones were returned to their original positions, and additional material was obtained from probably the same quarry which furnished stone for the original construction. The existence of an upper chamber was confirmed. It is now once again a most attractive site. Only the roof has been left incomplete, since we lack evidence to confirm how it was finished off: the drawing which Ramis published in 1818 is not convincing.

Even if we accept, tentatively, the theoretical division of these Balearic monuments into tombs (*navetas*) and dwellings (*navetiformes*) we must allow that they tend to merge one into the other. Confronted by a particular and often ruined example in the field, we cannot always be sure of its category. All this will explain our inability to establish chronological subdivisions.

The 'giants' tombs' of Sardinia have always been mentioned as possible prototypes for navetas, for the building techniques employed are similar. A connection with the underground tombs in Provence should also be recognized. The naveta is a stone rendering of the underground tomb; at the same time it reflects the form of the gallery grave in its tumulus covering. It is thus a Balearic version of an idea common to the Mediterranean.

We cannot be sure whether the boat-shaped house derived from the naveta-tomb, or vice versa. However, we should probably accept the hypothesis of Minorcan archaeologists, that development of the house form was relatively late.

Finally, we may mention some sites which exemplify the variations which link the *navetas* and *navetiformes*. Thus a boat-shaped structure, built in place of a square-based talayot, at Solleríc, Lluchmayor, on Majorca, had been classed as an almost perfect naveta; and Son Valent at Capdepera (Majorca) or Binimaimut near Mahon are for their part very close to being navetas. There are other such examples on both islands.

The excavations which took place while Els Tudons was being restored in 1959–60 gave far better results than had been hoped, seeing that the site is so well-known and constantly visited. There were still considerable deposits remaining in the main chamber, with hundreds of human bones lying on a layer of pebbles, in which it was possible to distinguish several strata. Among the finds, bone buttons with v-perforation and discs engraved with small circles seem to date fairly far back in Mediterranean chronology. The bronze objects, which included bracelets still encircling the bones of the arms they had adorned, were consistent with agreed datings.

Hypostyle courts. We now turn to another form of structure which archaeologists have distinguished among the cyclopean remains on Minorca, where the number of examples greatly exceeds the few known on Majorca. These are the so-called hypostyle courts or chambers – also known as 'megalithic caves' – for which we have proposed the name 'covered enclosures'. I would tentatively assume that they were intended for human occupation, or as enclosures for livestock. None has been properly excavated, and there are doubtless many more examples awaiting discovery. When the earth is cleared away, they no longer give the impression of underground chambers.

The sites are enclosures with walls and roofing of cyclopean character. The roofing is of particular interest, being composed of large natural slabs which rest on the walls or, when the space to be covered is too wide, are supported either by angular pilasters, or on pillars made of superimposed stones. It is a characteristic of these pillars that the smaller stones are used in the lower part, and Santa-Olalla has called this form the 'Mediterranean column', since it is a type found repeatedly in countries around this sea. Sometimes there is a large median stone beam, supported by the central pillars and the side walls. Usually the roof is low.

Plate 48

The ground-plans vary. Talatí de Dalt has an oval chamber, with a corridor, one central pilaster and another leaning against the back wall. In Toraixer de l'Amo en Pere (Villa Carlos) we find an irregular, elongated chamber and no less than five central pillars, with several others against the walls. Son Mercé de Baix could be included here, with its three central pilasters, though it is usual to class it with the navetas (an ascription which is questionable). Some of the hypostyle courts stand alone (Llumena den Salom, Binigemor, both at Alayor, etc.); others are found in settlements or round talayots (Torre d'En Gaumés, Torralba d'En Salort, Talatí de Dalt), or in proximity to other buildings (Son Carlá, Llucmassenet, Alcaidús etc.). It may be noted that the monolithic columns sometimes found in the centre could be thought of as small-scale models for the much larger uprights of the taulas, (discussed below), and this might support the hypothesis that these too had some structural function. According to Mascaró, a bank of stone was built on occasion as a facing against a side wall (for example at Binigaus nou). At times there are a few steps giving access to the chamber. A court may contain several chambers, though this is uncommon.

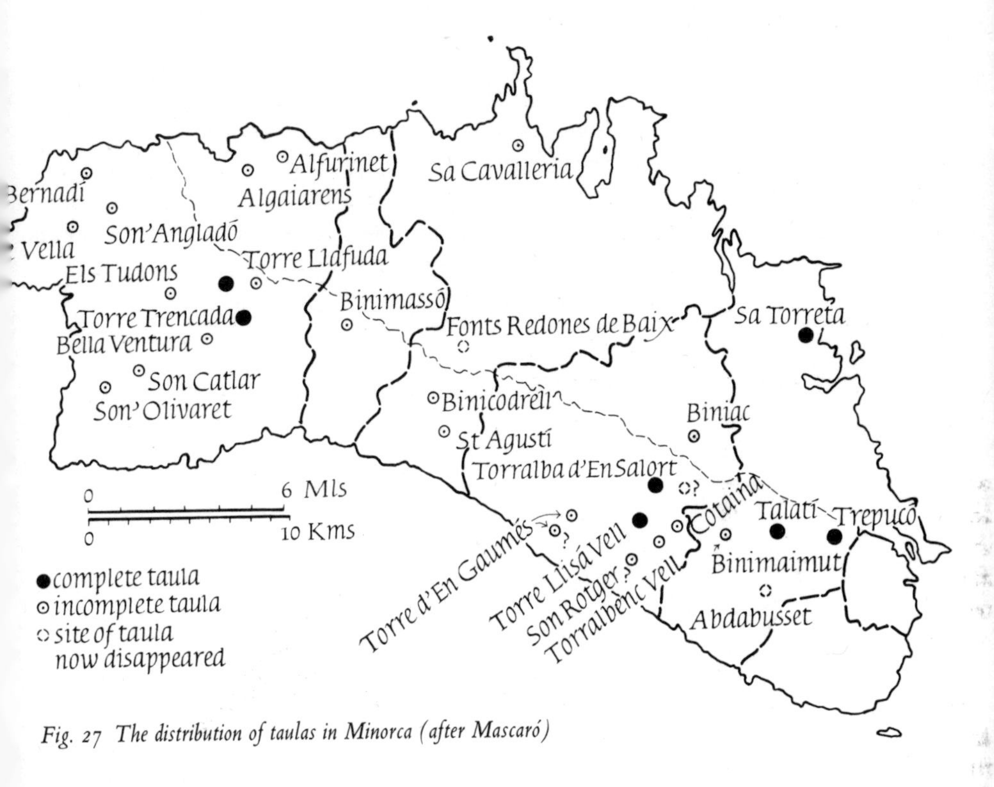

Fig. 27 The distribution of taulas in Minorca (after Mascaró)

The 'taulas'. The taula is one of the most distinctive monuments in Balearic archaeology; there is nothing comparable in any other part of the world. What is more, all known examples are confined to Minorca: although recently columns with a capital standing in the middle of an enclosure have been found on Majorca at Almallutx, which could represent a poor and late introduction of the Minorcan taula, I continue to believe that the taula did not spread to the other island, otherwise some evidence of its distinctive form would have survived.

Fig. 27

As the Catalan name implies, a taula is like a huge table set horizontally on a monolithic pillar, which is very wide in comparison to its limited thickness. The taula stands inside a wide, horseshoe-shaped enclosure, which generally has an opening in the middle of the straight side. The taula is not, however, exactly central, but displaced a little towards the northern wall. The front surface of the orthostat is turned towards this entrance of the precinct, which faces south. An exceptional arrangement is found at Binimaimut, where the precinct entrance is at the side, instead of being opposite the front of the taula upright. The supporting column is almost always rectangular, or occasionally slightly trapeziform, tapering towards the bottom. This monolith is from two to seven times wider than it is thick. In a single example (Trepucó) the front face, which is always more carefully dressed than the reverse, is decorated with oblique parallel lines. In some instances there is a more or less marked vertical ridge on the reverse face (Torralba d'En Salort, Sa Torreta, Son Carlá). In the Torre Trencada an additional pillar has been set against the centre of the main support. An even stranger arrangement is found at Talatí de Dalt, which has a second, oblique, support for the capital slab.

Fig. 28

Fig. 29

Fig. 30

Fig. 31

In better examples the horizontal slab is carefully prepared and trapezoidal in section. In some cases there is a hollow or groove in its lower surface to engage with the upright (Torre Llafuda, Torre Trencada); at other times it is the upright which is grooved, to receive the top slab.

The building technique applied to the characteristic taula precinct does not differ greatly from that used in the settlement walls. A line of pillars, which are shorter and less carefully prepared than the taula supports, is filled in with irregular intermediate walling, made up wholly or partially of large slabs. These pillars sometimes carry a capital, similar to those of the central monument.

According to Mascaró (1968) thirty-one taulas can be identified, of which seven are complete and three have now disappeared. The complete ones are Talatí de Dalt, Trepucó and Sa Torreta, in the district of Mahon, Torralba d'En Salort and Torre Llisá Vell in the Alayor district, and Torre Llafuda and Torre Trencada at Ciudadela. The horizontal stone is missing from the remaining twenty-one, although in some instances it lies where it fell. This is the case at Biniac and Torre D'En Gaumés at Alayor, Sa Caballeria, San Agustí Vell and Binicodrell nou at Mercadal and in the second taula of Torre Llafuda and in Bella Ventura at Ciudadela.

Plates 40–42

Trepucó is the largest taula known; its support stone reaches a height of 4 m., and a maximum width of 2.74 m. The supports of several other taulas are more than 3 m. high, and that of Bella Ventura is 0 57 m. thick. Smallest in size are those of the Torre Llafuda I, 1.70 m. high and Alfurinet (where the upper stone is missing), 1.03 m. The largest

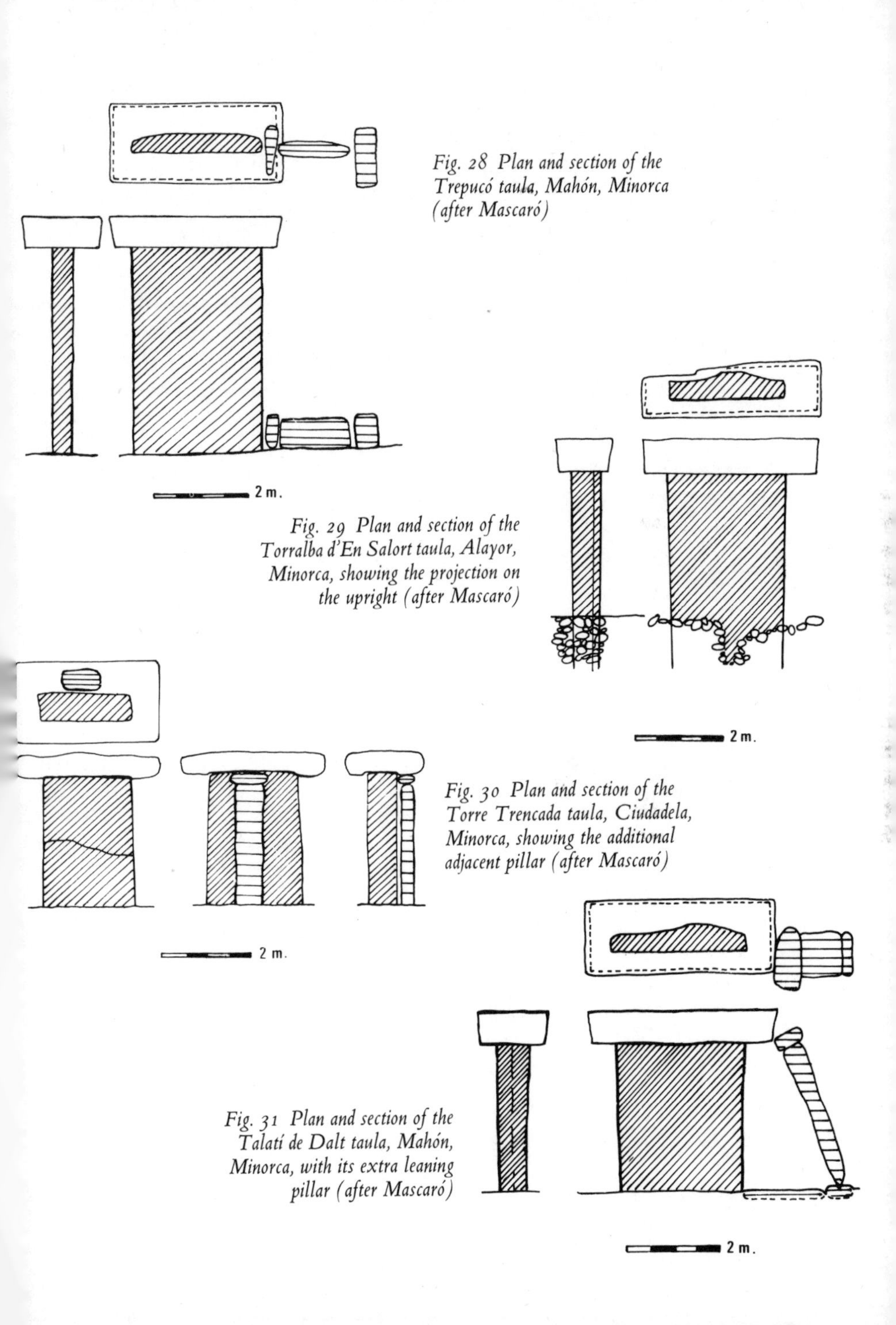

Fig. 28 Plan and section of the Trepucó taula, Mahón, Minorca (after Mascaró)

Fig. 29 Plan and section of the Torralba d'En Salort taula, Alayor, Minorca, showing the projection on the upright (after Mascaró)

Fig. 30 Plan and section of the Torre Trencada taula, Ciudadela, Minorca, showing the additional adjacent pillar (after Mascaró)

Fig. 31 Plan and section of the Talatí de Dalt taula, Mahón, Minorca, with its extra leaning pillar (after Mascaró)

horizontal slab is at Talatí de Dalt, measuring 4 × 1.53 × 0.68 m., followed by Trepucó, 3.75 × 1.84 × 0.61 m., and Torralba d'En Salort, 3.80 × 1.10 × 0.72 m. The smallest surviving horizontal stone is at San Agustí Vell, which is only 1.08 × 1.18 × 0.53 m.

There are indications that further taulas once existed apart from those which it has been possible to identify, though they have now completely disappeared. When only a portion of a monument remains it is difficult to determine whether it belongs to a true taula, or was part of some other structure. This applies to the supposed taula head-stones reported by Alcover in Majorca, or the stones noted by Miss Serra inside the Minorcan enclosure of Torelló. It is perhaps not unreasonable to suggest, however, that each village would have had its taula precinct, and that we are dealing with a monument far more specialized and rare than commoner forms like the talayot.

It remains to consider the essential question of what purpose the taulas served. One would have expected the study and excavation of their precincts to yield valuable information, but the only results which are in fact available are those obtained by Miss Margaret Murray at Trepucó and Sa Torreta, and these do little to solve the problem. Miss Murray thought the ashes found inside the enclosures were of a later date than the construction. The remains of several individuals came from an area near the Trepucó precinct. It is, however, quite certain that the taulas and their precincts occur in conjunction with talayots and settlement remains, and must have played some special role in the life of the community.

There has been endless discussion about the taulas, from the time when Armstrong in 1752 declared they were sacrificial altars and Ramis, in 1818, suggested that the sacrifices were of humans. There are two main schools of thought; one believes that the taula is no more than a further, albeit exceptional, structural feature of the sites, the other ascribes to it a transcendental character, relating to the religion of its builders.

The first hypothesis derives from the French scholar Emille Carthailhac, who published it in his well-known volume of 1892, after a visit to the islands. It was a reaction against some of the fantastic notions which had preceded it. The argument is based on the indisputable fact that pillars with capitals, rather like miniature taulas, are found in the so-called hypostyle courts and enclosures which are roofed by means of bridging beams, and that among these a large number are of imposing size, even though they are now often in a lamentably ruinous condition. The taula, then, would have served as a central support column for roofing its enclosure. A series of beams, of wood or stone, would have run from it to the lateral pilasters in the enclosure walls. At times these are not much shorter than the central taula. This view that the taulas were purely functional has been the most popular in recent years, among both Spanish and foreign scholars, and Florit believes he has found decisive arguments to support Cartailhac's thesis. The opposing view, accepted by a few scholars, is the one preferred by the amateurs.

The assumption that the taulas did not serve a merely structural function is based on their exceptional size (at least in the case of the most famous ones) and on particular features of their precincts, which it is impossible to confuse with the various plans of the covered courts, or enclosures roofed by beams. Furthermore, bridging timbers or stones would rest awkwardly against the central pillar if they had to slope downwards, sometimes as much as 2 m., to be supported by lateral pilasters in the surrounding walls, some of which are quite a distance out; and in the majority of cases the inclination of the capitals, where these are found on the lateral pilasters, is the reverse of what would be appropriate for receiving such roofing beams. Given the structure of the precinct walls, moreover, it is difficult to believe that the taula could possibly represent the central pillar of a huge chamber roofed by bringing the outside walls together in a false cupola. The case for any such constructions is further weakened by the fact that we do not find taula precincts filled with the remains of the material which would have been required. Broken stone is present in other types of monument where a pillar and beam roof has fallen. The taulas, furthermore, are distinct in their siting, their careful workmanship and restricted numbers.

The situation, then, is that some have thought the taulas were sacrificial tables, or tables for carving up the dead before burial (Vives). Others have suggested they were altars for sun worship (Camón), for a cult which was lunar (Flaquer) or simply astral (Fenn), or again that they were connected with funerary cults or practices (Hernández Sanz, Chamberlin, etc.). Miss Murray interpreted them as a symbol of the divinity, or at least a cult object. Santa-Olalla took the taulas to be cult centres, and supposed that part of the enclosure, though not the monument itself, would have been covered. More recently, Mascaró has put forward the suggestion that they were centres for bull worship, and has related the taula to all other manifestations of this cult found in the Balearics. He supposes the taula to be a schematic representation of a bull's head, with its horns.

For my part, I believe that the taula with its precincts has a symbolic or religious significance, rather than that its architecture was functional and formed part of a covered cult centre; and that there would have been one in every settlement. We are not in a position to say more. I do not deny that in form the taula resembles many of the monolithic pillars used to support the astonishing roofs of our covered and beamed hypostyle courts, which are perhaps the most fascinating of the ancient structures on Minorca. In this sense it would not be wrong to classify the taula as in appearance simply a pillar with a capital, though of an extraordinary size and unique in its siting and enclosure form. But though we could likewise say that a chalice is in one sense no more than a cup, we can recognize from details of its execution and design that in intention it is far more transcendental.

There is the further problem of whether the taula was current throughout the cyclopean phase of Balearic archaeology, possibly undergoing evolutionary changes, or whether it coincided only with the earlier or the later part of the period. Once more we are faced with the chronological difficulties inherent in Balearic archaeology.

There have been attempts to define earlier and later phases of the taula. It has been argued that originally the enclosure would have been formed by a surround of pillars, without the orthostatic or crudely built intermediate walls we find today. It has also been suggested that the taulas must be late, because there are relatively few of them. I cannot myself see any evidence which is decisive. I should provisionally accept that taulas began fairly early, about 1000 BC, developing at the time when oriental influence was at its height, though as an intrinsically Mediterranean tradition which finds a variety of expressions, some of the utmost originality, as a column cult.

Fig. 32

Plates 10, 11

Recently, at Almallutx (Escorca) at the foot of the Puig Major range in Majorca, B. Enseñat has found some enclosures with fallen columns, which it has been possible to restore. Provisionally at least I am inclined to class them as a version of the Minorcan taula. The columns are built

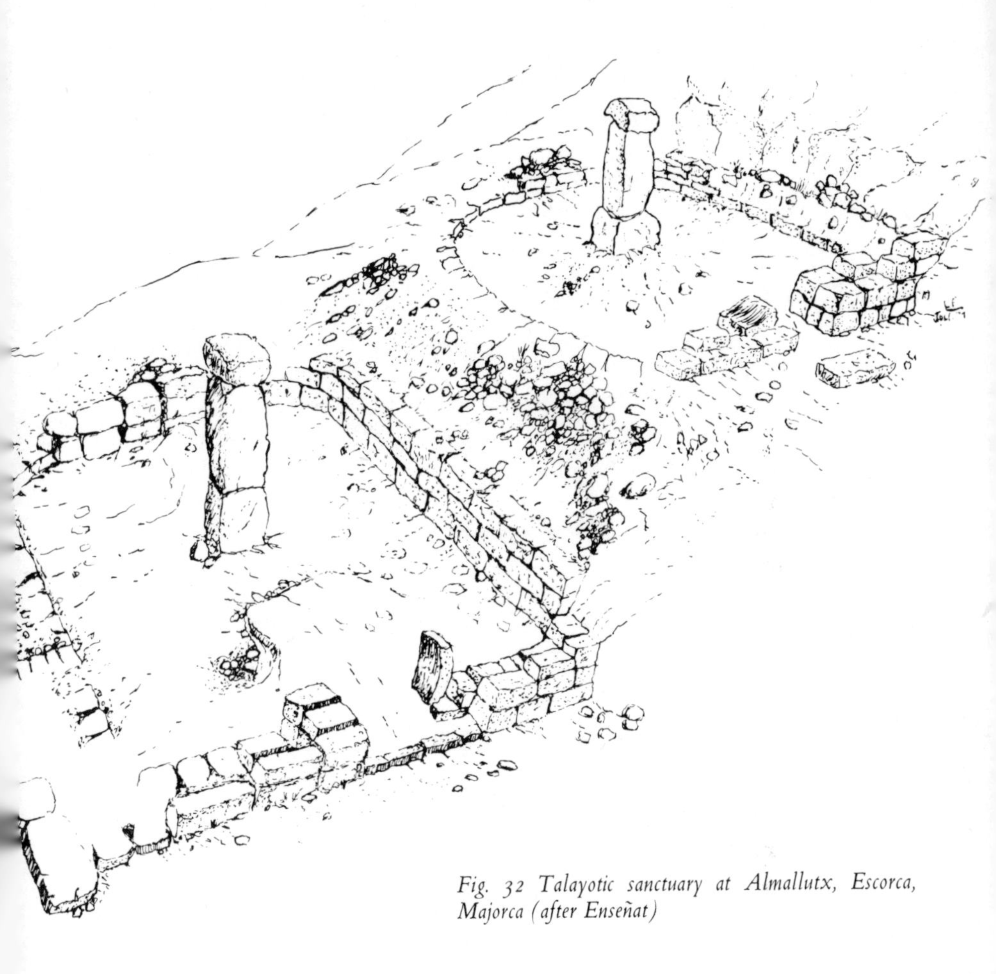

Fig. 32 Talayotic sanctuary at Almallutx, Escorca, Majorca (after Enseñat)

up of superimposed, roughly square, stones, supporting a capital, and they do stand in the centre of open, horseshoe-shaped enclosures. Admittedly, here the site is made up of a number of enclosures; but the idea is the same, or at least the desire to copy it is there.

Dolmens. Dolmens in the Balearics have also been the subjects of much debate. Professional archaeologists have long been reluctant to include in the Spanish megalithic culture certain monuments of dolmenic appearance on Majorca and Minorca, while they refuse to allow that they are true dolmens. I do not now think we can maintain this rigid position. Forms of dolmen, or megalithic tomb, do exist in the Balearics, although they occur in limited numbers. This is hardly surprising, remembering the islands' Mediterranean contacts during the period the tombs were built. Their scarcity and their evolved form, are the result of the relative isolation of the Balearics.

At present five examples are known. The only one in Majorca is Son Bauló de Dalt at Santa Margarita (published by Mascaró and Rosselló); it has an antechamber and remains of a stone barrow. Its maximum dimensions are 5.6 × 6.5 m.; the chamber measures 2.10 × 1.90 m. and the ante-chamber 1.60 × 1.15 m. Cova del Nenu at Santa Rita (Ferrerias) is the most dubious of the Minorcan dolmens. It is about a metre long and only slightly less wide, with thick walls made of several superimposed slabs; its massive appearance makes one suspect it was part of some cyclopean structure. The other examples in Minorca resemble the Spanish series more closely and have blocking stones with roughly ovoid apertures, less than a metre long. All three are in Alayor. Alcaidus den Fabregues seems to have a corridor and the remains of an ante-chamber. Montplé is a rectangular cist built of very thick slabs, 3 × 2 m., and faces west. The most classic example seems to be Sa Comerma de Sa Garita at Torre d'En Gaumés. It is perfectly rectangular in plan, built of slabs a uniform 25 cm. in thickness. The cover stones are missing (as in all the sites we have mentioned), and there are signs of a tumulus. The present height of some of its side stones is just over half a metre and the chamber measures 4.2 × 2.5 m.

The presence of these forms of megalithic tomb is clearly of interest, although the small number suggests sporadic and limited influences. It provides another clue for interpretation of the second-millennium period which preceded the time of cyclopean or talayot building.

Rock-cut caves. The artificial caves of Minorca are fairly similar to those in Majorca in the essential features of their main types, but for the most part the Minorcan caves occur in groups, in rocky gorges which run down to the sea. Here they form large cemeteries, which are far more imposing than anything found on Majorca.

A good example of a common type is Torre del Ram, at Ciudadela. It contains a doorway and a short antechamber, and the side walls of the rectangular chamber are slightly curved. A projection or bench runs the whole length of the chamber. Generally the caves are more complicated than this, with openings in the vertical or sloping cliff walls. More than thirty cave groups of this type are known in the island.

Over-all the plans and arrangement of these caves support the view that they represent an advanced form, later than the artificial burial caves we have described as pre-Talayot. Though we know a number of similar cave groups, no other site matches the wild beauty of Cales Coves, which is hidden from the sea. It is unlikely that many more have escaped attention, since they are visible from a distance. Son Morell is a spectacular group on the northern coast, and other similar cemeteries are found in the ravines of Biniparraitx, Son Bou and den Fideu (Coves gardes).

Plate 46

Plate 45

A good description of these sites is given by Hernández Sanz. Almost all the caves have the same features. Generally the entrance, which is always rectangular, is less than 2 m. high, framed with stone and rabbetted or stepped back. Inside, the spacious chamber is usually roughly circular, 5 to 10 m. in diameter, with central pillars or pilasters against the walls. Running from the floor to the roof at various points is a sort of rib, which becomes more prominent higher up; these projections suggest division of the room into several compartments. What looks like a handle cut in the rock face near floor level served some unknown purpose. The caves average more than 2 m. in height. At every site we have mentioned a large number of the caves contain several cells or compartments; but there are also caves with a single small chamber, with a semi-circular entrance or very short corridor. In some instances the caves are oval, like the majority of those we described in Majorca. The suggestion has often been put forward that these caves were inhabited, though they appear no longer to contain any remains. However there are reports of burials and funerary offerings which oblige us to interpret them as cemeteries. Their advanced date is demonstrated by the inscribed Roman tablets which have sometimes been found near the entrance.

On occasion the cave façade is slightly concave, recalling ancient megalithic practice. Some fifty human burials have sometimes been found under the floor of the caves themselves, for example among those in the Torreta Saura gorge, which is also evidence of an advanced date. Some of the entrances are more complicated. Thus in Cala Morell no. 9

there are steps for reaching the doorway, which is protected by a wide peep-hole cut in the rock, framing the whole opening.

It is my conviction that these vast Minorcan cemeteries were the chosen burial places of the Minorcan population at the time when the talayot culture was at its height. They would have come into use after the famous naveta family vaults, being nearer in their construction to the great megalithic tombs and excavated vaults of Provence. I believe that demographic calculation would support the idea that the majority of burials from the thousand years of talayot culture in Minorca took place in the two dozen or so ravine cemeteries we find along the island's coasts.

Finally, certain sites have been called underground caves which in fact are caves only in appearance. In fact they represent megalithic enclosures, with pilasters and pillars for roofing beams, which have become buried in soil. Some are approached by steps. In my view they should be classified, typologically and structurally, with the so-called hypostyle courts.

Rock engravings and paintings. We have several times mentioned the appearance of rock art, and there are repeated reports of it from caves and on monuments in the Balearics, both on Majorca and more especially on Minorca. It has led to speculation and a search for complicated symbolic meanings, mythological and cosmological designs, including astral cults, or other recondite explanations. Rock art has also been cited to confirm the theory of an early phase within the Balearic Bronze Age.

The sole paintings so far reported in Minorca are in the gorge of Santa Ana, Ciudadela. These are limited to a few examples in red, among which can be distinguished the profiles of two ships and an anthropomorphic cross. I do not believe we need to attribute to them any great antiquity. This applies also to the engraved signs, which are far more numerous. The motifs comprise human figures, reduced to the utmost degree of stylization, and some totally unidentifiable animal figures. In addition there are geometric signs: triangles, ladder and net patterns, a five-pointed star, and other more complicated and less obvious signs. An example of the last is the boat containing several persons, on a pillar in the N'abella d'endins at Els Tudons. In a cave quite near the Torre Llafuda settlement, Ciudadela, Mascaró has reported three rows of engraved signs, some of which resemble letters.

I believe these engravings in general are fairly late, dating at the earliest to the end of the Bronze Age, or else to the Iron Age or historical times.

Other monuments in Minorca. The explorations of so many amateur archaeologists on such a small island as Minorca have inevitably brought to light other monuments whose purpose we have not been able to determine. Particularly interesting are the megalithic enclosures or redoubts. These are roughly walled enclosures found in positions difficult of access, near the sea or a spring and, apparently, not far from the large cemeteries of artificial caves. There are examples at Cala Morell, Cales Coves, Son Bou, Caparrot de Forma and Es Castellaret, Macarella. The last site stands just above tidal rocks, and there are steps cut in the rock wall for descending into a pit. These enclosures could have been places of occasional refuge in dangerous times, and as such we may compare them with the fortified enclosures in the mountains of Majorca, referred to earlier and likewise imperfectly studied.

The archaeologist F. Camps has studied certain monoliths or rough pillars which stand alone at the top of cliffs and are called *fares* or *frares*. These are either cut in the living rock which supports them, or built of piled boulders, to form a crude pillar.

A great deal has been written about the oval cavities which have been found hollowed out of the rock, generally elliptical at the mouth and flat or concave at the bottom. Local fantasy would ascribe them to the dreadful Moors, bashing the stone with their heads (*capades de Moro*)! The maximum size is 75 cm. high by 65 cm. across and 45 cm. deep. Several hundreds are known and they generally occur in groups, sometimes of up to fifty (Santa Ponça). Some have a notch in the rim, for securing a blocking stone; they are either cut in the rock face itself or in stone which has been used for walling. Examples have been found in the encircling wall at Son Carlá and in the Montefí talayot, and this has been offered as proof that the cavities must ante-date the main Talayot period. This conclusion would be supported by the date proposed by Mascaró for a find of archaic pottery from near a group at S'Almudaina, Alayor.

It has been suggested that the cavities served some funerary purpose, as a receptacle for infant burials, or bones of fully-grown skeletons, or for an urn with bones and ashes. These arguments are doubtful, and I prefer to think the cavities are a fairly late phenomenon.

The Balearic Islands

FIRST CONNECTIONS WITH THE CLASSICAL WORLD

The earliest textual references to the Balearics. However much interest and enthusiasm is aroused by the numerous and splendid finds of archaeology, we cannot dispense with the evidence from written texts which has reached us through classical authors. These are actual reports, which tell us of customs and ways of life which often could have left no tangible remains. We may only regret that the references are so sparse and inadequate, and often merely confirm what has been learned from the archaeological material.

What, then, are the first references we have? It is well known that we are rather short of early texts mentioning Spain, so that there is little hope of a clear toponymy before 500 BC. Nonetheless we do get a glimpse of these times from the famous and much discussed Massaliote Periplus incorporated in the *Ora Maritima* of Avienus, and for this we have good reason to accept a date, as proposed by Schulten, in the second half of the sixth century BC. In a description of the coasts of Alicante and Valentia, after recording the boundaries of the Tartessians, it speaks of the Gymnetes as though they occupied a neighbouring region. The island of Gymnesia is then mentioned, and it seems here to mean Ibiza, although the name is used by Diodorus and Strabo to refer to all the Balearics, or to Majorca and Minorca in particular. The two later verses in the *Ora Maritima* which mention the Pityusae in distinction to the Balearics seem to be an interpolation, possibly by Ephorus, or from Punic sources.

Of greater value are two references from the geographer Hecataeus of Miletus, written about 500 BC and preserved for us in the works of Stephanus Byzantinus. These refer to two islands off Iberia, Kromyoussa and Meloussa. Both names have the termination *oussa*, which seems appropriate to an ancient route from Italy to the Iberian peninsula and would thus appear to derive from Greek navigators of before 500 BC. It would be logical to assume the names apply to Majorca and Minorca, though it is not easy to confirm this hypothesis. The names could signify, respectively, 'the island of the onions' and 'the island of the apples'.

The oldest certain reference to the Balearics comes from a text of Diodorus relating to the year 406 BC and the recruiting of mercenaries by the Carthaginians for their great campaign on Sicily. We find Balearic mercenaries mentioned again in connection with the famous revolt of 240 BC at the end of the first Punic War, savagely suppressed by Hamilcar Barca. Both these passages, however, are cited in authors who wrote later than the events reported. The first known author to use the name *Baliares* was Polybius, in the second half of the second century BC. This is doubtless a rendering of a native name, and there have been proposals to relate it to, or derive it from, the Greek *balein*, meaning to throw from a sling, or the Basque *balar*, a sling-thrower. There may be a connection between it and certain *Balari* on the island of Sardinia. In the third century Timaeus for his part tells us that there were certain Boeotians from the islands, which earned them the name of *Xoirades*. For Strabo, on the other hand, it was the Rhodians on their return from the Trojan war who colonized the islands of *Gymnesiai*, the Greek name and that most widely current, being already used, as we have seen from Avienus, in the sixth-century Periplus. The name would seem to derive from the islands' denuded appearance or lack of vegetation (at least in summer), though Hübner would interpret it as 'those who go lightly armed'.

The brief descriptions of the Balearics we have from ancient authors tend to cover much the same ground, and there is a great deal of repetition. The areas given for the islands, and their distances relative to each other and to Spain, are approximately correct. In general the islands are described as fertile. Lycophron described the people as clad in sheepskins and barefoot. Other authors have told of their living in the hollows of rocks and digging caves in the cliffs or, in many places, subterranean refuges for shelter and safety. They anointed their bodies with the resinous oil of the mastic tree (turpentine). An instance of their uncouth habits was a marriage custom, like that of the Libyan Nasamones, according to which at the wedding the bride was first possessed by the friends and relations of the bridegroom, who gave gifts in exchange. Prohibition on the import or use of gold and silver is evidence of the rarity of precious metals. Timaeus, who gives these accounts, also says that funerary customs included breaking the corpse with wooden clubs and casting the pieces into an urn, over which was raised a heap of stones.

We are told that the men of the Balearics liked to return from their expeditions bringing women and wine, to which they were much addicted, in preference to riches in metal. To avoid being left without women they chose rather to ransom one of them, if these were carried off by their enemies, even surrendering three or four men of rank in exchange.

We learn most about the activities of Balearic sling-throwers abroad in connection with the second Punic War. A good number of them were included among the many mercenaries Hannibal enlisted, from all over Spain, when preparing his campaign. Polybius relates that he sent Hispanic troops to Africa, bringing African troops to Spain. The number of Balearic slingers sent was 870, while 500 stayed behind. If we reflect that he took a further good detachment with him to Italy, we arrive at a total of at least two or three thousand mercenaries from the islands, which is high when compared with the figure of thirty thousand given by Timaeus as their over-all population.

At Trebia we know that Balearic slingers were in the vanguard and that it was they who opened the battle by attacking the Roman forces with missiles. In 208 BC Mago, who commanded the last Carthaginian forces in the peninsula, went to the Balearics to recruit men. Cadiz fell in 206, and seeing no hope of restoring Punic power in Spain Mago left with his fleet and was well received in Pityousa (Ibiza). When he attempted to land on Majorca, however, he was met with a hail of stones, and retired to Minorca. There he was able to disembark, occupying a strong-point above the harbour at Mahon, which took its name from him (*Portus Magonis*). From here, and without opposition, he took possession of the island, recruiting two thousand auxiliaries. At the battle of Zama in 202 we still find Balearic mercenaries fighting on the side of the Carthaginians.

We have no more information about the islands until the Romans undertook their conquest. Meantime, for several decades, their inhabitants lived peacefully, freed from Carthaginian dominion.

Greek finds in the Balearics. We should like to know what role the Greeks played in the cultural development of the Balearics, and this problem will be discussed when we come to the question of origins and influences. Greek trade with Tartessos, however, which may have been initiated near the start of the first millennium, must undoubtedly have used a route from Magna Graecia that would have sought out the Balearics as staging points for reaching the Iberian peninsula. In this way, as we have said, we get archaic Greek names with the termination *oussa*, which run from Pithekoussa and Ichnoussa through Kromyoussa and Meloussa to Cotinoussa (Cadiz) and Ophioussa (Spain). We may be sure there were even earlier links with the Aegean; and if the classical authors have not misled us on the subject of trade with Tartessos, we should be able to find indications of the route which was followed.

Such evidence does exist. There are first of all the influences apparent in Iberian art in south-eastern Spain, and, more particularly, the use of an archaic Greek alphabet in the region of Alcoy. In the Balearics there are actual Greek finds, though they always occur singly and thus help little in dating local material.

The most sensational finds are the bronzes. According to Garcia Bellido, half of all such bronzes found in present-day Spain come from the Balearics; which is surprising when we remember that as far as is known there was no permanent Greek colony on the islands, and that finds of contemporary pottery there are sparse compared with what is known from the mainland. Bellido thinks most of the pieces must have been looted by the Carthaginians, especially from the cities of Sicily after the end of the fifth century, and brought to the Balearics by returning mercenaries.

Plate 38

Plate 26

What we take to be the oldest of the bronzes is a representation of an archer (*toxotes*) 12 cm. high, found in 1919 in a Lluchmayor talayot. It is a somewhat crudely rendered nude figure of an athlete, unhelmeted, with a quiver, although the bow is missing. It may be classed as Dorian sculpture from Sicily or south Italy and dated about 560 BC. A boar found near Torelló, Mahon, could be from Asia Minor and should be dated about 500 BC, and a similar date may be given to the figure of a running athlete from Rafal del Toro in Minorca, and to a bird with a woman's head. There are numerous fifth century bronzes, reproducing archaic forms. The list includes the handle of a patera from Son Corró, Campanet, several representations of Athene Promachos, from Porreras and an unknown site in Minorca, and a further Athene from Santanyí, a helmeted naked warrior from Sineu, a warrior putting on his armour, from an unknown site in Majorca, a young man making an offering from Santa Eugenia, a satyr 'basket-bearer' from Establiments, a female figure and a satyr in Lluchmayor, and a figure believed by Bellido to represent Ulysses found at San Luis, Minorca. There are a further half dozen bronzes in a poor state of preservation.

I have left more recent finds until last. Near the Son Favar talayot, Capdepera, four bronzes were found in 1941 and 1945, the first by chance and the others in excavations by Amorós. These magnificent bronzes are in the Artá Museum. The largest, 50 cm. high and weighing 4 kg., represents a nude warrior, with a large helmet and shield, and with tenons on the feet. The spear he brandished in the right hand has been lost and must have been of iron. The helmet is of Phrygian type, with a large crest. The figure retains its limestone pedestal. This bronze may be dated to the end of the fourth or to the third century, and in the view of Garcia Bellido it is a rendering of an Italic Mars, in the Greek manner (Mars Balearicus). Another of the bronzes, also a nude and helmeted warrior in the same style, is about 30 cm. high and weighs two kilogrammes. A third, 25 cm. high, represents a bearded warrior with a helmet, shod in high boots. Lastly there is a small head, which must have come from another warrior. In 1944 a figurine similar to these finds was found at Son Carrió, together with Hellenistic and Roman pottery and a bronze horn, and recently there have been further examples found, notably the crudely executed warrior figurines from Roca Rotja at Soller. We cannot be sure of the provenance of a fine bronze springing deer, reputably from Campanet. There is a sixth-fifth century archaic head of a panther from Son Mari at Santa Margarita.

Plates 53, 57
Plate 56
Plate 57
Plate 54
Plates 39, 43
Plate 28

No examples of stone sculpture of Greek origin have been found in the Balearics, although there is a rich collection of clay sculpture from the cemetery at Ebusus. Pottery is abundant. The oldest Greek find known in the Balearics is an *oenochoe* in the collections of Ramis y Vives, which was apparently discovered in Minorca at the beginning of the nineteenth century. This is a beaked jug (*Schnabelkanne*), 17 cm. high and whitish in colour, with dark bands. I do not think there is much foundation for the doubts about its Minorcan provenance. Its interest lies in its Cycladic character, its date (early second millennium BC), and its resemblance to a similar find at the Bassin du Carenage, Marseilles.

Plate 4

The Greek pottery from Puig des Molins, Ibiza, includes some indubitably early pieces, like the Naucratic *aryballos* and an Attic black-figure *lekythos*. Then from the fifth and fourth centuries there are a good number of those globular or pointed forms of scent bottle which served as unguent jars for funerary use, though there are none of the large Attic or Italic *kraters* or mixing bowls, which are so common on the mainland. Pottery and lamps of Campanian type are much in evidence. In Majorca and Minorca there are also quantities of Sherds of Hellenistic

Greek ware, at least from the fourth century on. These finds are useful for dating one phase of the native culture.

Of great interest is the wealth of Greek gold and silver work from Majorca, including a series of ear-rings of great beauty. Several come from Alcudia and may be of fourth-century date, although the types persisted until Roman times. They include representations of goat, carnivore and lion heads, or present more intricate work, such as floral patterns, small female heads or Cupids, set on discs or in the round. An exceptional Nike figurine in gold found with a golden crown of leaves and flowers may be from Alcudia. Measuring 5.5 cm. in height and weighing 10 grammes, it is made from a small plaque of gold, with the wings soldered on, and must have been intended for use as a pendant. In style, however, it corresponds to known types of Hellenistic goldwork.

Plate 69

Finally, there are not infrequent finds of Hellenistic and Greek coins.

LIFE IN THE TALAYOT PERIOD

By combining the results of archaeological research with the evidence of textual sources we obtain a reasonably complete picture of the life of the people responsible for our cyclopean culture.

Houses. We are fairly well informed about the layout of settlements, thanks to the numerous excavations which have taken place, and it is not necessary to summarize their results again. By good fortune the finds include carbonized remains of the wood used for roof supports, so that we have evidence of the way the buildings were covered, when they were not corbelled. Floors were flagged, or of trodden earth. A simple central hearth of stones was found to be sufficient.

Clothing. We have here to contend with the difficulty of accepting that the name *Gymnetes*, the naked people, should signify an absence of clothing. It could mean merely that the men fought without armour, which would contrast sharply with practice among classical warriors. We find several references to skin clothing (Lycophron). Apart from using hides, the peoples of the islands spun and wove, and for this purpose they had not only wool from their sheep but the fibres which grow wild in Mediterranean lands, flax, esparto and the dwarf fan-palm (palmetto). There is archaeological evidence for this last material from the talayot of Son Serralta. Esparto would have been used for the formidable slings, as it still is by shepherds in the mountains of Valencia.

Strabo records that it was the Carthaginians who taught the people of the Balearics to dress in broad-striped tunics or shirts. The poet Philitas (*c.* 300 BC) writes of the wretched and dirty tunics of the Balearic slingers.

It is more difficult to get an idea of the women's clothing. I do not think it would have differed greatly from what was worn on the mainland, though there may have been differences of detail. Women's ornaments would also have been similar, and we find necklaces of paste beads which suggest the trinkets of Punic commerce. There are also metal bracelets, plain and spiral, a variety of fibulae, and different pendants, including discs and bells. A lead plaque, decorated with circles, which is found in several shapes, including a very summary outline of a bull is something of a curiosity. These plaques were attached to clothing, and must have been a native product since moulds have been found for making them.

Fig. 33

Agriculture and herding. Agriculture and herding were the basic economic activities. I think it improbable that we shall discover a hunting and gathering stage, though finds from inhabited caves in particular are characterized by absence of pottery, which might denote an archaic economy. We have adequate evidence of agriculture, from analysis of remains: the cultivation of cereals such as wheat and barley, for instance, as also vetch; doubtless there were also crops of the vegetables which commonly grow wild in Mediterranean countries. As on the Spanish mainland, acorns were of great importance. We do not know at what point cultivation of the vine was introduced for wine-making. According to Diodorus, the inhabitants of the islands set great store by it, and their wine was famous. The resin from another distinctively Mediterranean species most abundant on the islands, the mastic tree (*Pistacia lentiscus*), and from the closely related terebinth, must have been available from the earliest times, but the olive seems to have been a Punic introduction which was grafted onto the wild or tree olive, another characteristic feature of the Majorcan and Minorcan landscape. Dioscorides refers to the use of an arum rhizome (*drakontium*) for making pies, by cooking its starch with plenty of honey. Scillas (*urgines*) were abundant.

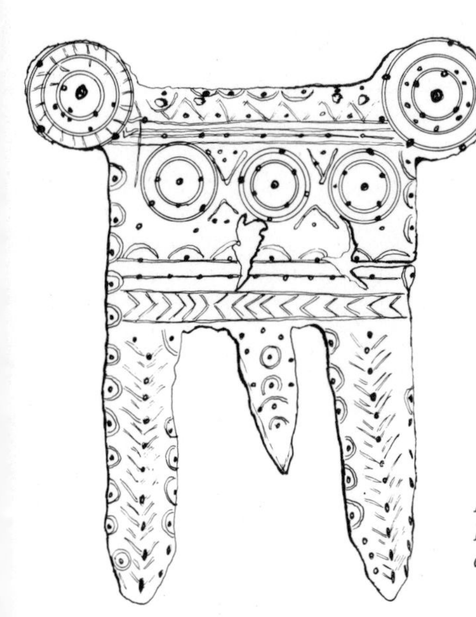

Fig. 33 Lead plaque from Son Juliá, Lluchmayor, Biniali, Majorca (after c. Enseñat). 1 :3

There have been no great changes in agricultural implements since those early times. Sickles and, more especially, querns are still used. With the Romans, a rotary, circular quern came into use, replacing the ancient oval type, which was worn concave across one face by rubbing.

We cannot say at what periods the various domestic animals, known from their remains in settlements or from ancient texts, were introduced. Full use was made of herds of cattle, sheep and goats, and milk and cheese were obtained from them. There were large quantities of pigs, of a breed which is still distinguishable from later importations; while the mules of Minorca were praised by Diodorus for their great size and strength. The rich cave, Cometa dels morts at Lluch, produced a bronze figurine of a cock, a pertinent fact when tracing the bird's introduction into the west, after its initial domestication in the Asiastic east.

Food. The traditional practices of hunting and gathering retained their importance throughout antiquity. We have already mentioned the acorn, which was ground into a meal for making cakes, mastic oil (turpentine), etc. It is also thought that man exterminated the *Miotragus* antelope from the Balearics. It is more difficult to allow that deer could have been hunted in Majorca in ancient times, despite mention of them in the

Middle Ages. The rabbit, which was so abundant in Spain from the Palaeolithic onwards, does not seem to have reached the islands until Roman times. Among birds, there is evidence of the sea-raven or cormorant, the coot, falcon and a species of small crane (*vipio*).

Fishing was practised near the shores, and we cannot be sure that the inhabitants were not able to venture farther out to sea, on rafts, in canoes or hollow dug-outs, or even more elaborate craft. Molluscs and crustaceans were naturally daily fare, as they are all round the shores of *Mare nostrum*. Present-day activities in underwater archaeology should produce further evidence of this.

It remains to mention the problem which is still serious in the islands, namely that of water. We find wells and tanks that must go back to the Talayot period, and these betoken great effort and much practical talent. Almost no other installation of this kind can compare with the great stepped well near to the site called Na Patarrá, Alayor, on Minorca. A well like this has naturally attracted attention in all periods, and it has given rise to many legends. It bears a likeness to installations described in ancient oriental sources. To be specific, I believe there is a clear parallel in the fountain or well of the biblical Gideon in Palestine, and that the well at Megiddo was not dissimilar. If these are valid comparisons, they would suggest a date around the eighth century BC. The Na Patarrá well might be another feature to reach the Balearics with peoples from Palestine who migrated here when the Talayot culture was at its zenith.

Household goods. The most prominent feature of Balearic archaeology is the great abundance of pottery sherds which are found. Unfortunately, this ware turns out to be very poor in both fabric and decoration, being both coarse and plain. The finest ware is that which was acquired from Greek traders (as was also the case with bronze figurines). Greek painted vases, and others of Punic origin, provided a luxury ware which was zealously preserved by the natives. Other domestic crafts would have been basket-making and weaving. We have already mentioned the importance of wood for making equipment in Talayot times.

Fig. 34

Metallurgy. The metal finds encountered in the Balearics present a special problem. We have always believed that the islanders were parsimonious with their metal, which would be natural since it was

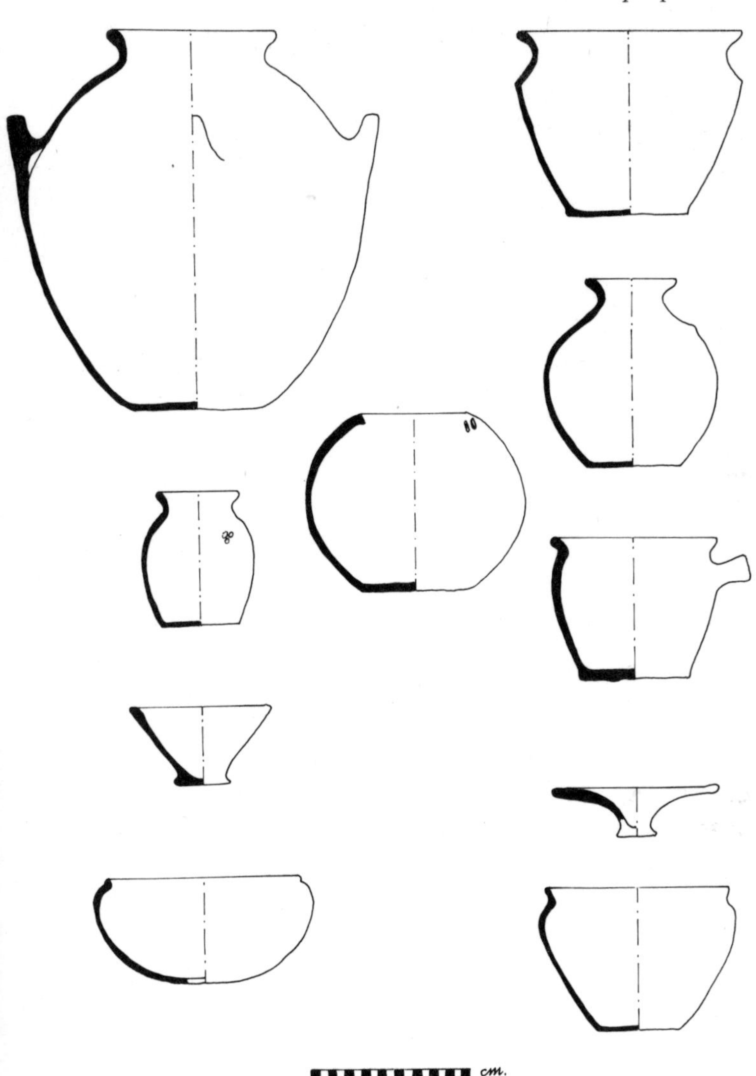

Fig. 34 Talayot pottery forms (after Rosselló Bordoy)

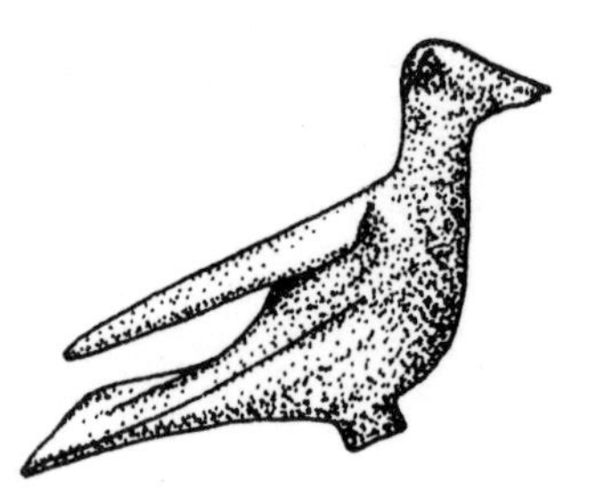
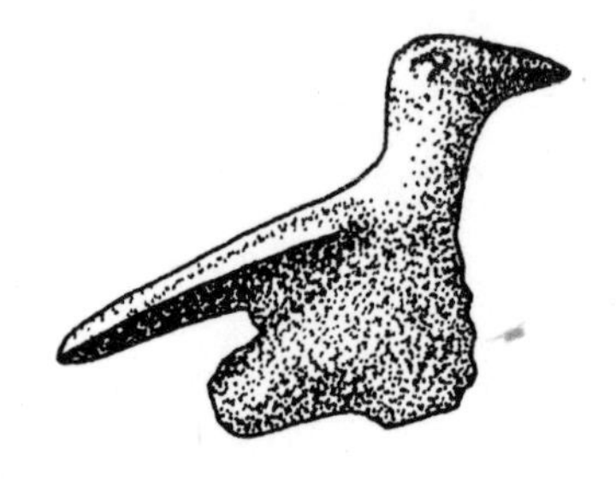
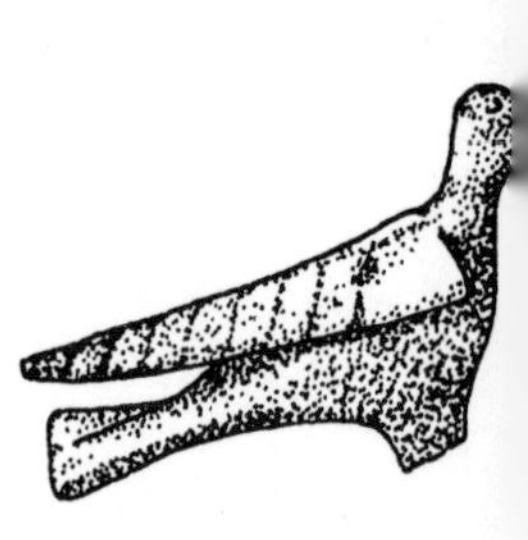

Fig. 35 Pigeons or small birds of bronze, Son Cresta, Lluchmayor (after Font). 1 : 2

difficult to procure. This assumption may be wrong, however. When we survey the sum of the evidence accumulated from both the official and the numerous amateur excavations on the islands during the last century, we may need to modify this pessimistic conclusion, and attribute the sparsity of known material rather to the incontestable fact that many of these, predominantly casual, finds have been either destroyed or lost.

It is possible that both Majorca and Minorca were a source of some raw materials, a little metal which could have been exploited from remote times. We know several mineral deposits which have yielded small quantities of copper, lead and iron at least; and, it has even been said, of tin. Vitruvius spoke of red lead (vermilion) from the Balearics, and said that consequently snakes could not live there. Imports traded from other Mediterranean countries, though arriving irregularly during the pre-Roman period, would have had to supplement these supplies, and this would have meant that metal was at times sparingly used by the inhabitants. As in all aspects of Balearic archaeology, the most difficult problem with metal finds is their dating. There is always the danger that different series have become confused, and that we attribute to advanced or Roman periods forms which in fact belong to the Talayot phase, at least in the first half of the last millennium BC.

Fig. 36 Bronze figurine of a bird on the end of a shaft, Son Cresta. 1 : 3

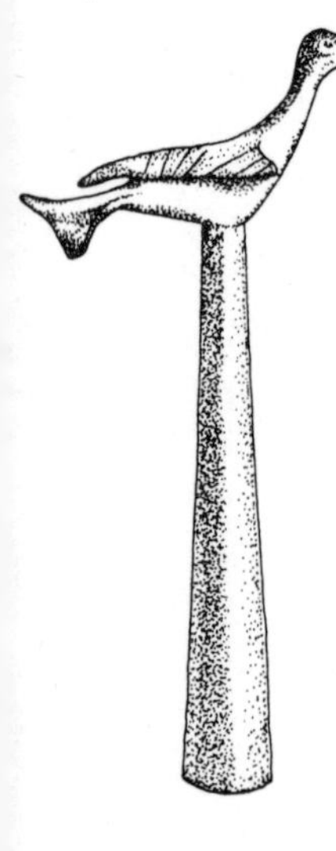

There is nothing outstanding about Balearic metallurgy, and techniques were rudimentary. The forms were cast in moulds and we have found those used for making the lead plaques. It may be that crude human figurines, horns, birds on long rods, bull protomes and possibly some of the large bull's heads were the work of local craftsmen. Bulls' heads like the three found in the talayotic sanctuary of Son Corró

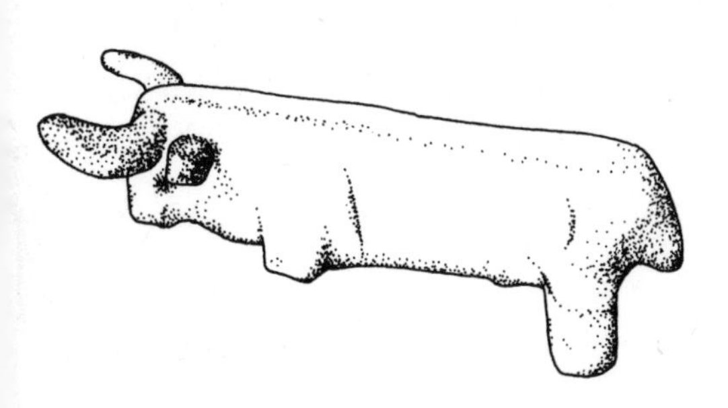

Fig. 37 Small bronze bull, found at Son Cresta, Lluchmayor (after Font). Actual size

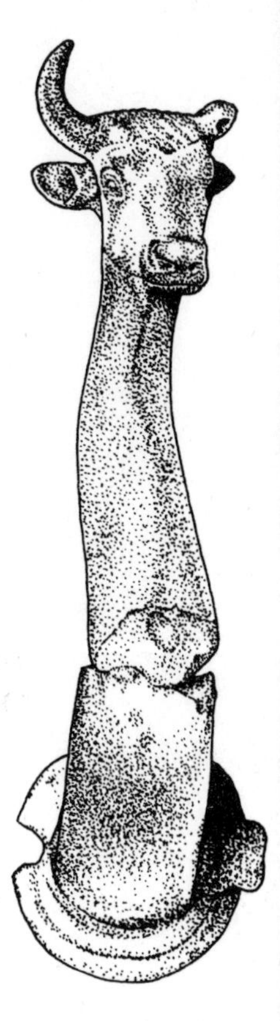

Fig. 38 Bronze head of a bull, from Can Peloní, Valldemosa. Reconstruction.

(Costitx) are impressive, and show new techniques. The treatment of the eyes indicates their late date.

Metal finds from the pre-Talayot phase have already been described. This was followed by what we may term the classic phase, during which bronze became more abundant and a wide variety of forms appear. A third phase, distinguishable only with difficulty from the second, takes us up to Roman times, and in it we find a profusion of metalwork, among which it is often impossible to differentiate imports from native work. The iron sword found in the Talaya Joana has been held to mark the beginning of the Iron Age in Majorca.

The more simple types which occur repeatedly in the classic phase of the Balearic Bronze Age are rings and bracelets, swords and daggers, spear- and arrow-heads, flat axes with a curved cutting-edge, and made in double moulds, socketed axes, side-lugged axes, chisels and gouges.

At the height of the Balearic metal age in the last centuries BC art objects such as figurines appear among the now richer metal finds. At the same time, however, local industries were developing a range of expression which, though reflecting outside influences, penetrated deeply into native life, to give the period its strangely diverse character. We find a wealth of figurines of an obviously religious nature.

In addition we find purely decorative objects in profusion. These are rather late in date, and doubtless achieved their greatest currency in the final centuries BC, at the time when iron was coming into regular use. Among them are the strange lead objects with geometric relief decoration, and an outline which has been interpreted as a schematic representation of the horns or head of a bull, recalling a Minoan altar. To judge from their holes, these little plaques may have been sewn onto clothing.

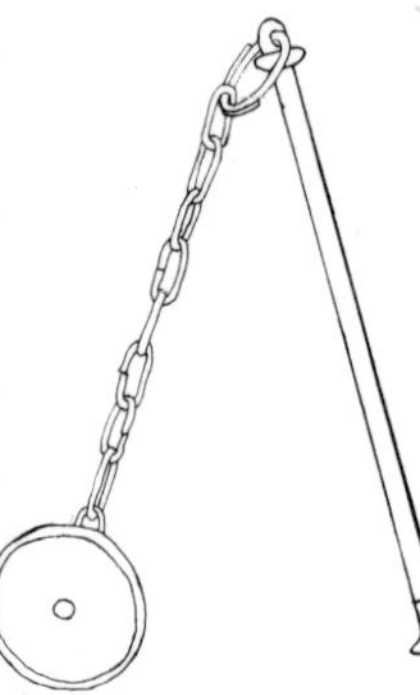

Fig. 39 Rod with chain and bronze disc, from Cometa dels Morts (after Font)

Another form encountered in this late phase has been called the *tintinabulo*, or jingle. It consists of several cast or beaten bronze discs, sometimes with *pointillé* decoration in strange patterns, attached by chains to a bronze rod. It has been supposed that the handle would have been placed between the hands of the deceased, and a disc laid over the mouth. This explanation assumes that the objects were symbols of prestige or authority. They have been found in a great number of places, especially in burial caves, since in the final stages of Balearic independence burial in natural caves came back into fashion (if indeed it had not been practised throughout).

Ornaments, like bronze or iron bracelets, having plain, spiral, or more complicated star-shaped or spiked forms, are extremely abundant. Also found are bronze models, including little eagles. One curious form is a composite bronze collar of juxtaposed strands, very similar to contemporary nordic *Halskragen*. The best of these come from Lloseta, as does a magnificent bronze belt. We are told of the prohibition on the import or use of gold and silver.

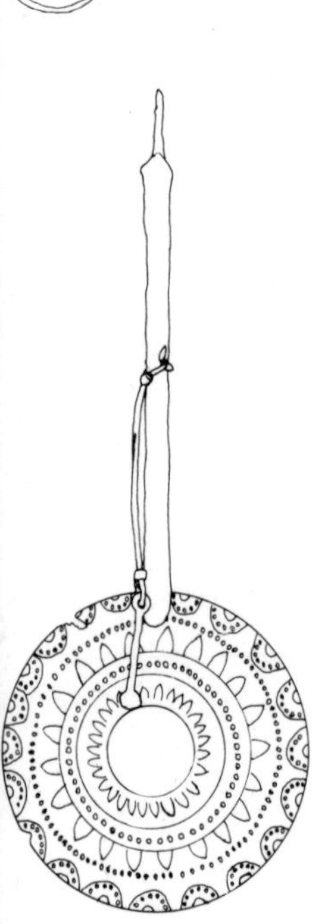

Fig. 40 Repoussé disc of bronze, from Cometa dels Morts (after Veny). Approx. 1:6

Weapons. All the authors who wrote about the Balearics were in agreement on one point, that the inhabitants were expert with the sling. This would be natural for a people who were constantly handling stone and were skilful in adapting it to their purposes. Strabo and Timaeus tell us that they hurled stones (pebbles and possibly baked clay or lead shot) from the sling with the force of a catapult and with great accuracy, hitting the mark at up to six hundred paces, wounding those who were on the far side of walls and smashing their armour and helmets. Three sizes of sling were used, according to distance, and they were carried wound round the head or with one on the head, one in the belt and one in the hand. The throwers' skill was the result of training, to which they were subjected from boyhood: mothers used to place their meals in a tree, and they had to bring them down with a sling stone. The slings themselves were made from sinew, skin, rushes or other vegetable fibres, and excellent ones could be made from the esparto grass which is still used for the purpose by shepherds in the mountains of Spain. As mercenaries the sling-throwers were particularly useful for opening a combat by demoralizing their opponents or for attacking the defenders of a wall. According to Caesar, the usual weight of sling-stones was one pound.

Fig. 41 Bronze discs, from the cave of Son Taxaquet, Majorca (after Colominas and Font). Approx. 1 :3

Other weapons also are represented. There are wooden darts with fire-hardened points: examples with an iron point are rare, since this metal is scarce. After the daggers of the early Bronze Age, we pass to solid-hilted swords of Mediterranean or Mycenaean type, a form which also occurs as a dagger. Some of the swords bear comparison with the European Möringen type, and with other Late Bronze Age forms. These are followed at a later date by some antennae swords or daggers, generally of iron. There are also curved swords of Greek origin.

Plate 29

Plates 31, 32

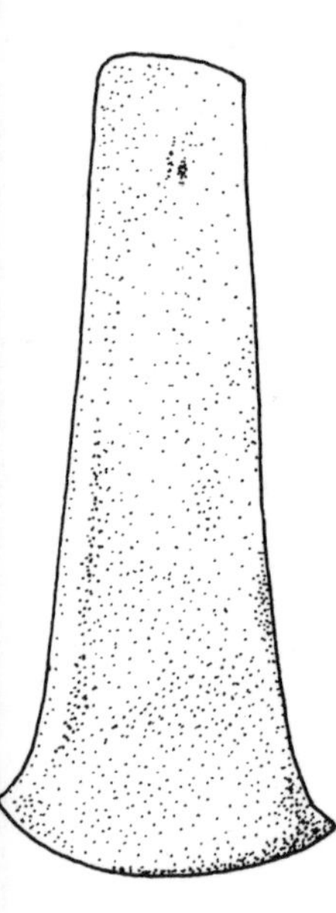

Fig. 42 Bronze axe, Cas Corraler, Felanitx. Majorca Museum

Other finds include spear-heads, ranging from crude forms, which may be local or more primitive, to perfectly made examples. There have been some examples of the *pilum*. By way of defensive armour, apart from what is shown on the Greek warrior figurines, we have several bronze helmets (for example from Ses Paisses, Artá).

Trade and transport. We must assume that trade would have been as active as transport difficulties would allow. It is comparatively easy to trace typical remains of Roman roads, and we may suppose that in part they followed older tracks. Those in Minorca in particular have been the subject of study by Mascaró. More of a problem are secondary roads, which may belong to much later periods.

Land transport would have utilized rudimentary methods, but these must have been effective, since otherwise it would not have been possible to shift the stone used for building purposes.

There is no doubt that like all good inhabitants of the Mediterranean the Balearic islanders practised piracy, and for this the islands were admirably placed. Movement by sea undoubtedly took place, though we have no exact references to the types of craft employed. The one passage where Balearic craft are actually mentioned, describing them putting out against ships of Metellus Balearicus during his conquest of Majorca, can be interpreted as referring only to simple rafts. It would, however, be difficult to see how the Balearic people came to deserve their fame as pirates without having more sea-worthy craft. We are led to suppose they were more skilful at sea than the Iberians; although belief in that people's naval ineptitude has been much weakened in recent times, at least if we are speaking of the whole of Spain.

Personally, I believe that seafaring was one of the most important of Balearic activities, and that communication between the islands was active. There would have been frequent passage between Majorca and Minorca, not only on peaceful errands but on warlike missions – to judge from the imposing defensive structures we find and the uncomfortable hidden passages in so many of the talayots.

Religion. To understand any culture it is essential to know its religion; yet in archaeology any such study is especially difficult and hazardous. It must involve a search for basic concepts and attitudes, which generally

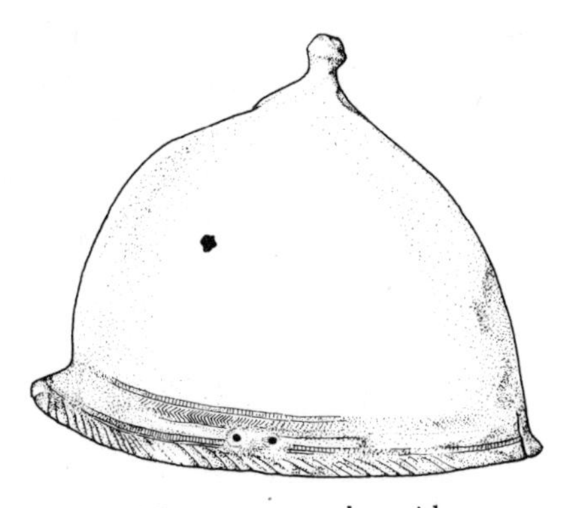

Fig. 43 Bronze helmet of a type common in the Balearics. Found at Llubi. Majorca Museum. Approx. 1 : 5

lie hidden in the human mind, and their significance cannot be evident from material remains. For this reason we are quite unqualified to reconstruct the remote religious past of the Balearics, being without the appropriate evidence for the centuries before Christianity was introduced.

We may, however, draw some conclusions from archaeological data, even at the risk of falling into dreadful confusion. Thus, I feel tempted to assign a religious significance to the group of naked warrior figurines, which we summarized when discussing the influence of Greek sculpture. These figures, some up to 50 cm. high and 4 kg in weight, would seem to be votive offerings, and to come from temples or native sanctuaries. Their style seems fairly archaic, whilst the warrior from Son Taxaquet is dated by his helmet and crest to the fourth century BC.

Plate 58

We might then allow the cult of a warrior god in the last millennium BC, and agree he should be called *Mars Balearicus*. Possibly this cult would have been brought back by mercenaries who had fought in Sicily.

The idea that there was a bull-worshipping cult on the Balearics has been mooted, and it might, indeed, be assimilated to the cult of the warrior-god, the bull being one of his symbols. The abundant evidence furnished by native and imported bronzes such as those we have described, in particular the famous find of bulls' heads from Costitx, would appear to support this hypothesis. Not only does the bull's head seem to have a religious import, but also figures of doves and eaglets, as well as the single horns found, in association with spears (*hastae*) at Son Corró and Cova Monja.

Plate 55
Plate 27

Both the possible bull cult and such remains as link the Balearics with religious rites in other Mediterranean countries find parallels in Biblical texts, and no interpretation can afford to ignore all these factors. The symbolic figurines provide a particularly good example.

The many other aspects of religious life in the Balearics, and further possible divinities there, at present elude us, although some of the enclosures in our settlements must have had a religious purpose. We may mention the square building in which the splendid Costitx bulls were discovered, and, in the village of Els Antigors, Ses Salines, a horseshoe-shaped building which is 5 m. across and has a roof supported by four pillars. Small vases of *ex voto* character were found on the top of stones, together with a thick layer of ashes, animal bones, jawbones of pig and goat, and goat horns. No less important in this context is the building at San Mari, Santa Margarita, though this already contained Roman finds. News of a find, not yet published, of wooden bulls' heads, is very interesting indeed.

It also seems difficult to deny that the taulas had some religious significance; I believe, for my part, that this enigmatic structure could not have been purely functional in purpose. There are some writers who suggest that the taula, too, is linked with a bull cult; but this notion is as questionable as any which concerns ancient symbolism and rites. In certain cases, apart from animal sacrifices, there might be some evidence of pottery offerings (*cf.* the find at Sa Mola and Santa Ponsa).

There can be no doubt that the care lavished on the construction of monumental tombs was linked with ideas of life beyond the grave. I have already given a sufficient account of the evidence from the different types of cave cemetery. The Son Maimó cave, near Petra, excavated by L. Amoros, has yielded a great deal of information on this theme. Coffins were found hollowed from the trunks of pine, olive and wild olive, though unfortunately these disintegrated on exposure to the air. The series of metal goods we have already listed completed the equipment of the graves. It is obvious that we still have more to learn about these matters when we consider recent discoveries in the Son Real cemetery in Majorca, which revealed, as already described, finely constructed tombs built from well dressed stone blocks, circular, squared, or like a small boat (*navetiforme*) in plan.

Cave burials. It is remarkable that natural caves should not only have been used as burial sites throughout the Talayot period, but have continued in use far into Roman times. It is worth while describing some of the finds from these caves.

One of the sites to produce the most abundant material is Son Cresta at Lluchmayor, discovered in 1895 and excavated by the Institut d'Estudis Catalans in 1917. The main cave measures 18 × 11 m., with a 'vestibule' of 14 × 7 m., and contained three crude columns. There were a great number of burials, with inhumation and cremation in stone urns, which had either flat or peaked covers.

Great quantities of grave goods were found including hand-made biconical, ovoid and cylindrical pots, as well as much wheel-turned ware, lamps and unguent jars of the second century. As a selection from the rich metal finds we may cite a bronze figurine of a warrior girding on his armour (a Greek work of the fifth century BC), a resting bull, a small bull's head in the style of the Costitx finds, sixteen birds mostly on rods, numerous rings, of which twenty are spiral, bracelets, bells, embossed and plain discs, lead plaques, three further bulls, a gold ring, and two coins of Augustus.

Similar lists, some shorter, others even longer, could be compiled for finds from the caves of Son Juliá, Lluchmayor, and those of Els Fiters, Muro, or from the cave of Sa Cova at Arta, S'Albaraiet at Campanet (where fifteen skulls were found), Sa Torre Redona at Palma, Son Vaquer at Rivera, Son Danús and Sa Madona at Santañí, Santa Ponsa at Calviá, Sa Pleta at Mandía, Es Rafal at Montuiri, Son Serra at Felanitx, to name the most important sites. This brief account will give some idea of the comparative richness of sites of this type, and of what we may still hope to find in the future. Unfortunately, by their nature the finds are usually dispersed before they can be adequately studied. The difficulty of dividing the finds into pre-Roman and post-conquest is also apparent, since obviously there was no break between the periods. It can be shown, too, that bronze was far more widely used than iron. It is remarkable that we do not find more tools suitable for stone-working, when we remember the enormous effort, in quarrying and dressing stone, implied by the sometimes huge blocks and squared building stones encountered on the islands.

ANTHROPOLOGY

The course of migration from other islands of the central Mediterranean can be clarified only by anthropological evidence. There is adequate material for such studies from the hundreds of inhumation burials on the

Balearics. Work on it has barely begun, however, and has been cut short by the untimely death of Dr Miguel Fusté, who had undertaken the task. There is no complete study of the skeletal remains of the several hundreds of Balearic dead, from over two thousand years of antiquity, for comparison with similar surveys from other islands or the Mediterranean coastlands. In these circumstances we can simply record some of the features of the early Balearic population.

It is hardly surprising that results published to date (Aranzadi, Alcobé, Fusté, Pons) agree in confirming a gracile people of Mediterranean race with some admixture of Eurafrican and Cro-Magnoid elements and, especially, of features of the Dinaric-Armenoid race, that is, of brachycephalic groups from the eastern end of the Mediterranean.

Genetic studies too are likely to play an increasingly important role. It may be recalled that it has been possible to identify an illness peculiar to Minorca, *favismo*, or an allergy to broad beans, which could only have been brought in by a group of human carriers from some other Mediterranean region where the disease still exists.

If we wish to end with an estimate of population, we may argue from figures given in ancient texts about mercenaries from the Balearics. The numbers quoted for detachments of islanders recruited on various occasions suggest that a good proportion of the employable men emigrated. These figures have enabled us to put the population of Minorca at about five thousand, which compares with the figure of about four thousand which Tarradell obtained for Ibiza, based on the number of burials. This allows us to assume that the more fertile island of Majorca might have had twenty to thirty thousand inhabitants.

ORIGIN AND CONNECTIONS OF THE TALAYOT CULTURE

We now come to the question which the reader will no doubt have been asking from the beginning: Who were these crazy people responsible for the stone structures on the Balearics, and where did they come from? This is exactly what archaeologists and amateurs alike have been considering over the years. Let us set out the evidence which has a bearing on the problem, even though from the outset it must be admitted that there is no satisfactory solution.

It is easy to see that there was a certain community between all the islands of the Mediterranean, although by definition none was exactly like the others and each modified or developed characteristics which distinguishes it from its fellows (a similar process can be observed among the Canary Islands.) In the Balearics the process terminated inexplicably in a definitive separation of the Pityusae, the islands of Ibiza and Formentera, from their larger neighbours. Even these two islands, however, exhibited differences which cannot easily be explained, certain features being found on one that are not found on the other. A further point which soon becomes evident is that the Balearics were not in close contact with the Iberian mainland; indeed it may be that connections were entirely sporadic, and almost without consequence. It was not until later that the islands became incorporated into Spain, though even in the classical period relations were minimal.

We are no less uncertain about relations between the two larger islands during the thousand years of their cultural zenith.

At the same time it is perfectly clear that everything about Balearic archaeology reflects not the Western world but the Near East, with its exuberant creativity. This influence was spread principally by sea, since only competent navigators could have colonized our remote islands, bringing with them seeds for crops and the basic flocks and herds.

When we attempt to emerge from these generalities and be more specific as to origins and dates, our ignorance is almost complete. We have already remarked that links with Spain must be supposed to have been weak, although the lack of cultural connections between the mainland and Ibiza is quite odd. With the south of France there must have been cultural interchange over long periods, especially at the time of the Provençal artificial chamber tombs, which were copied by the local population.

Sardinia is the island nearest to the Balearics, which explains the close cultural contacts between them. Moreover Sardinia, almost a small continent in size, exceeds the area of Majorca and Minorca together; numerous features of our archaeological record belong equally in a Sardinian context. It is evident that the Balearic pre-Talayot phase derives from a Sardinian Eneolithic, with incised ware and beakers, as well as other comparative material. The pottery parallels in turn lead us to the caves of the Ligurian coast, which also has other features in common with the Balearics, such as v-perforated bone buttons. I think the Sardo-Italian origin of these is obvious, and though there are others in Catalonia, they will have come overland from Italy. More than a century ago the Italian archaeologist Dell Marmora compared our Balearic talayots with the *nuraghi* on Sardinia (though these are more grandiose), and that island's 'giants' tombs' with the Minorcan naveta. Along with the various parallels which may be traced to Sardinia, I am inclined to accept that the cyclopean mode of building could have come to the Balearics from this source.

In recent years there has been additional evidence to take into account. The island of Corsica has at last been properly studied, showing that there were cultural similarities with neighbouring islands. The French archaeologist R. Grosjean has established a number of periods, one of which, characterized by tower-like structures (*torri*), corresponds to the Talayot period, and its connections with the Balearics have been recognized. Sicily, too, had close relations with other islands, especially in earlier periods. We may suppose that links between Sicily and Spain and the Balearics were stronger at certain times than at others, although we cannot establish any agreed chronology for such contacts.

Further afield, the small island of Malta (with less than half the area of Minorca or Ibiza) rivals its larger neighbours in the density and splendour of its monuments. There are significant parallels with the Balearics, notably in the special and unusual layout of the houses or enclosures of oval plan in the Alcaidús settlement at Alayor in Minorca.

Other parallels are found in countries such as Egypt, Tunisia, where what is called the Sirtes culture includes structures not unlike the talayot, or other lands to the east. Linguistic evidence has so far been of no assistance for tracing connections, since no native texts are known; nor can we discern any extensive indigenous vocabulary through the repeated occupations to which Majorca and Minorca have been subjected. Certain hypotheses have, nonetheless, been put forward. The name *Baleares* might have connections with the *Balari*, a tribe on Sardinia. On Sardinia, too, there was the town of Nora, said to have been founded by the Tartessian king Norax – a strange account which perhaps contains an important historical fact. 'Nura' seems to be precisely the name given by the people of Sardinia to Majorca (Minorca may have been called 'Clumba').

As we have already pointed out, the study of the skeletal remains of the ancient Balearic people, based on the abundant evidence of the tombs, is still to be pursued. The islands' early peoples did not differ fundamentally from their present-day inhabitants, and a basically Mediterranean population had been established by Neolithic times. Oriental elements seem to have been present as well, though not to a degree which allows any real distinction to be made between the earliest inhabitants of the Balearics and the race of those who have since then occupied Spain, or the western Mediterranean generally.

In essentials the cultures of Majorca and Minorca developed virtually parallel with those of their neighbours. A more exact analysis, however, will require careful study of the classifications which have in recent years been proposed for each of the other islands – that of Evans for Malta, Bernabò Brea for Sicily, Pallottino and Lilliu for Sardinia and Grosjean for Corsica – as is clear from the account I have given.

There are, moreover, signs that the Balearics were influenced from farther afield. Certain features might be classed as Cycladic, or come from even farther off, if Florit is right in his views on the idol he discovered at Ciudadela. We should not lose sight of the fundamental fact that for millennia the valley of the Nile was the source from which megalithic building techniques were diffused throughout the world.

We are less able to visualize exactly what impulses were necessary to stimulate the development of the Talayot culture, and to account for its special characteristics.

CHAPTER IV

The Punic Islands: Ibiza and Formentera

While there are many geological connections between the Balearic islands we have been studying and the two, lying nearest to the mainland, which the ancients called the Pityousae (the pine islands), archaeologically – which is in this instance to say historically – there is a distinct gulf between them. The western Balearic Islands and their antiquities have been studied for a shorter time, and less intensively, than their neighbours.

It is difficult to account for the complete absence of Neolithic or early Bronze Age remains on Ibiza and Formentera, but the fact remains that they are not found. Equally, it may be recalled that the antiquities of Majorca and Minorca show practically no Iberian influence. This being so, there are strong arguments in favour of seeking a source for the Balearic cyclopean culture in islands further to the east; the same applies to the impulses responsible for pre-Talayotic culture, despite certain parallels which are known in the Iberian peninsula. Any cultural interchange between Spain and Majorca would have been bound to leave traces in Ibiza, an unavoidable landfall in this period of uncertain navigation. Our ignorance of the actual mechanism of cultural relationships in the past once again constitutes a stumbling block.

IBIZA

The history of Phoenician colonies on the southern coasts of Spain is well known. We accept that about 1000 BC, or a little later, Phoenicians were relying on a trading-post in distant Gadir (Cadiz), and that many of their merchants lived on the coast of Andalucia. The traditional date for the foundation of Carthage is 814 BC; its rise to dominance in the western Mediterranean on the fall of Tyre, and the consequent increase in rivalry with the Greeks, preceded the Carthaginian colony on the island of Ibiza and in neighbouring Formentera, which dates, according to the tradition handed down by Diodorus, to 654 BC. It is a little surprising that the Greeks, who were already familiar with the route from Italy and Sicily to Tartessos by way of the Balearics, had not established themselves on Ibiza earlier, since they were trading with Majorca and Minorca.

The subsequent history of the Carthaginians in Spain was largely the outcome of the battle of Alalia (about the year 535 BC), which secured their hegemony in the western Mediterranean and the expulsion of Greek traders from the coasts of Spain. The destruction of Tartessos about 500 BC led to the closure of the Straits of Gibraltar and hindered free passage into the Atlantic for two hundred years. The policy of restoring and extending Punic power in Spain undertaken by the Barcas, despite the loss of Sicily and Sardinia as the result of the First Punic War, led to some years of intensified Carthaginian hegemony and to its final collapse shortly afterwards, after the second Punic War. The archaeological evidence indicates that Ibiza survived the misfortunes of the Carthaginian empire, and maintained its Punic character for a considerable time. Cadiz, and other cities in southern Spain, were Phoenician while Ibiza was Carthaginian.

Diodorus, in his account, no doubt based on Timaeus, of the island Pityoussa, fixes its position at three days' and three nights' sail from the Straits of Gibraltar, one day and a night from the African coast, and only a day out from the peninsula. The name of the colony is given as Ebusos, with varying forms in different authors. The name may be of native origin, or more likely from the Punic word which also meant 'pine island'. On coins we find the form IBUSIM.

There is some information in Roman texts about contemporary Ibiza. We find descriptions of its capital (the town of the same name) with its walls and market place, and of the comparative fertility of the countryside, with picturesque hills where, with the vine, the true olive was cultivated, having been grafted onto the wild tree. Strabo and Mela speak of rich cereal crops, and of an abundance of rabbits, which was also a feature of other Balearic islands. Pliny praises the dried figs which Ibiza produced, and also its bulbs. He refers, too, to rich fisheries and mentions that in contrast to other countries dried cod was appreciated there, because it was cooked only after being softened. Several references mention that the island did not support dangerous animals. There must have been many salt-workings, a speciality of the Carthaginians, which would compete with their many sites on the mainland coasts of Spain.

We know very little of the history of Ibiza during the long period of Carthaginian dominion. It appears to have played no important part in the second Punic War, although Livy records that Scipio attacked it with a fleet. In 206 BC, after defeat on the Spanish mainland, the Carthaginian commander Mago led his fleet to the Balearics and, as might be expected, was well received in Ibiza. At the end of the war the island may have been accorded recognition with a status similar to that of Cadiz (which Pliny calls a federate city) and enjoyed a period of freedom during which coins reminiscent of Sicilian Greek models, and bearing the legend EBUSITANORUM, were minted. The best known of the coins from Ebusos, found in contemporary trading-centres in peninsular Spain, is a small and rather crude bronze coin with a Cabiros device. Another common device is a bull.

After the conquest of the Balearics by Q. Caecilius Metellus Baliaricus in 123 BC Ibiza must have shared the fate of the larger islands and gradually become Romanized and absorbed into the general life of Hispania. After the vicissitudes of the Middle Ages it finally became, like them, incorporated into Spain with subjection to the Kingdom of Aragon.

Principal archaeological sites. The comparatively uniform finds so far known from Ibiza and Formentera do not allow us to say with any certainty when the islands were first settled, or even whether there were already any inhabitants when Punic colonists arrived in the middle of the seventh century. We may suppose they were not entirely uninhabited, though there is hardly any archaeological proof of occupation, and certainly none of the impressive monuments of human endeavour which confront us on Majorca and Minorca.

There are, it is true, a few finds which may antedate Punic colonization. These include sherds of hand-made pottery, one with relief cordon decoration and another with a small vertically perforated handle and impressions, from the bottom layer of the well-known Cova des Cuyeram; three truncated conical pots with lugs were also found at different sites. There is a bronze axe with side lugs, and a socketed axe found with a bronze ingot from Formentera, with two other axe fragments from the site of Les Salines. From its position, the stratified pottery could be fairly early, but there is no certain evidence of a Neolithic phase, which some have suggested, or even of a Bronze Age occupation contemporary with the pre-Talayot or Talayot period. The finds could well derive from the seventh century BC, and might even be later than the first Punic colonies.

It has been usual to cite a group of figurines in baked clay as the earliest finds from the colonial period. They were found on the islet of Illa Plana, called Triquadra in antiquity and nowadays linked to the mainland by harbour works at Ibiza. The foundations of a small temple were uncovered there in 1907, with a central column and remains of a capital. Numerous pieces of several curious figurines were found in a nearby pit, together with sherds of pottery and ostrich egg shells. The figurines are archaic in appearance and show traces of painting; they have been made on a wheel, though with the surface modelled by hand. Similar fragments have turned up at other sites on the island.

Plates 59, 60

The group includes thirty-five complete figures and fragments of as many more. They are from 16 to 25 cm. high, apart from one which must have measured about 50 cm. when it was complete. The figures are ovoid or bell-shaped, and the general impression is markedly crude, making them look grotesque. In a recent study Maria E. Aubet has distinguished four types, the first being the crudest, with male and female bell-shaped figures. The second comprises bird-headed figures, with marked masculine attributes and wearing a sort of cap; the third type is generally masculine, ovoid in form, with the arms on the belly and wearing a clay necklet. The fourth type is an open bell-shape, masculine, holding up a double-spouted Punic lamp in the right hand. Most of the figurines have a hole in the base, possibly to help in the firing.

The Illa Plana figurines have been presented as a group contemporary with the first Punic colonists, but Miss Aubet argues for a revised and much lower chronology. Her first type has clear parallels in Sardinia, Carthage and the eastern Mediterranean and will indeed be from the eighth or seventh century BC. The fourth type however dates to the fifth century, while the third (though with less certainty) might be as late as the third or second century. Miss Aubet's second type, too, is probably late. In addition there were a few pieces and fragments found nearby which are undoubtedly late products, being better made and showing classical influence. We may suppose the site was a sanctuary where votive offerings accumulated in the pit, perhaps dedicated to the god

Eshmun, who has been identified with the Greek Asclepius, the god of medicine.

The cave sanctuary of Es Cuyeram found in 1907 in the Sant Vicens district near the bay of Mayans contrasts with the Illa Plana site. It is difficult to reach, though more spacious inside. In addition to pottery and fragments of copper and iron, excavation produced cremated human bone and a great number of baked clay figurines. There have recently been new excavations there, directed by E. de Fortuny.

Plate 64

The older find there included over six hundred figurines and some thousand heads of the same type, as well as censers in the form of female busts. There was also a small ivory model of a lion, which had been carbonized, and other figures in stone. The figurines sometimes show signs of painting, and even gilt. Most of them were bell-shaped and represent a praying woman dressed in a tunic and mantle. She usually has a head-dress of cylindrical form, occasionally with flowers, and a necklace with, below it, a rose. Her breast is adorned with a lotus flower, caduceus, solar disc or moon crescent and, in rare cases, she seems to be seated on a throne. The figurines are not more than 25 cm. high and usually take the form of busts, the diameter across the elliptical base being at most 10 cm. Depiction is exact, though we cannot claim they were portraits. One type of figure is flat and worked only on the front, has a cylindrical head-dress and holds a dove or other sacred bird in the left hand.

Another class of statuette seems identifiable as a goddess, to judge from form and attributes: triple necklet with amulets, torch, veil, pomegranate, pig. This could only be Tanit, successor to the Phoenician Astarte. A large collection of small heads in a variety of styles from the Cuyeram cave completes this splendid array of figurines, which show obvious signs of Greek influence. We may imagine the cave was a sanctuary of the goddess Tanit during Hellenistic, and even advanced Roman, times, and that the ashes of the priestesses would be kept there.

A third sanctuary is known on the Puig den Valls, a hill 2 km. from the town of Ibiza, which was excavated in 1906 by the Ebusos Archaeological Society. Traces of houses were uncovered, with two temples, one of which was underground. Among the finds were pottery, including cylindrical jars for offerings, modelled heads, ornaments such as beads and amulets, glass unguent jars etc. Greek influence is obvious in both the pottery and equipment, and this has led to the suggestion that we may have here evidence of a Greek trading post on Ibizan soil.

Cemeteries. Three important cemeteries are known on Ibiza. That of Purmany preserves in a corrupt form the ancient name of Portus Magnus, originally borne by the magnificent bay of San Antonio. It belongs to the Roman period, as is evident from the urns, pottery and other material, as well as from the coins, found in the tombs, which are almost invariably earth graves.

Another considerable cemetery was found in the suburb of Talamanca, very close to the island's capital. The Cas Curoné cave had already been discovered here in 1896, and had produced the bust of a woman 23 cm. high and worked only on one face; it is one of the finest examples to come from Ibiza. Excavation in 1906 and 1907 revealed a typical Punic cemetery of the type of Puig des Molins, which we describe below. The finest find was a baked clay figurine of a woman in a long tunic, with a cylindrical head-dress, emerging from a shell which encompasses her. Other small cemeteries, such as Cala d'Hort, are also interesting.

All the sites we have mentioned are, however, surpassed in splendour and riches by the Puig des Molins cemetery on a hill ('Windmill Hill') alongside the modern town of Ibiza. It covers the whole northern slope, from the summit to the foot. This is a classic example of a Punic cemetery, consisting of underground tombs cut in the rock to various depths, with narrow shaft entrances. Being so near the town, it is natural that its position should have been long known; consequently, when conditions were favourable for treasure-hunting while the island was governed by the Moors, the tombs were plundered and passages tunnelled between them. The extent to which grave deposits have been disturbed, the number of tunnels dug, combined with finds of Arab lamps show how persistently the tombs were combed, leaving us to deplore the loss of treasures.

Fig. 44

Despite these depredations, enough material has been salvaged to furnish several museums: there are rich collections in Ibiza, Barcelona and the National Museum in Madrid, as well as smaller groups, for example at Valencia. About four thousand tombs are known, and there must still be some undiscovered. They are closed by large stone slabs, and are quite shallow, without descending steps. The normal tomb is about 3 m. long, and each one may contain between one and six burials. The bodies were laid in stone coffins, which are smooth-surfaced when they are made in the sandstone (*marés*) which forms the underlying stratum of the island. These coffins, cut from a single block of stone, are of various sizes, though it has been noticed that many of them have a length of 2.28 m. They do not have lids, but normally there are several hollows for standing amphorae or round-based jars, as well as cavities in the region of the corpse's head and feet. Only a small number of complete skeletons remain, and valuable information concerning the physical type of the local population has thus been lost.

The quantity of grave goods which has been recovered is none the less enormous, the most abundant finds being of pottery. The Ibizan clay is excellent, and furthermore it was believed that it had the power to cure illness and ward off beasts of prey, a fact which may account for the development of the pottery industry and for the extensive export of its products.

There are numerous amphorae, the most typical form being pointed, with either one or two handles, a wide mouth and sometimes a projecting rim. Imported ware is represented, and is either Punic, with bands of painting, or Greek, with the usual rich decoration, predominantly Italiote. In the Roman period the practice of cremation explains the appearance of frequent urns and funerary dishes for holding ashes. Other pottery forms are vessels with a long spout, generally taking animal forms (bull, sheep, dove, or, in one example, a human head), circular open lamps with from one to four spouts, unguent and extract containers, as well as *terra sigillata*. There are crude *ex votos* of baked clay representing parts of the body, and disc-shaped clay loom weights with two perforations.

There is also a quantity of glass ware. Though round-based vessels and fine pieces are very rare, there are large numbers of extract containers, which are most attractive with the iridescent patina of age. Very numerous are glass and paste beads, generally spherical in form, either smooth or with relief work and in a variety of colours (green, blue, white or red). There are flasks for perfume enamelled in blue and green, and a great variety of tiny pendants for necklaces, in the shape of small amphorae, Cabiri, sphinxes, tortoises, winged beasts, human heads, acorns, etc. Scarabs are found in the same materials, showing the Egyptian influence

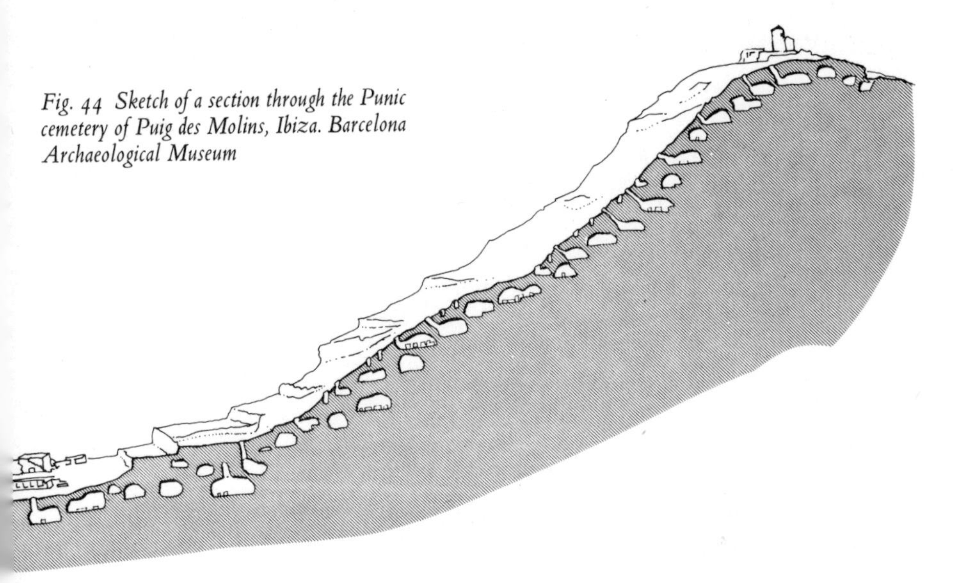

Fig. 44 Sketch of a section through the Punic cemetery of Puig des Molins, Ibiza. Barcelona Archaeological Museum

which Punic commerce spread throughout its ventures in the western Mediterranean.

A wide variety of objects were fashioned in ivory and bone: buckles, punches, trinkets and amulets which again include sphinxes, Cabiri, acorns and modelled heads, as well as combs and hemispherical perforated buttons.

Scarab-seals are commonly made from agate, carnelian and malachite, and have various interesting scenes cut in the flat lower face. Female figures are rare, though we find priests at sacrifice, human heads with exaggerated or grotesque features, riders, warriors, four-horse chariots, sphinxes and winged beasts, cupids, scenes from mythology or inscriptions.

Notable among the metal finds are lead perfume boxes, circular mirrors of burnished bronze, rings, bracelets, seals, pincers, spatulas, spoons, bells, needles, buckles, little boxes, razors, fish-hooks, etc. As may be expected when the tombs have been so badly rifled, few gold or silver objects have survived, although there are some silver rings, ear-rings, bells and other pendants. Gold finds include rings, pendants, and ear-rings which are usually plain hoops. The pendants are sometimes quite tiny, and they are often found fixed to the ears and nostrils of the baked clay figurines we shall examine below. Very rare finds are the gold mountings for scarab-seals; these gripped the edges of the seals so that a finer impression could be gained by rocking.

Plates 61, 62

The most frequent and characteristic finds at Puig des Molins however are the baked clay figurines, which were deposited in enormous quantities as offerings at the cemetery. Among them we can distinguish divinities, sacred animals, masks and portraits of the deceased. The figures were made in moulds, and most are female. There are traces of polychrome painting and sometimes gold ear-rings or nose pendants (*nezem*). Occasionally they demonstrably represent the goddess Tanit, the Punic Artemis, or her priestess. Seated on a sort of throne, with a dove on one hand or at her feet, the tall figure in elegant drapery might even be compared to a Tanagra statuette. In a few instances the reverse of the figure is also modelled. In other examples a seated or standing woman may be suckling some creature, pressing a disc to her breast, lifting up a sphere in her left hand, or holding doves, torches, necklets or discs, etc. Many of the more crudely made female figures are wearing a cylindrical head-dress and a long mantle which covers the arms. These must represent the dead. Facial features, down to details, are rendered on the one-sided busts. Some moulded female heads have been found, to add to the variety of finds. Male figures are far fewer and less carefully made; notable among these are representations of the god Baal, with a head-dress and necklet, and of a Cabiros seated on a throne, wearing a conical cap and with a mace in his left hand. A limited number of figures have been hand-modelled, instead of cast, but they betray the imperfect work of the unskilled. Miriam Astruc drew attention to relief work on vases from Ibiza, and to casts and reliefs in baked clay. Among the clay reliefs, which were sometimes used to decorate pottery, we find the figures of Silenus and Bes, birds and animals, horsemen, floral patterns, ribs, and a whole series of amulet pendants. Of no less interest are the masks which imitate Greek models, with features of the satyrs or Sileni, to frighten off possible violators of the corpse.

Both Colominas and Garcia Bellido have produced systematic classifications of the principal styles represented among this mass of material. The largest group derives clearly and directly from the Greek, either Hellenic or Hellenizing; Sicily will doubtless have played an important role in transmitting these influences. The Roman style represents a continuation of this movement. Punic and Egyptian-influenced styles are also evident, though here there is always a Hellenizing substratum. The comparative crudity of these last styles is further proof of the Phoenicians' and Carthaginians' artistic sterility.

Other minor sites and casual finds on Ibiza have provided further examples of the forms we have described.

Coins have been found in considerable numbers. In addition to foreign issues, in particular Hellenistic coins from the east and Roman coins, the finds included a quantity of small copper pieces from the Ibiza mint, usually under five grammes in weight. The devices include a Cabiros, squatting or with his symbols (snake and hammer or mace), and an attacking or standing bull, and there are short legends. These types achieved wide currency in the trading centres of peninsular Spain. They are easily identified and show the extent of Punic commerce at its height, in the period just before the Roman conquest.

I have left until last one of the more curious finds from Puig des Molins, the ostrich egg shells, which are a link with Africa. Despite their fragility it has been possible by patient search to find and restore some of the shells to their original form. In addition to plain shells there are the far more interesting examples which have been painted, almost always in red. Mademoiselle Astruc in particular made a study of the motifs. There are occasional shells which have been engraved, in one instance in a sort of *bas relief*. In the very rich collection from the Ibiza site some shells were cut to three-quarter height to form a jar, for holding colouring material. Others were cut in half, to make bowls or, very rarely, masks. There would seem to be no finds of whole eggs which show the hole through which they were blown.

Decoration on the ostrich shells is principally of plant patterns, or geometric. Often running plant designs link bands of leaves, flower buds, which sometimes open into tulips, palmettes, or flowers which are difficult to identify; or we may find floral motifs, predominantly palmettes or lotus flowers, grouped into metopes. There are elegant alternations of rosette and lotus, and the oriental style of this decoration is evident. The rosettes have up to sixteen petals, some of which are coloured. They alternate with a winged eye (*udja*). A few instances of animal designs (including the sphinx) are found, as well as occasional geometric figures on the half-shell bowls. Shell fragments with summary paintings of a smiling face are rare, as are shells bearing plastic relief.

The sum of the evidence dates the use of the great Puig des Molins cemetery from the end of the sixth century, and it continued well into Roman times, at least until the first century AD.

Others finds. The time is ripe for increasing our knowledge of Ibizan archaeology, what with the greater interest the subject now attracts and the new work continuously undertaken, which includes the use of underwater archaeology. Substantial wrecks have been discovered by this means, notably the one found in the bay of San Antonio. Although as might be expected underwater archaeology has so far yielded mainly Roman finds, there is every likelihood that remains of Carthaginian ships and their cargoes will come to light, thus helping us to clear up this important aspect of the Punic colony. We still do not know enough about houses and villages, and there are as yet no sites with stratigraphy. It is also to be hoped that one day the relationships of the Pityusae with the people of the Balearics proper will be understood. While we have as yet no evidence of contacts, such isolation is scarcely credible, given the navigational skills of the Carthaginians on the one hand, and the piratical tendencies of the inhabitants of Majorca and Minorca in antiquity on the other.

FORMENTERA

Close beside Ibiza is the small, flat island of Formentera, called Ophioussa by the Greeks, or later Columbraria. They described it as deserted and occupied by beasts of prey, and especially by snakes. There was a fanciful legend that to fend them off it was enough to surround oneself with a pile of earth from Ibiza, which frightened them away and was harmful to them. In fact even at this period Formentera was already important for its salt deposits, which provided material for salting food, a great speciality among the Carthaginians.

There has been little archaeological exploration. Finds of Punic or Roman remains are poor, though there are more from the time of Arab domination, including several cemeteries with a quantity of pottery and tombstones. A cave at a place called Portusalé found by chance in 1906 contained human skeletons with pottery, which was said to be 'archaic'. The report cannot be confirmed, since the material has been lost. Two bronze axes, one socketed and the other with side lugs, were found while constructing a road from the port of La Sabina to Es Caló. Punic and Roman coins, small pots of different types, cremation urns, etc., have turned up by chance from time to time around La Mola and in the parishes of San Francisco and San Fernando. On Formentera too the number of finds is increasing, and we may hope that this impression of relative poverty will be modified, with no repetition of the lamentable history of lost and forgotten material. Recently the German archaeologist Niemeyer has explored several sites (Isla de Alga, Sa Cova, and Estany del peix) which have produced pottery ranging from Massiliote types to Late Empire.

CHAPTER V

The Close of Ancient Times

AFTER THE ROMAN CONQUEST

Caecilius Metellus conquered the islands for Rome in the years 123–122 BC. The pretext for occupying them was piracy on the part of the inhabitants, who ventured out in fragile craft to make daring attacks on whatever vessels came near. They even presumed to attack the vessels of Metellus's fleet, showering them with a hail of stones. The general, however, had taken the precaution of covering the decks of his ships with skins, and with his galleys and darts made the attackers flee to the coast, where they took refuge in what Florus calls tumuli, though he doubtless means the numerous talayots, with their narrow passages. We are told it was necessary to seek them out there, in order to vanquish them. According to Orosius there was great slaughter, and Strabo relates that three thousand Roman colonists were brought in. The islands submitted, and their subsequent Romanization was successful, to judge from the abundant harvest of Roman remains, especially pottery, which archaeologists are constantly bringing in from all quarters; some of the authors also make boastful claims about the pacific character of the population shortly after the conquest.

Plate 30

Quintus Caecilius Metellus, to match the honours accorded to his father and his brother who were named Macedonius and Creticus respectively, was dubbed Baliaricus, and two cities owe their foundation to him: Palma and Pollentia, one in each of the bays on the coast of Majorca. Excavations at Pollentia have revealed a talayot building just beneath Roman works of the first period of the colony's foundation. In fact, native life went on undisturbed in many respects; the old settlements continued to be occupied and their cults observed. This fact has given rise to errors in dating some of the finds.

The Balearics are again mentioned in texts concerning the wars between Caesar and the sons of Pompey. In 47 BC Gnaeus Pompey left Africa for the Balearics, occupying Majorca and Minorca without difficulty, though needing to use force to take Ibiza. Gnaeus fell ill but was able to cross to Spain, where the battle of Munda and his death in flight put an end to his career.

Thenceforth the history of the Balearics for several centuries is a tranquil one; the land underwent remarkable development, and foundations were laid for an agriculture and industry which were long to survive. There are some interesting accounts, of a more or less anecdotal nature, about the Balearics in Roman texts. Strabo relates what happened about their rabbits. This animal has thrived in peninsular Spain since Palaeolithic times, to the point where it is probable that the present name, 'Spain' – from the Semitic root *span* – derives from it. However, some authors think the animal was imported from Africa. One story goes that a pair was taken to the Balearics, and there multiplied to such a degree that the inhabitants entreated the Romans to be transferred to another land. Pliny asserts that the rabbits brought famine, and that a delegation was sent to Augustus asking for soldiers to help put them down. Strabo, who gives the islands' names, details of their size and positions, also describes the inhabitants, saying that the fertility of the soil made them peaceful. Friendship with the pirates had been the fault of a few, for which all had paid, by being conquered by the Romans. He praises the fine harbours, though noting that reefs near their mouths called for careful navigation.

He also records the fact that Metellus after the conquest brought three thousand Romans from Spain as colonists. With these (though Balil has questioned this interpretation) he peopled the two cities, Palma, which commemorated his victory, and Pollentia ('the city of strength'), adjacent to present-day Alcudia; the name is, however, preserved in the modern Pollensa nearby. These were not true *coloniae* but, according to Pliny, bore the title of *municipia civium romanorum*.

It is also Pliny who gives us the names of three other cities on Majorca, which are not certainly located. These were Guium (Pliny wrote Cinium, but an inscription requires us to make this rectification), Tucis and Bocchorum or Bocchoris. This last must have been on the bay of Pollensa, a site well-known for the find near that town of two patronage tablets which name it. The name is also preserved in present-day Boquer. Guium and Tucis enjoyed Roman law, and Bocchoris was federated.

On Minorca, Pliny speaks of Iamno, which also appears in other authors and is doubtless Ciudadela, of Mago (Mahón), which received its name from the Carthaginian general Mago, and of Senisera, which is assumed to be Santa Agueda. Iamno and Mago are quoted by Mela as being simple *castellae*. On Ibiza, the town of Ebusus was also federated.

The island of Capraria is also cited by Pliny and must be Cabrera, since its distance from Majorca is fairly accurately given. He says further that facing Palma the islands of Menaria, Triquadra and the still smaller Anibal's are visible – a statement which has tempted some scholars to the fanciful interpretation that Cabrera was the birthplace of Hannibal.

The activities of archaeologists, in the nineteenth century and later, have produced a great quantity of Roman material which it is not always possible to arrange in chronological order. One could almost say it is impossible to walk on Balearic soil without treading on Roman pottery. A good number of epigraphic pieces are also found. These confirm the normal pattern of life in the islands under Roman rule. Ancient Pollentia, with its theatre and extensive remains, is being scrupulously excavated under the patronage of the Bryant Foundation. As for Palma, the destruction of medieval times has resulted in confusion on the site of the ancient town; but recently there have been convincing finds of buildings of Republican date. An inscription naming a duumvir, abundant Roman pottery, the classical street plan, the Roman aspect of the Almudayna gate, continuity of the site through the Moorish town (Madina Maiurka), and other minor factors adduced by Rosselló Bordoy and J. Camps confirm the identity of ancient and modern Palma.

Plate 66
Fig. 45

We know of few historical events connected with the Balearics during the Roman period. The actual process of Romanization and transformation of the 'talayotic' way of life is hidden from us. But there is soon evidence that the delights and advantages of the islands came to be appreciated by the epicurean Roman. Thus Tacitus relates that the notorious informer L. Suillius Rufus was banished by Nero in AD 58 to the Balearics, known as the scene of a *copiosa et molli vita* which today we call the *dolce vita*. Shortly afterwards, when Galba rebelled against Nero, Suetonius tells us that he got in touch with the exiles on Majorca, which suggests there was a group of them.

The old sanctuaries and living-sites, and the caves where burials had taken place for centuries, naturally continued in use. Older religious traditions and customs took on novel forms.

Some traces of the old customs and superstitions, and some toponymous elements (only eleven for Majorca and three for Minorca have been

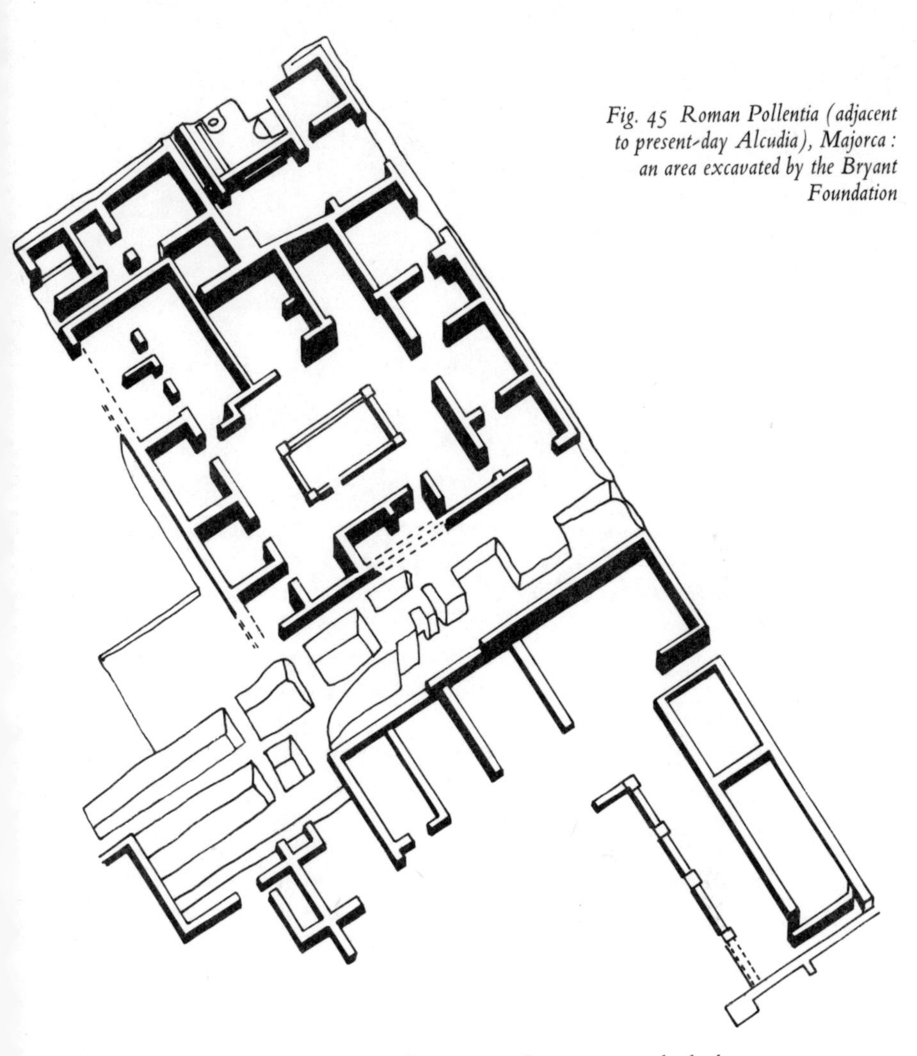

Fig. 45 Roman Pollentia (adjacent to present-day Alcudia), Majorca: an area excavated by the Bryant Foundation

recorded) must doubtless have come down to us; but as yet we lack the criteria to recognize them. It should, on the other hand, be possible to make a detailed study of the pottery, which would demonstrate the whole evolution of the famous *terra sigillata* up to its development into Late Roman ware, and also of the sculpture, which also was imported in great quantity. Certain surviving bronzes are excellent examples of Roman art.

Plates 68, 70

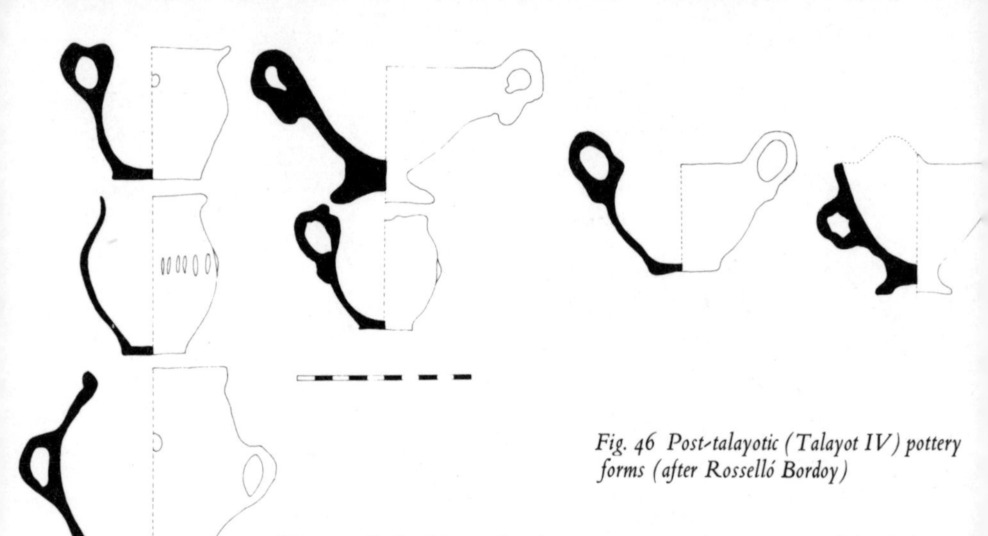

Fig. 46 Post-talayotic (Talayot IV) pottery forms (after Rosselló Bordoy)

We conclude this section by returning to the question of the Balearic language. From what we know of the indigenous population ethnically, it must evidently belong to the presumed linguistic substratum common to all coastal regions of the Mediterranean. However, language is the most nebulous aspect of Balearic history: a succession of imported tongues, Latin, Arabic and Catalan, has at all events so obliterated the native tongue that we can have no notion of what contacts it could have had with Indo-european or Hamito-semitic groups. Linguists like Juan Colominas will in due course furnish us with a small fund of place and proper names from the Balearics of prehistory. These will enable us to make the comparisons and hypotheses which for the present are out of the reckoning. There is no doubt that the peculiarities of present-day phonetics have roots in the past. The passage of seventy generations has not sufficed to eradicate them.

UNDERWATER ARCHAEOLOGY

It is quite understandable that underwater explorers should have been attracted to our islands, since there are some thousand kilometres of coastline. Unfortunately, it has until very recently not been possible to control this exploration, and the sites have largely been pillaged for the benefit of collectors.

At present more than a hundred underwater sites are known, as reported by Mascaró, of which sixty are round Majorca, fourteen round Minorca and eleven off Cabrera. A recently formed association of enthusiasts and archaeologists together has encouraged more rigorous control than was previously possible in the usual, and even dangerous, circumstances of the finds.

For the most part our knowledge of this type of find is rather precarious. There are reports of amphorae, which were used on Roman vessels for transporting cargoes of wine, oil, wheat, almonds and hazel nuts and of shafts of lead anchors, and of mill-stones. The amphorae are of common Greek, Roman or Punic types, with their local variants, but on occasion other pottery has been recovered. Ingots of metal and sounding-leads, as well as ships' timbers have been located. These are sometimes well enough preserved to establish the form of the craft. Some of the finds date from the fourth or third century BC but there are more from the time of the Roman Empire in the first centuries of our era, when trade increased.

It is off the south coast that the majority of the wrecks are found. It has been suggested that these derive as much from attacks by pirates as from accidents, though I do not believe that pirates were the chief cause. In the bay of Palma, where one of the ancient ports was situated (another would have been at Alcudia-Pollentia), valuable pieces of bronze of considerable size have been obtained from a wreck, but have been dispersed among private collectors, or even taken out of Spain. A *dolium* has been dredged up in Palma harbour, and a marble female head was found near the small island of Toro. Important finds have been made near San Jorge, including a ship 25 m. long and another with a cargo of lead ingots, stamped with the names of the mine controllers, of which 1600 kg. have been recovered. In shallow water at Porto Cristo lay the remnants of a ship with its timbers clad in lead, the principal cargo being lamps bearing Christian symbols; a vessel sunk in the bay of Sant Vicens has the same lead sheathing. The famous fragment of the decree tablet concerning the municipality of Bocchori came from a wreck in the bay of Pollensa. A wreck near the Illa Redona ('of the eels' or 'burbots'), close to Cabrera, contained lumps of bronze and tin ingots, weighing 60 kg. Near Conejera, flat ingots of tin were found together with lead ingots. The coasts of Ibiza have produced similar finds, especially round the bay of San Antonio, as we have already noted.

Underwater exploration is without doubt a field which will yield surprising results, once sufficient resources are directed to the task, under the control of competent archaeologists. We must nonetheless be grateful to the pioneer amateurs who began diving for the thrill of making archaeological discoveries.

CONCLUSION

In Diocletian's provincial reorganization the Balearics probably became part of the *provincia Carthaginensis* (diocese of Hispania, prefecture of the Galliae). Later, between 369–385, they were made into a province, the seventh in Hispania, governed by a *praeses*. The first mention of the names Maiorica and Minorica is in a third-century text of St Hippolytus.

The outstanding feature of the period was the spread of Christianity, which was quickly adopted in the islands. Apart from historical accounts and some inscriptions, we have the remains of several Early Christian churches to show the advances of the new faith in late imperial times. Details of their construction and decoration confirm that primitive Christianity in the Balearics derived from African sources. It was also asserted that Saint Paul visited the islands.

On Minorca these churches include Son Bou, discovered in 1951 near the southern coast and dating from the end of the fifth century, Fornás de Torelló, near Mahon, with magnificent mosaics, discovered in 1956, the older find (1888) on the Isla del Rey in the bay of Mahon, also with important mosaics, Cap des Fort (Fornells), discovered in 1958 and still being excavated, a church near the harbour of Ciudadela, found in 1918 but destroyed, and the latest discovery (1967) on the island of Colom.

Plate 67

Early Christian churches in Majorca have been known for a longer time, but in general they are less well preserved. Son Peretó at Manacor (1912) is pre-eminent for the beauty of its mosaics. In the same district there was once the basilica of Sa Carrotja, of the fourth-fifth century, found in 1908 and now destroyed. Despite its interest, the same sad fate befell Cas Frares, at Santa Maria del Camí, found in 1833. The cave sanctuary of San Martin at Alcudia may also date back to this early period.

There has been much dispute over the authenticity of an encyclical letter attributed to Severus, a bishop of Minorca in the first half of the fifth century, which reports a dispute with the Jews, ending in the conversion of many of them.

It was not long before the tranquillity of the Balearics, in which doubtless the new faith was fervently observed, was broken by attacks from the northern tribes the Late Empire could not contain. About AD 426, according to Idatius, Vandals under the command of Gunderic ravaged the islands after conquering the east coast of Spain, where they must have built a fleet. On the death of Valentinian III, Gaiseric with his Vandals gained control from north Africa of all the west Mediterranean islands, including Majorca, Minorca and Ibiza. Son Peretó was burned, and as an Arian Gaiseric persecuted the Catholics until his death in 477. His cruel son Huneric called the Council of Carthage in 483, and we learn that the Balearics formed a province as a dependency of the governor of Sardinia. Each island sent a bishop to the Council; Macarius from Minorca, Elias from Majorca and Opilius from Ibiza. The four hundred and sixty six bishops present were then persecuted and many suffered martyrdom. Freedom was not restored to the Catholics until 494, under Guntamund. It is not known to which Metropolitan church the Balearic bishoprics belonged.

Already in the fifth century a monastery was established on the small island of Cabrera, and it was visited by Orosius. In 603 Gregory I sent a legate to deal with the indiscipline there.

The Balearics were again invaded in the mid-sixth century, this time by Byzantine forces under the command of Apollinar. Together with reconquered Spanish territories and Ceuta they were formed into a second Mauretanian province. We know the names of several wealthy and powerful Jews of the time, and we hear of theological discussions, such as that between Licinianus, bishop of Carthage, and Vicente, bishop of Ibiza, who preached the authenticity of a letter written by Christ, which fell from heaven onto the shrine of St Peter at Rome. St Isidore and other contemporary texts use the names Maiorica and Minorica; but others call the islands the Aphrodisiades, a name derived from ancient Greek tradition.

It is not known precisely when the Byzantine empire in the western Mediterranean came to an end. It must have been near the end of the eighth century. There is an account of the first Muslim expedition which plundered the islands, in AD 707. It has been supposed that the Moors, who had been established on the mainland since 711 and the years following, finally subjected the islands in 798. It would appear that the facts were rather more complex, and that there were a number of expeditions against the Balearics. This is not to say, however, that they were not in some way tributary to the caliphate (a punitive expedition was ordered in 848 by Abderrahmen II), or that they escaped pressure both from the Carolingian emperors and from the Counts of Ampurias during the ninth century. Majorcan churches at this time were subject to the church of Gerona. Rosselló Bordoy maintains that the Balearics were not definitely annexed by the Caliphate of Cordova until AD 902–3. At the beginning of the eleventh century the *valí* of Denia took over Majorca and Ibiza. A century later (1114) a Pisano-Catalan expedition set free many thousands of Christian slaves.

It is a curious fact that the last known medieval reference to the Balearics, in Suidas's tenth-century history, emphasized their skill with the sling. This had been the *leit-motif* of classical writings, which at times had led to the exaggeration of supposing that slinging – a common enough device among primitive peoples – had originated there. Sergius Grammaticus asserts this, in his fourth century commentaries on the *Georgics*.

We have now reached the end of surviving references to the Balearics and their inhabitants in ancient texts. Though not very numerous, they do help us to visualize something of the life and vicissitudes of the early population, and their role in the history of the western Mediterranean. Only the Romans can claim to have involved the islands in the life of the Hispanic province. Later, under Vandals and Moors, they were again cut off, until King James I of Aragon conquered Majorca in 1229 and Ibiza in 1231. Minorca he made a feudal dependency in 1235, and it was finally incorporated in the kingdom by his grandson, Alphonso III, in 1287.

Bibliography

ABBREVIATIONS

AEA	*Archivo Español de Arqueologia. Madrid*
AIEC	*Anuari de l'Institut d'Estudis Catalans. Barcelona*
Amp	*Ampurias. Barcelona*
AMSEAEP	*Actas y Memorias de la Sociedad Española de Antropologia, Etnografia y Prehistoria. Madrid*
Ant.J	*Antiquaries Journal*
BACAEP	*Bulletí de l'Associació Catalana d'Antropologia, Etnologia i Prehistoria. Barcelona*
BSAL	*Boletín de la Sociedad Arqueológica Luliana. Palma de Mallorca*
BSHNB	*Boletín de la Sociedad de Historia Natural de las Baleares. Palma*
BSPF	*Bulletin de la Societé Préhistorique de France. Paris*
CHPH	*Cuadernos de Historia Primitiva del Hombre. Madrid*
CIA	*Congreso Internacional de Arqueologia*
CICPP	*Congreso Internacional de Ciencias Prehistóricas y Protohistóricas*
CNA	*Congreso Nacional de Arqueologia*
DAM	*Deyá Archaeological Museum*
EAE	*Excavaciones Arqueológicas en España. Madrid*
H de M	*Historia de Mallorca, J. Mascaró, ed. I, Palma, 1970*
IBS	*Instituto Bernardino de Sahagún, Madrid-Barcelona*
MM	*Monografias Menorquinas. Ciudadela*
NAH	*Noticiario Arqueológico Hispano. Madrid*
OCB	*Obra Cultural Balear. Palma*
PB	*Panorama Balear. Palma*
RABM	*Revista de Archivos, Bibliotecas y Museos. Madrid*
RM	*Revista de Menorca. Mahón*
St.S	*Studi Sardi. Sassari*
Tal	*Colección Talaiot. Palma*
TMP	*Trabajos del Museo de Palma. Palma*
Tr.P	*Trabajos de Prehistoria (Instituto Español de Prehistoria, del Consejo Superior de Investigaciones Científicas, Madrid.)*

CHAPTER I

ALCOVER, M. *El hombre primitivo en Mallorca*, 2 vols., Palma, 1941.

ALMAGRO, M. *Manual de Prehistoria Universal*, 2nd ed., Madrid, 1970.

ALMAGRO GORBEA, M. Las fechas del C14 para la Prehistoria y la arqueologia peninsular, *Tr.P.* 27 (n.s.) 1970.

ARMSTRONG, J. *The history of the island of Minorca*, London, 1752. Spanish translation of the 2nd English ed. (1756) by J. VIDAL MIR and S. SAPIÑA. Mahón, 1930.

BOSCH-GIMPERA, P. *Etnologia de la Peninsula Ibérica*, Barcelona, 1932.

— and COLOMINAS ROCA, J. *Les fouilles de Majorque et la Préhistoire des Iles Balears,* Barcelona, 1935.

CARTAILHAC, E. *Monuments mégalithiques des Iles Balears,* Toulouse, 1892.

COLOM CASANOVAS, G. *Biogeografia de las Baleares. La formación de las islas y el origen de su flora y de su fauna.* Palma, 1957.

COMAS CAMPS, J. *Aportaciones al estudio de la Prehistoria de Menorca,* Madrid, 1936.

CHAMBERLIN, F. *The Balearics and their people,* London, 1927.

FERGUSON, *Rude stone monuments*, London, 1878.

KOPPER, J. S., WALDREN, W. Balearic Prehistory. A new perspective. '*Archaeology*' 20, 2, 1967, p. 108.

LILLIU, G. I monumenti primitivi delle Baleares, *St S.* 28 (1962).

LLOMPART MORAGUES, G. *Bibliografia arqueológica de las Islas Baleares (Mallorca y Menorca)*, Palma, 1958. (Supplement by G. LLOMPART and J. MASCARO) *BSAL.*, Palma, 1964.

MALUQUER DE MOTES, J. La Edad del Bronce en las Islas Baleares, in *Historia de España* ed. by R. MENENDEZ PIDAL, vol. I, Madrid, 1947, p. 715.

MASCARÓ PASARIUS, J. *Mapa arqueológico de Menorca,* Ciudadela, 1947–51.

— *Mapa general de Mallorca*, Palma, 1952–62.

— *Prehistoria de las Balears*, Palma, 1968.

MAYR, A. Uber die vorrömischen Denkmäler der Balearen, *Sitzungberichte der K. Bayerischen Akad. der Wissenschaften, Phil. kl.*, 1914, VI Abhandlung, 1916.

PERICOT GARCIA, L. *La España primitiva, Barcelona*, 1950 (French trans., *L'Espagne avant la conquête romaine,* Paris, 1953).

— *Historia de España*, t.I,3a ed., Barcelona, 1967.

RAMIS Y RAMIS, J. *Antigüedades célticas de la Isla de Menorca desde los tiempos más remotos hasta el siglo V de la Era Cristiana*, Mahón, 1818.

ROSSELLÓ BORDOY, G. *La Prehistoria de Mallorca,* Palma, 1972.

— and LLOMPART, G. Prehistoria y Protohistoria de Mallorca. *OCB*, mon. 3, Palma, 1965, p. 5.

SERRA RAFOLS, J. de C. *Las islas Baleares*, IV CIA, Barcelona, 1929.

VARGAS PONCE, J. *Descripciones de las Islas Pithiusas y Baleares*, Madrid, 1787.

WALDREN, W., KOPPER, J. S. A nucleus for a Mallorca chronology of Prehistory based on Radiocarbon analysis. *DAM*, no. 4, Deya.

CHAPTER II

AMOROS, L. Ariany, Petra (Mallorca), Sa Canova. *NAH.* 2, 1953, p. 17.

CAÑIGUERAL CID, P. J. Los primeros habitantes de Mallorca, La cueva de Sa Canova de Ariany. *Ibérica*, Barcelona, 1951, p. 348.

CANTARELLAS CAMPS, C. *Ceramica incisa en Mallorca,* Palma, 1972.

ENSEÑAT, B. *Los problemas actuales de la Historia primitiva de Mallorca*, Palma, 1953.

— *Noticias sobre el hallazgo en Mallorca de unas cerámicas incisas del estilo del vaso campaniforme.* VII CNA., Barcelona 1961 (Zaragoza, 1963, p. 184).

— *Aportaciones al conocimiento de los primitivos pobladores de Mallorca*, X CNA, Mahón, 1967 (Zaragoza, 1969).

— El hombre primitivo de Mallorca, in *Historia de Mallorca* ed. J. MASCARO, Palma, 1970.

HEMP, W. J. Rock-cut tombs in Mallorca and near Arles in Provence, *Ant. J*, 13, London, 1933.

— Some rock-cut tombs and habitation caves in Mallorca, *Archaeology*, 76, Oxford, 1927, p. 121. Trans. J. MASCARO, *Tal.*, n.l, Palma, 1959.

FLORIT PIEDRABUENA, G. El Myotragus coexistió con los primeros habitantes de Menorca, *Diario Baleares*, Palma, 20, 1, 1965.

KOPPER, J. S. and WALDREN, W. Balearic Prehistory. A new perspective, *Archaeology*, 20, 2, 1967 p. 108.

MASCARÓ PASARIUS, J. *Cuevas Prehistóricas de Mallorca*, Palma, 1962.

MARTINEZ SANTA OLALLA, J. Jarro picudo de Melos hallado en Menorca (Baleares), *CHPH.*, Madrid, 1948, p. 37.

ROSSELLÓ BORDOY, G. Cerámicas incisas de Mallorca, *St. S.*, 16, 1958–59, p. 300.

— La facies 'cueva cultural' en la cultura pretalayótica mallorquina, *Amp.* 1960–61, p. 263.

— *Cuevas mallorquinas de planta sencilla*, VII CNA. Barcelona, 1961.

— Excavaciones en la necrópolis de cuevas artificiales de Son Sunyer, (Palma de Mallorca), *EAE.*, n. 14.

— Informe sobre el hallazgo de cerámicas pretalayóticas en la cueva natural de Son Maiol, *NAH*, VI, 1962 (1964).

— Cuevas mallorquinas de múltiples cámaras, *St. S.*, 18, 1962–63.

— Ultimas aportaciones a la cultura pre-talayótica mallorquina. VI *CICPP.*, Roma, 1962. (1965). p. 416.

—, WALDREN, W. H. and KOPPER, J. S. Análisis de Radio Carbono en Mallorca, *TMP.*, 1.

— and MARTIN TOBIAS, R. *Un nuevo tipo de cerámica pretalayótica mallorquina*, VII CNA. Barcelona, 1961.

VENY, P. C. La cueva de Ariany, *BSAL* 31 1953, p. 35.

— La necrópolis cueva 'Cometa dels morts', cerca de Lluch, en Mallorca *AEA.*, 20, 1947, p. 46.

— La cueva dels Tossals verts (Mallorca), *Saitabi*, XI, Valencia, 1961, p. 201.

— *Las cuevas sepulcrales del Bronce antiguo de Mallorca*, Madrid, 1968.

WALDREN, W. H. Los materiales encontrados en la cueva de Muleta, *BSHNB*, 12, 1962, p. 47.

— *El Myotragus balearicus*, X CNA, Mahón, 1967 (*DAM.*, n. 5).

— A unique prehistoric weapon from the balearic island of Mallorca, *DAM*, 6, 1970.

— Beaker ware from the Balearic island of Mallorca, *DAM*, n. 7 1970.

WALDREN, W., KOPPER, J. S. *Preliminary study of the cave of Muleta*, Deiá, 1968.

— *Informe preliminar sobre análisis de radiocarbono en Mallorca*, X CNA. Mahón, 1967, (Zaragoza 1969).

—, and ROSSELLÓ BORDOY, G. *Complejo norte de Es Figueral de Son Real* X CNA. Mahón, 1967, (Zaragoza 1969) p. 83.

CHAPTER III

Talayot culture in Majorca

ALMAGRO, M. *Inventaria Archaeologica-España*. 6 Madrid, 1962.

AMOROS, L. Contribución al estudio de la

Edad del Hierro en Mallorca, cueva de Son Bauzá. *BSAL*. 22, 1929, p. 290.
— La Edad del Bronce en Mallorca, *PB*. 23, 1952.
CAMPS COLL, J. Cerámica de tipologia indígena hallada en Conejera y Cabrera, *BSAL*. 1962.
— *et alia* Notas para una tipologia de la cerámica talayótica mallorquina, *TMP*, 6, 1969.
COLOMINAS ROCA, J. L'Edat del Bronze a Mallorca. Les investigacions de l'Institut, *AIEC*, 6, 1916–20, p. 555.
— Els bronzes de la cultura dels talaiots de l'illa de Mallorca, *BACAEP*, I. 1923, p. 88.
— Gli scavi di Majorca, *Atti Conv. Arch. Sardo*, 1962, p. 115.
COMISARIA DEL PATRIMONIO ARTISTICO NACIONAL *Monumentos prehistóricos y protohistóricos de la Isla de Mallorca*, Madrid, 1967.
ENSEÑAT, B. El Puig d'en Canals, *NAH*, 3–4, 1953–55, pp. 37.
FONT OBRADOR, B. *El ciclo cultural prerromano balear. El especimen hueso tallado en las necrópolis de Mallorca y Menorca.* X CNA, Mahón, 1967 (Zaragoza, 1969) p. 146.
— Los ciervos de bronce de Lloseta (Mallorca), *AEA*. 31, 1965.
— Mallorca protohistórica, in *Historia de Mallorca*, Palma, 1970. (ed. J. MASCARO).
—, ROSSELLÓ BORDOY, G. *El poblado prehistórico de Capocorp Vell (Lluchmayor)*, Lluchmayor, 1969.
—, MASCARÓ, J. *Tipologia de los monumentos megalíticos de Mallorca*, Tal. 3, 1962.
FREY, H. O. *Trabajos de la Universidad de Marburg am Lahn, en Mallorca*, X CNA, Mahón, 1967. (Zaragoza, 1969) p. 86.
— Els closos de can Gaiá, *TMP*. 2.
HEMP, W. J. The navetas of Mallorca, *Ant. J* 12, 1932–33.
LILLIU, G. Primi scavi del villaggio talaiotico di Ses Paisses (Artá-Maiorca). *I. Naz. d'Arch.e Storia*, n. ser. 9, 1960.
— La missione archaeologica italiana nelle Baleari, *Arch St. Sardo* 28, 1962.
— Cenno sui piú recenti scavi del villaggio talaiotico di Ses Paisses ad Artá-Maiorca Baleari, *Arch St. Sardo* 28, 1962.
—, BIANCOFIORE, F. Primi scavi nel villaggio talaiotico di Ses Paisses (Artá-Maiorca) *Ann. Fac. Lettere*, Cagliari, 27, 1959.
RIPOLL PERELLO, E., ROSSELLÓ BORDOY, G. Grabados rupestres en Sa Cova de Betlem (Deyá) *Amp*. 1959.
ROSSELLÓ BORDOY, G. Los nucleos talayóticos de Puigpunyent. *BSAL*, 1957.
— *El túmulo escalonado de Son Oms, Palma de Mallorca.* Barcelona, 1963.
— Excavaciones en Es Vincle Vell, Palma de Mallorca, *EAE* n. 15, 1962.
— Excavaciones en el conjunto talayótico de Son Oms. *EAE*. 35, 1965.
— Las navetas en Mallorca. *St.S*. 19, 1966.
— Arquitectura ciclópea mallorquina. *Simposio sobre arquitectura megalítica y ciclópea catalano-balear*, Barcelona 1965.
—, CILIMINGRAS Observaciones tipológicas en algunos talayots de la Sierra de Mallorca, *BSAL*, 1958–59.
—, FREY, H. O. Levantamiento planimétrico de S'Illot (San Lorenzo), Mallorca, *EAE*, 48, 1966.
ROSSELLO COLL, G., MASCARO, J. Premier dolmen découvert a Majorque, *BSPF*. 1962, p. 100.
TARRADELL MATEU, M. La necrópolis de Son Real y la Illa dels Porros, Mallorca, *EAE*. 24, 1964.

— *Problemas de la cronologia de la última fase talayótica,* X CNA Mahón, 1967 (Zaragoza 1969).
—, WOODS, D. The cemetery of Son Real. *Archaeology*, 12, New York, 1959, p. 194.

Talayot culture in Minorca

CAMPS MERCADAL, F. De los talayots, *MM.* n. 53, 1961.
COLOMINAS ROCA, J. El problema del vas de doble fondo de Menorca, *BACAEP.* 4, 1926.
COMISARIA GENERAL DEL PATRIMONIO ARTISTICO. *Monumentos prehistóricos y protohistóricos de la Isla de Menorca.* Madrid, 1967.
FLAQUER FABREGAS, J. Navetas de tipo intermedio, *RM*, 11, 1916, p. 161.
— Excavaciones en Torre d'En Gaumés (Menorca) *RM*, 29, 1942.
— Sobre la procedencia menorquina de una Schnabelkanne, *AMSEAEP*, 1944, p. 151.
— Alayor (Menorca) Torre d'En Gaumés, Excavaciones de 1952, *NAH*, 1952, p. 99.
FLORIT PIEDRABUENA, G. Hallazgo en Ciudadela de una nueva naveta, *RM*, 1962, p. 193.
— La funcionalidad de las taulas revelada por un viesjo texto, *RM*, 111, 1969.
— Consideraciones sobre la forma externa original de la Nau dels Tudons, *RM*, 1966, p. 66.
— *Introducción al conocimiento del megalitismo y de sus manifestaciones en Menorca*, 1968.
HERNANDEZ MORA, J. Menorca prehistórica. Notas descriptivas, *RM*, 1949, p. 241.
HERNANDEZ SANZ, F. *Monumentos primitivos de Menorca*, Mahón, 1910.
MARTINEZ SANTA OLALLA, J. Elementos para el estudio de la cultura de los talayots en Menorca, *AMSEAP*, 14, 1935, p. 5.
— L'Etat actuel de l'Archeologie dans l'ile de Minorque. *Comiss. Int. por l'étude de la Preh. de la Medit. Occident*, Barcelona, 1937.
MASCARÓ PASARIUS, J. *Els monuments megalítics a l'illa de Menorca,* Barcelona, 1958.
— *Las Taulas*, Mahon, 1968.
— *El talaiot de S. Agustí vell,* Palma, 1963.
MURRAY, M. *Cambridge excavations in Minorca. II.* Sa Torreta, London, 1934.
—, GUEST, E. M., AINSWORTH, M. G., WART, T. J. *Cambridge excavations in Minorca*, London, 1832.
—, CAMERON, A., BECK, J. *Cambridge excavations in Minorca.* Trapucó, part II, London, 1938.
SERRA BELABRE, M.L. De Arqueologia menorquina, *RABM.* 69. 2, 1961.
—*Limpieza y excavación de la estación talayótica de Alcaidús, Menorca.* VI CNA. Oviedo 1959, Zaragoza 1961 p. 122.
— Canteras y pozos prehistóricos en Menorca. *Amp.* 25, 1963, p. 186
— *Menorca, piedra y Arqueologia*, Mahón, 1964.
— La naveta oriental de Biniac (Alayor, Menorca), *Pyrene*, 1, Barcelona, 1965, p. 73.
— Arquitectura ciclópea menorquina, *Simp. Arq. meg. y cicl. cat. balear*, Barcelona, 1965.
— De Arqueologia menorquina: Puertas de elementos dobles, *RM.* 1965, p. 279.
— *Contribución al estudio de las taulas. Talatí y Torre Llafuda*, X CNA. Valladolid, 1965 (Zaragoza, 1966, p. 17).
—*La naveta d'es Tudons*, X CNA, Mahón, 1964.
VENY, P. C. Un avance sobre la necrópolis de Cales Coves, *Tr. P.* ns, 27, 1970 p. 97.

The Balearic Islands

Connections with the Classical World

AMOROS, L. Capdepera (Mallorca) Son Favar, *NAH.* 2, 1953, p. 11.

— El bronce de Son Taxaquet, *BSAL.* 31, 1955–56, p. 266.

— El bronce de Son Carrió, *BSAL*, 29, 1944–46, p. 359.

—, GARCIA BELLIDO, A. Los hallazgos arqueológicos de Son Favar, *AEA.* 36, 20. 1947, p. 3.

FONT OBRADOR, B. La cabeza de pantera en bronce procedente de Son Mari, *AEA*, 36, 1958, p. 213.

— Los ciervos de bronce de Lloseta (Mallorca), AEA, 36, 1965, p. 214.

GARCIA BELLIDO, A. *Los hallazgos griegos en España*, Madrid, 1936.

— *Fenicios y cartagineses en Occidente*, Madrid, 1942.

— *España y los españoles hace 2000 años segun la Geografia de Estrabón*, Madrid, 1948.

— *Hispania Graeca*, 3 volumes, Barcelona, 1948.

— Los mercenarios españoles en Cerdeña, Sicilia, Grecia, Italia y Norte de Africa. *Hist. de España* ed. MENENDEZ PIDAL; I, II Madrid, 1952, p. 647.

—*La Peninsula Ibérica en los comienzös de su Historia*, Madrid 1953.

SCHULTEN, A. *Fontes Hispaniae Antiquae*; vols. I-IX, Barcelona 1922–47.

— *Iberische Landeskunde, Geographie des antiken Spanien,* Strasbourg 1955. Spanish trans: *Geografia y Etnologia antigua de la Peninsula Ibérica.* Madrid, 1959.

Life in the Talayot period

BLANCO FREIJEIRO, A. El toro ibérico. *Homen. C. de Mergelina*, Madrid 1961–62, p. 163.

BORRAS REXACH, C. Los honderos baleares, *H de M*, Palma, 1970.

LLOMPART, G. Mars balearicus. *Bol. Sem. A.Arq.* Valladolid, 26, 1960.

— La religión de los honderos baleares, *MM*, 57, Ciudadela, 1963.

— La religión del hombre prehistórico en Mallorca. *H de M*, Palma, 1970.

GOMILA SIREROL. *Na Patarrá*, Mahón, 1950.

PARIS, P. Les bronzes de Costig au Musée Archéologique de Madrid. *Rev Arch.* 3 serie, 30. Paris 1897. p. 138.

MASCARO, J. *La taula como símbolo taurolátrico.* X CNA. Mahón 1967 (Zaragoza 1969).

PRITCHARD, J. B. *The water system of Gibeon.* Un. Pennsylv., Philadelphia, 1961.

TARRADELL, M. El poble dels talaiots a Mallorca i Menorca. El indígenes de les Balears vistos pels autors clàssics. *Hist. dels catalans* ed. F. SOLDEVILA, Barcelona, 1962.

Anthropology

BARRAS DE ARAGON, F. Notas sobre restos humanos prehistóricos y antiguos de España, *AMSEAEP*, 9, 1930, p. 38.

FUSTER ARA, M. Estudios sobre unos cráneos de la cultura helenístico-romana de Baleares, *IBS*, 9, 1950, p. 37.

— Cráneos de la Edad del Bronce procedentes de una cueva sepulcral de Son Maymó en Petra (Mallorca) *IBS.* 12, 1951, p. 153.

GARRALDA, M. D. Restos humanos hallados en el poblado de Almallutx (Escorca Mallorca), 'Trabajos de Antropologia', *IBS*, 16, 2, 1971, p. 63.

MARTINEZ SANTA OLALLA, J. La naveta de Biniach y el estudio antropológico de algunos restos humanos por el Dr Aranzadi, *BACAEP*, 1, 1923.

PONS, J. Cráneos de la época romana procedentes de la necrópolis de Son Taxaquet (Mallorca). *IBS*, 12, 1951, p. 11.

VERNEAU, R. *Notice sur les ossements humains des anciennes sepultures de Minorque*, in E. CARTAILHAC, *op. cit.*

Origin and connections

BOSCH GIMPERA, P. I rapporti fra le civiltá mediterranee nella fine della etá del Bronzo, II *Convegno, arch. in Sardegna*, 1926.

COLOMINAS ROCA, J. Cascos etruscos de La Tène en Mallorca, *Amp.* 11, 1949, p. 196.

EVANS, J. D. The prehistoric culture-sequence in the western Mediterranean, *Bull, Inst. of Arch*, 1955–56.

— The prehistoric culture-sequence in the Maltese archipelago, *Proc. Preh. Soc.* London, 1953 (1954), col. XIX, 1, p. 41.

— Two phases of prehistoric settlement in the western Mediterranean, *Bull, Inst. of Arch.*, 1955–56.

— La civilización de las islas maltesas y sus relaciones con las demás culturas con arquitectura megalítica en la cuenca occidental del Mediterráneo, *Amp.*, 22–23, 1960–61, p. 129.

GROSJEAN, R. Les Balears et leurs rapports avec la Mediterranée occidentale *L'Anth*, 65, (1961), p. 500.

— *La Corse avant l'Histoire.*, Paris, 1966.

LABORDE, M., Aballarri, las Baleares y sus honderos, *Munibe*, San Sebastián, 1950.

LILLIU, G. Las nuragas, *Amp.*, 24, 1962, p. 67.

— Rapporti tra la cultura 'torreana' e aspetti pre e protonuragici della Sardegna, *St. S.*, 20, 1966.

MARMORA, A. della *Voyage en Sardeigne*, Paris-Turin, 1840.

MULLER, M. Die Kultur und Handelsbeziehungen der Balearen zur Bronzezeit, *Zeitschrift für Ethnologie* 84, 1, 1959, p. 124.

PALLOTTINO, M. El problema de las relaciones entre Cerdeña e Iberia en la Antigüedad prerromana, *Amp.*, 14, 1962, p. 135.

SERRA BELABRE, M. L. *Los círculos de Alcaidus. Su relación con los monumentos de Malta.* VIII CNA., Sevilla-Malaga, 1963 (Zaragoza 1964), p. 243.

CHAPTER IV

ALMAGRO GORBEA, M. J. *Excavaciones arqueológicas en Ibiza*, Madrid, 1967.

— *Un quemaperfumes en bronce del Museo Arqueológico de Ibiza,* Madrid, 1968.

—, E. DE FORTUNY Excavaciones en la cueva des Cuyeram (Ibiza), *NAH.*, XIII-XIV, 1969–70.

AMO, M. del. *La cerámica campaniense en Ibiza,* Tr.P., 1970. p. 201.

ASTRUC, M. Empreintes et reliefs de terre cuite de Ibiza. *AEA*, 30, p. 975.

AUBET, M. E. *Los depósitos votivos púnicos de Isla Plana (Ibiza) y Bithia (Cerdeña)*, Santiago de Compostela, 1969.

— *La cueva des Cuyram, Ibiza.* Barcelona, 1969.

BLAZQUEZ, J. M. Coroplastia prerromana del Puig des Molins, *AEA*, XXXVII, 1964.

FORTUNY, E. de *La cueva des Cuyram en Ibiza*, X CNA. Mahón, 1962 (Zaragoza 1964) p. 136.

GARCIA BELLIDO, A. *Fenicios y cartagineses en Occidente*, Madrid, 1942.

MACABICH LLOBET, I. *Historia de Ibiza. Antigüedad*, Palma, 1957.

MAÑA DE ANGULO, J. M. Actividades arqueológicas en Ibiza y Formentera, *AEA*, 24, 1951.

NIEMEYER, H G Archaeologischen Beobachtungen aus Formentera, *Madrider Mitteilungen*, 1965, p. 91.

PLANELLS, A. *El culto a Tanit en Ebyssos*, Barcelona, 1970.

TARRADELL, M. El impacto colonizador de los pueblos semitas, *I Simposio de Prehistoria Peninsular*, Barcelona, 1960, p. 257.

VIVES ESCUDERO, A. *Estudios de Arqueologia cartaginesa. La necrópolis de Ibiza*, Madrid, 1918.

CHAPTER V

AMOROS, J. L., ALMAGRO, M., ARRIBAS, A. El teatro romano de Pollentia (Alcudia), *AEA.*, 27, 1951, p. 261.

BALIL, A. *Notas sobre las Baleares romanas*, CNA, Valladolid, 1965 (Zaragoza 1966).

CAMPS COLL, J. *Primeros hallazgos arqueológicos en las islas de Cabrera y Conejera*, VII CNA, Barcelona 1961.

— *En torno al problema de Palma romana*, X CNA. Mahón, 1967.

CAMPANER Y FUERTES, A. *Numismática balear*, Palma, 1879.

COROMINAS, J. *Estudis de Toponimia catalana*, Barcelona 1966.

FONT OBADORS, B. Depósitos arqueológicos subacuáticos de los alrededores de la Isla Dragonera, *AEA*, 36, 1958.

MARTI CAMPS, F. La basílica paleocristiana de Son Bou, *MM.* 9, 1954.

MARTIN, G. *Conclusiones preliminares del estudio de la terra sigillata clara de Pollentia (Alcudia)*, Mallorca, X CNA., Mahón 1967 (Zaragoza 1969) p. 146.

MARTINEZ SANTA OLALLA, J. La cerámica ibérica pintada de Menorca, *RM.*, 19, 1924, p. 121.

MASCARÓ PASARIUS, J. El tráfico marítimo en Mallorca en la Antigüedad clásica *Bol. Cám. Ofic. de Comercio y Naveg. de Palma de Mallorca*, 136, 1962, p. 173.

— Yacimientos arqueológicos submarinos de Mallorca. *Congr. Arq. Subm.* Barcelona. 1961.

PALOL, P. de. Basílicas paleocristianas en la isla de Menorca, Baleares, *Festschrift Fr. Gerke*, Baden-Baden, 1962, p. 39.

PEREZ, L. Mallorca cristiana, in *Historia de Mallorca*, Palma, 1970.

PINYA, B. El Museo arqueológico y la basílica primitiva de Manacor, *PB*, 1953.

ROSSELLÓ BORDOY, G. La evolución humana de Palma en la Antigüedad. I. Palma romana, *Bol. Cám. Ofic. de Comercio y Naveg. de Palma de Mallorca*, Palma, 1961, pp. 121, 182.

— *Varia posttalayótica*, X CNA. Mahón, 1967.

— *L'Islam a les illes Balears*, Palma, 1968.

SEGUI VIDAL, M. *La carta-encíclica del obispo Severo. Estudio crítico de su autenticidad, con un bosquejo histórico del cristianismo balear anterior al siglo VIII*, Palma, 1937.

— Las Baleares romanas, *BSAL*, 1939–43, p. 333.

— La basílica descubierta de Son Bou y los orígenes del Cristianismo en Menorca, *Analecta Gregoriana* 70, Rome, 1954.

—, HILLGARTH, J. N. La 'Altercatio' y la basílica paleocristiana de Son Bou de Menorca, *BSAL*, 31, 1953, p. 69.

VENY, P. C. *Corpus de inscripciones baleares hasta la dominación árabe*, Rome 1963.

Sources of Illustrations

PLATES

Courtesy of Archaeological Museum, Barcelona: 24, 25, 29, 36, 37, 59, 60, 68, 69, 70; courtesy of Artá Museum: 28, 35, 53, 56, 57; courtesy of Bryant Foundation: 16, 20, 21, 22, 31, 63, 65, 66; courtesy of Deyá Museum: 3, 34; courtesy of B. Enseñat: 10, 11; courtesy of B. Font: 6, 7, 17, 18, 26, 27, 58; courtesy of Prof. G. Lilliu: 13, 14; courtesy of Mallorca Museum (G. Roselló Bordoy): 4, 5, 9, 30, 39, 43, 51, 52; courtesy of Mahón Museum: 44; courtesy of J. Mascaró: 15, 19, 23, 33, 42, 45, 46, 47, 48; courtesy of Prof. P. de Palol: 67. Foto Mas: 61, 62, 64.

FIGURES

Figs 1, 3, 11, 12, 22, 23, 27 drawn by Shalom Schotten; figs 9, 24, 26, 32, 33, 39, 40, 41 drawn by Luis Fullola-Pericot; figs 2, 8, 35, 37, 38, 42, 43 drawn by Susan Mercer; figs 13, 19 drawn by Janet Hartley; fig. 44 drawn by David Eccles.

The tables on pages 30 and 40–41 are by courtesy of P. Cristobal Veny and G. Rosselló Bordoy. All other photographs and line drawings are by courtesy of the author.

1

2

3

4

5

6 7

8

9

10

12

13

14

15

16

17

18

20

21

19

22

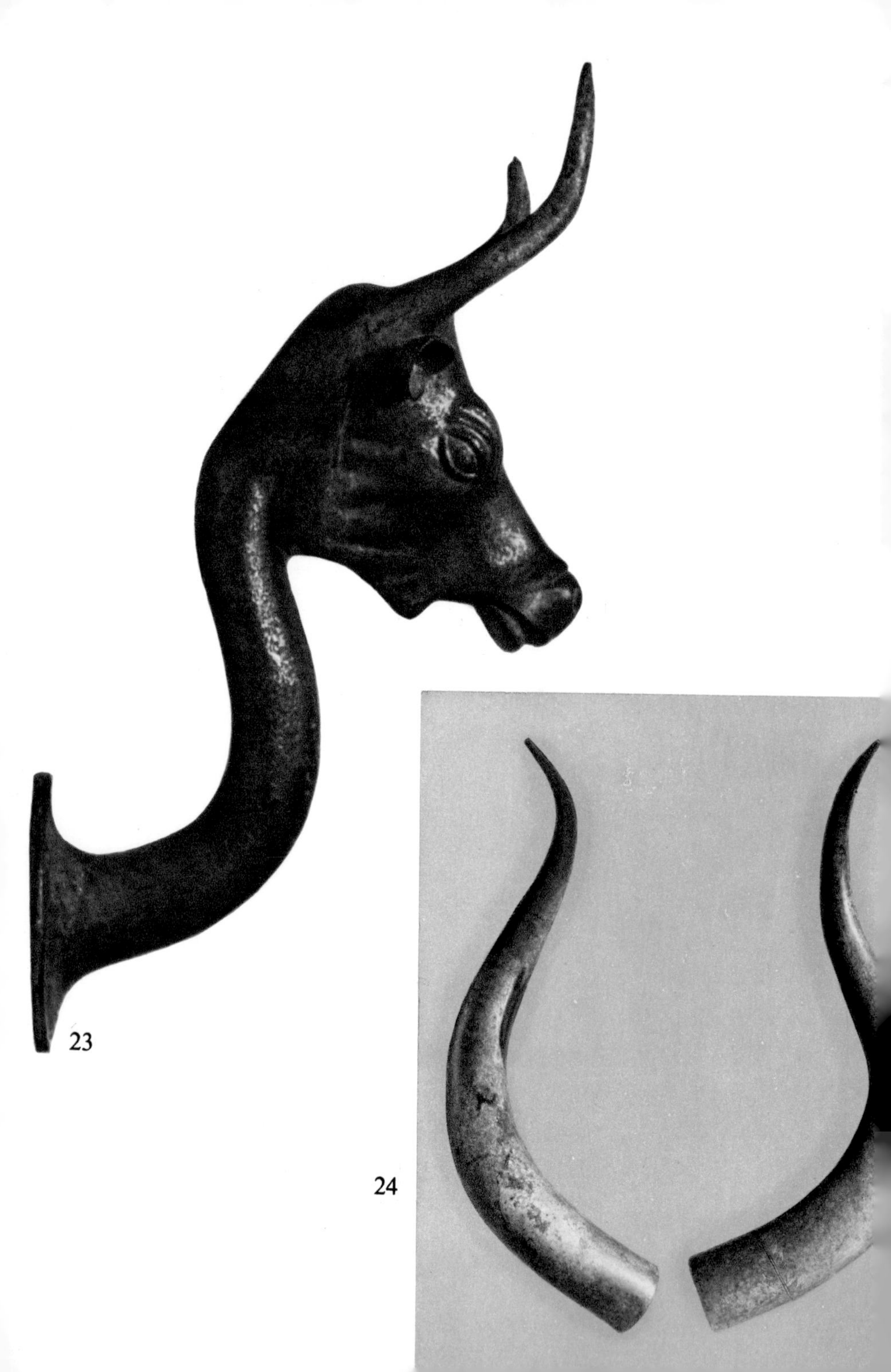

23

24

25

26
27
28

29

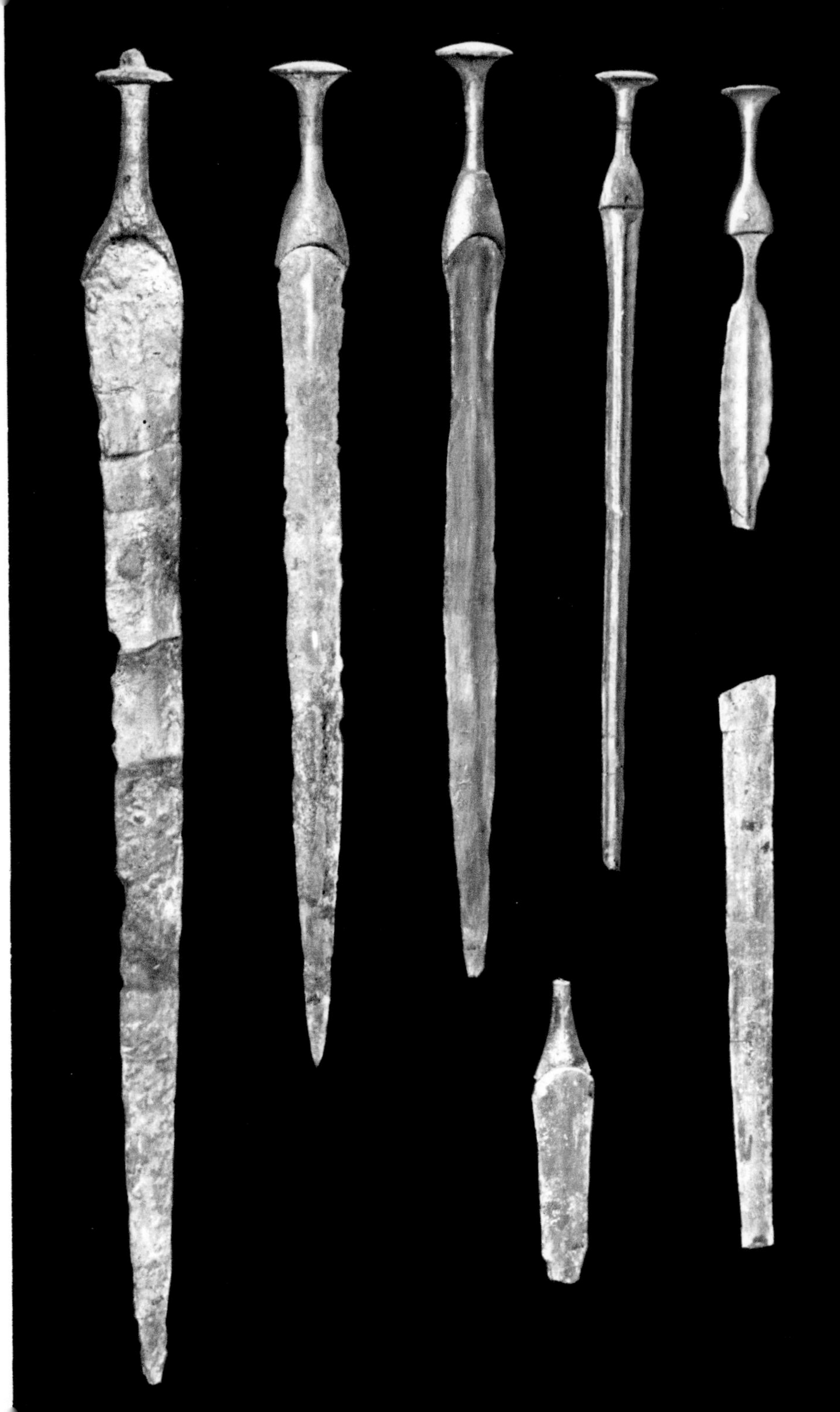

30

31

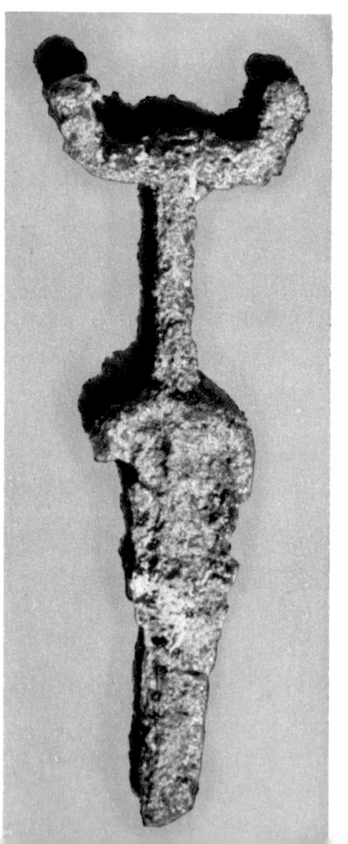
3

33

34

35

36

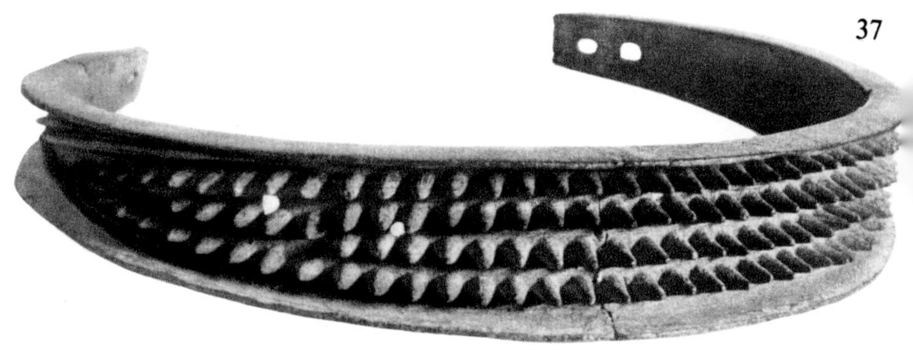

37

38

39

40

41

42

43

44

45

46

47

48

49

50

51

52

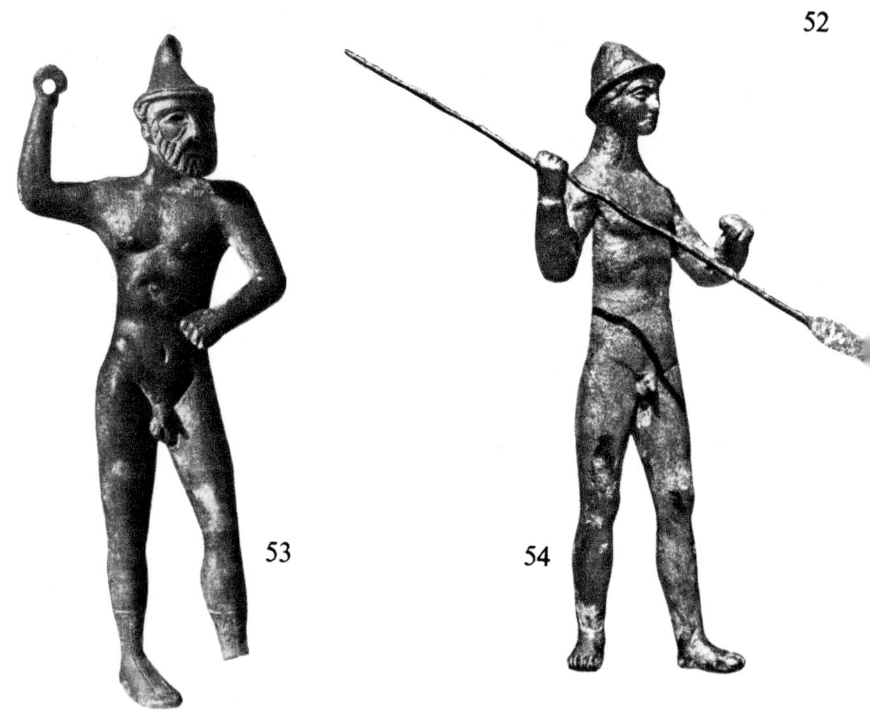

53

54

55

56

57

58

63

64

65

66

67

68
69
70

Notes on the Plates

1 Flint knife from the Majorcan pre-talayotic culture, from Tossals Verts. 1:2.

2 Bronze knife from the pre-talayotic culture of the Minorcan caves. 3:4.

3 Small bowl (incomplete) with Beaker-type decoration. Deyá Archaeological Museum. Actual size.

4 Beaked jug (*schnabelkanne*) from Minorca. Minorca Museum. 2:3.

5 Interior of an artificial cave at Sant Vicens, Pollensa, Majorca. Majorca Museum.

6 Entrance to the rock-cut cave of Son Boscana, Lluchmayor.

7 Entrance to the rock-cut cave of Son Hereu, Lluchmayor.

8 One of the enclosures in the settlement of Sant Vicens de Alcaidús, Minorca.

9 Aerial view of the Son Oms talayot complex, Palma de Majorca.

10 The sanctuary enclosure of Turixant, Almallutx, Escorca.

11 Sanctuary enclosures at Almallutx, Escorca.

12 Central column of the Sa Canova talayot, Artá, Majorca.

13 An entrance to the walled enclosure at the talayot settlement of Ses Paisses, Artá, Majorca.

14, 15 Hypostyle courts excavated by Professor Lilliu in the Ses Paisses settlement, Artá.

16 The Son Real cemetery at Can Picafort, Santa Margarita, Majorca.

17 The Son Noguera talayot, Lluchmayor.

18 A house with pillars at Capocorp Vell.

19 The square talayot of Sa Canova, Artá, Majorca.

20 Navetiform tomb in the Son Real cemetery, Can Picafort, Santa Margarita, Majorca.

21, 22 Tombs in the Son Real cemetery, Can Picafort, Santa Margarita, Majorca.

23 Bull's head in bronze from Vilar de Talapi, Buger, Majorca. 1:2.

24 Bronze bull horns from Son Mas, Inca. Barcelona Archaeological Museum.

25 Bull's head in bronze from Costitx, Majorca, National Archaeological Museum, Madrid. 1:5.

26 Bronze head of a helmeted warrior from Es Pedregar, Lluchmayor. Private collection. Length 8 cm.

27 Bronze bird on a rod, from Cometa dels Morts, Escorca. Approx. actual size.

28 Panther's head in bronze from Son Marí, Majorca. Artá Museum. 5:4.

29 Solid-hilted swords from Majorca. Barcelona Archaeological Museum. 1:5.

30 Post-talayotic vase with undulating rim. Majorca Museum. 7:8.

31 Iron antennae sword from the Son Real cemetery, Majorca.

32 Iron antennae sword from Son Bauçá, Palma, Majorca. 1:4.

33 Sandstone mould from Cas Canà, Sencelles, Majorca.

34 Bronze implement or point from the Talayot I level at Son Matge. 1:5.

35 Bronze axe, spear-head and collar from San Llorens des Cardessar, Majorca. Artá Museum.

36 Bronze pectoral, Lloseta, Majorca. Barcelona Archaeological Museum. 1:2.

37 Bronze belt, Lloseta, Majorca. Barcelona Archaeological Museum. Approx. 1:2.

38 Warrior in bronze (*Mars Balearicus*) from Torelló, near the great talayot of Torellonet Vell. Pons Soler collection.

39 Bronze figurine, *Mars Balearicus*, found on the site of Roca Rotja, Soller, Majorca. Palma Museum.

40 Minorcan landscape: in the centre the taula of Talatí de Dalt, Mahón.

41 The Trepucó taula, Mahón, Minorca.

42 The Torralba d'En Salort taula, Alayor, Minorca.

43 Bronze figure representing *Mars Balearicus* from Roca Rotja, Soller, Majorca. Majorca Museum. Approx. actual size.

44 The entrance gateway to the Torellonet Vell enclosure, Mahón, Minorca.

45 Pilaster in a burial cave at Cala Morell, Ciudadela, Minorca.

46 The vast cemetery of burial caves at Cales Coves, Alayor, Minorca.

47 The Trepucó talayot, Mahón, Minorca; one of the largest known examples. No entrance survives.

48 Mediterranean type column at Binigaus nou, Minorca.

49 The façade of the Els Tudons naveta, Ciudadela.

50 The apsidal end of the Els Tudons naveta, after restoration.

51 The chamber of the Rafal Rubi Nou naveta, with the entrance in the background. Alayor, Minorca.

52 Façade of the Rafal Rubi Nou naveta, Alayor, Minorca, after restoration.

53, 57 Bronze warriors from Son Favar, Capdepera, Artá Museum. 2:5, 1:2.

54 Bronze warrior with helmet and spear from Son Carrió at Can Amer, Sant Llorenç, Majorca. 2:5.

55 Bull's head in bronze from Cas Concos, Felanitx, Majorca. 5:7.

56 *Mars Balearicus* figurine in bronze from Son Favar, Artá, Majorca.

58 Bronze *Mars* found at Son Taxaquet, Lluchmayor, Majorca. 5:8.

59, 60 Baked clay figurines of archaic appearance from Illa Plana, Ibiza. Barcelona Archaeological Museum. 2:5.

61 Punic baked clay figurine, 'La Dama de Ibiza', from the necropolis of Puig des Molins, Ibiza. National Archaeological Museum, Madrid.

62 Male figurine in baked clay from the necropolis of Puig des Molins. National Archaeological Museum, Madrid.

63 View of a burial from a late phase of the site of Illa dels Porros, Can Picafort, Santa Margarita, Majorca. Excavated by Tarradell, with the support of the Bryant Foundation.

64 Punic figurine in baked clay; Cueva des Cuyeram, Ibiza. Barcelona Archaeological Museum.

65 Late tombs on the Illa dels Porros, Can Picafort, Santa Margarita, Majorca, opposite the Son Real cemetery. Excavated by Tarradell with the support of the Bryant Foundation.

66 View of the portion of Roman Pollentia (near present-day Alcudia), Majorca, excavated by the Bryant Foundation.

67 Mosaics in the Christian basilica of Es Fornás de Torelló, Mahon.

68 Roman bronze handle from a small vase found in ancient Pollentia, Alcudia, Majorca. Barcelona Archaeological Museum. Approx. actual size.

69 Hellenistic figure of Victory in gold, found in Majorca. Barcelona Archaeological Museum. Length 5.5 cm.

70 Roman bronze figurine from Pollentia, Alcudia, Majorca. Barcelona Archaeological Museum. Length 8 cm.

Index

Aegean 23, 95
Alayor 73, 75, 88, 112, *passim*
Alcaidús (Sant Vicens d') 19, 61, 70, 72, 80, 112, 127
Alcaidús den Fábregues (Alayor) 88
Alcobé, S. 67, 110, 113
Alcover, J. 61, 79
Alcudia 14, 61, 97, 127 (vid. Pollentia)
Alfurinet (Ciudadela) 82
Almagro, Maria J. 20
Almallutx (Fornalutx) 80, 81
Amorós, L. 10, 34, 64, 96, 108
antennae swords 66
Aphrodisiades 133
Aranzadi, T. de 110
Arene Candide 24, 28
Argar, El 27, 28, 37, 54
Ariant, cave, (Pollensa) 31, 38
Armstrong, J. 17, 84
Arribas, A. 10, 64
Artá 13, 50, 58, 59, 96, *passim*
artificial tombs 111
Astarté 118
Astruc, Miriam 20, 122, 123
Atzeni, E. 10, 50
Aubet, M. E. 117
Augustus 109, 127
Avienus 92, 93

Baal 122
Balari 54, 112
Baliares 93
Balil, A. 127
Banyalbufar 12
Bassin du Carenage (Marseille) 96
Bate, Dorothy 25
beakers 24, 31, 36, 42
Bella Ventura (Ciudadela) 43, 44, 82
Bellver ric (Mahón) 58
Binimelis, J. 16
Bernabó Brea, L. 113
Biancofiore, F. 10, 50
Biniac (Alayor) 75, 78, 82
Biniaiet (Mahón) 70, 72
Biniatzen (Mercadal) 73
Binicalaf (Mahón) 72
Binicalsitx (Ferrerias) 73
Binicodrell nou (Mercadal) 73, 82
Binicodrell de Dalt (Mercadal) 73
Binigaus nou (Alayor) 80
Binigemor (Alayor) 80
Binimaimut (Mahón) 42, 79, 82
Biniparratx (San Luis) 89
Boquer (Pollensa) 59, 127
Bochorum (Bochoris) (Pollensa) 127, 131
Bosch Gimpera, P. 18, 27, 54
Bover, J. M. 17
Bronze Age 27, 38, 114, 117, *passim*
Brown, M. 10
Bryant Foundation 8, 10, 19, 64, 128
bull cult 103, 107, 108, 109
Byzantine 133

Cabrera (Capraria) 11, 13, 128, 130, 131
Cadiz (Gadir) 94, 115
Caecilius Metellus Balearicus, Q. 21, 106, 115, 126, 127
Caesar 94, 115
Cala Morell (Ciudadela) 89, 91
Cala Sant Vicens (Pollensa) 12, 29, 31, 33, 38, 42, 59, 131
Cala Sa Nau (Felanitx) 38
Cales Coves (Alayor) 14, 89, 91
Calviá 12
Camón Aznar, J. 85
Campanari dels moros (Es Rafal, Montuiri) 58
Campanet 96
Campos 17
Camps, F. 91
Camps, J. 10, 128
Can Roig Nou (Felanitx) 60, 61
Cañigueral, P. J. 24, 28
capades de moro 91
Caparrot de Forma (Mahón) 41
Capdepera 13
Capocorp (Lluchmayor) 18, 47, 54, 55, 58
carbon-14 19, 21, 22, 25, 27, 31, 40, 46, 54
Cartailhac, E. 18, 46, 84, 85
Carthaginians 92, 95, 98, 114, 115, 123, 133
Cas Curoné (Ibiza) 119
Cas Frares (Sa Maria del Camí) 132
Cas Hereu (Lluchmayor) 29, 30, 37
Catalonia 11, 12, 37, 112
cattle 99

cereals 98
Chamberlin, F. 18, 85
Christianity 107, 131, 132
Cinium 127
Ciudadela 14, 26, 43, 113, 127, *passim*
Clumba 112
coins 17, 123
Coll de Sa Batalla (Lluchmayor) 31
Colominas, J. 18, 27, 30, 45, 46, 47, 54, 61, 122
Columbraria 124
Conejera 11, 13, 131
Confessionari dels moros, cave (Felanitx) 31
corbelled roof (false cupola) 54, 55
Corsica 11, 23, 54, 112
Costitx 102, 107, 108, 109
Cotaina (Alayor) 75
Cotinoussa 94
Cova calenta (Felanitx) 31
Cova de Sant Martí (Alcudia) 132
Cova de Santueri (Felanitx) 18
Cova de Son Mulet (Lluchmayor) 42
Cova del Lledoner (Pollensa) 42
Cova del Nenu (Sta. Rita, Ferrerias) 88
Cova dels Bous (Felanitx) 42
Cova des Cuyeram (Ibiza) 116, 118
Cova fonda (Felanitx) 38
Cova Monja (Biniali, Sentcelles) 107
Cova murada (Ciudadela) 43
Coves gardes (Minorca) 89
Coveta dels Morts (Son Gallard, Deyá) 31, 36, 38
cremation 31, 41, 120
Crespi, A. 33
Curnia 73
Cycladic 96, 113

Dameto, J. 17
Dehn, W. 19, 50
Deyá 12, 19, 25, 31, *passim*
Diocletian 132
Diodorus 92, 98, 99, 114, 115
dolmens 21, 54

Ebusus, Ebusos 95, 115
Egypt 18, 112
Els Antigors (Les Salines) 18, 50, 108
Els Fiters (Muro) 109
Els Tudons (Ciudadela) 75–78
Eneolithic 27, 28, 31
Enseñat, B. 10, 24, 28, 31, 64, 86
Ephorus 92
Es Cabás, cave (Sta. Maria del Camí) 38
Es Castellet (Macarella) 21
Es Coll (Manacor) 61
Es Figueral (Son Real, Sta. Margarita) 55
Es Mestall (Mercadal) 74
Es Pedregar (Lluchmayor) 46
Es Rafal (Palma) 36, 60
Es Rafal (Montuiri) 109
Es Rafalet (Manacor) 32
Es Rossells (Felanitx) 30, 42, 50
Es Torrent (Ses Salines) 55
Escorca 12
esparto 98
Establiments (Palma) 95
Estany del peix (Formentera) 125
Evans, J. 113

fares, frares 91
favism 110
Fenn, W. 85
Fergusson, J. 18
fibulae 98
fishing 100
Flaquer, J. 71, 85
flint 28, 38, 42
Florit Piedrabuena, G. 10, 26, 43, 85, 113
Florus 126
Font Obrador, B. 10, 47, 88
Fontsrodones de Baix (Mercadal) 73
Formentor (Mallorca) 12, 14
Fornás de Torelló (Mahón) 132
Fortuny E. de 118
Frey, O. 19, 50
Fusté, M. 110, 113

Gaiseric 133
Galba 128
Garcia Bellido, A. 95, 96, 114, 122
Garonda (Lluchmayor) 58
giants tombs 19, 112
Gideon 100
glass ware 120
goats 99
Gozo 17
Grasset de St Sauveur, A. de 17
Greece; Greek and Hellenistic influence, 17, 23, 26, 71, 96, 97, 106, 107, 109, 114, 115, 122
Grosjean, R. 112
Guium 125, 127
Gunderic 133
Guntamund 133
Gymnesiae, Gymnesiai 11, 16, 92, 93
Gymnetes 92, 97

halskragen 104
Hamilcar Barca 93
Hannibal 94, 128

Hecataeus of Miletus 92
Hemp, W. 33, 34
Hernandez Mora, J. 10, 18, 74
Hernandez Sanz, F. 85, 89
honey 98
horseshoe-shaped enclosure 81, 108
Hübner, E. 93
Huneric 133
hunting 99
hypostyle courts 90

Iamno 128
Iberian mainland 26, 27, 92, 111
Ibizan clay 120
Ibusim 115
Ichnoussa, 94
Idatius 133
Illa Plana (Ibiza) 117, 118
Illa redona (Ibiza) 131
Illot dels Porros (Son Real) 61, 67
Isla de Alga (Formentera) 125
Isla del Rey (Mahón) 132
Island of Colom (Mallorca) 132
Island of Toro (Mallorca) 131
Italy 92, 111, 112

Kessler, F. 18
Kromyoussa 92

lamps 120
La Mola (Formentera) 125
La Sabina (Formentera) 125
lead plaques 98
Licinianus 133
Liguria 24, 28, 111
Lilliu, G. 10, 19, 20, 46, 50, 51, 52, 53, 113
Livy 115
Lloseta 61
Llucamet, cave (Lluchmayor) 40
Lluch (santuario de) 12
Llumassanet (Mahón) 73, 80
Llumena d'en Montañés (Alayor) 75
Llumena den Salom (Alayor) 80
Lycophron 93, 97

Macabich, I. 20
Macarius 133
Madina Maiurka 128
Magna Graecia 94
Mago (Mahón) 10, 70, 94, 115, 127, 128
Malta 11, 17, 23, 112, 113
Malverti, J. 18
Mañá de Angulo, J. 20
March Foundation 8, 19, 78
Marmora, A. della 17, 112
Marola (Lluchmayor) 58
Mars balearicus 96, 107
Martinez Santa-Olalla, J. 18, 80, 85
Martorell y Peña, F. 18
Mascaró Pasarius, J. 10, 19, 32, 55, 58, 59, 71, 75, 80, 82, 86, 88, 91, 130
Mayans bay (Ibiza) 118
Mayr, A. 18
Meloussa 92, 94
Menaria 128
mercenaries 53, 92, 94
Mediterranean column 58, 71, 74, 80
megalithic caves 80
Megiddo 100
Mela, 115, 128
micro-naveta 64
mineral resources 16, 102
Montblanc, cave (Maria de la Salut) 38
Montefí (Ciudadela) 91
Montplé (Mahón) 88
Mitjá gran (Ses Salines) 50
moors 119, 133, 134
mules 99
Muleta cave (Deyá) 25
Murray, M. 18, 84, 85
Myotragus balearicus 25, 26, 27, 43, 99

N'abella d'endins (Els Tudons, Ciudadela) 90
Na Fonda, cave (Sa Vall, Ses Salines) 38
Na Patarrá well (Alayor) 73, 100
native tongue 130
naveta 54, *passim*
Naveta des Tudons (Ciudadela) 9, 19, 36, 75, 76, 78, 79
navetiformes 36
navigation 100
Neolithic 23, 26, 27, 114
Nero 128
Niemeyer, H. G. 125
Norax 54, 112
Nura 54, 112
nuraghe 53, 112

Oleo y Quadrado, R. 18
Oliva, M. 59
Ophioussa 94, 124
Orosius 126, 133

Pagenstecher, H. A. 18
Palestine 23, 100
Pallottino, M. 113
Palma 14, 18, 126 *passim*
Palol, P. de 10
Pell, Barbara 10, 60

Petrus, María 8, 10
Philetas 98
Phoenicians 114, 123
pilum 106
piracy 106
Pithekoussa 94
Pityusae 11, 16, 92, 94, 111, 114, 115, 124
Pla, E. 64
Pliny 115, 127, 128
Pollentia (Alcudia) 8, 19, 64, 126, 127, 128
Polybius 93
Pompeius, Cn. 126
Pons, J. 110
Pons y Soler 18
Pont den Cabrera (Algaida) 42
Porreras 95
Porto Cristo (Mallorca) 131
Portus Magonis, *see* Mago
Portusalé (Formentera) 124
pottery 100, *passim*
Provence 11, 12, 33, 79, 111
Puig den Nofre (Capdepera) 67
Puig den Valls (Ibiza) 118
Puig des Molins (Ibiza) 19, 64, 96, 119, 122, 123, 124
Punic influence 66, 98, 115, 117, 120, 121, 122, 123
Purmany (Portus magnus) 119

Quadrado, J. M. 17
querns 99

rabbits 100, 127
Rafal del Toro (Mercadal) 95
Rafal roig (Manacor) 74
Rafal Rubí (Alayor) 75, 76, 78
Ramis y Ramis, J. 17, 75, 76, 79
Randa (Lluchmayor) 13
resin 93, 98
Rhodians 93
Ripoll, E. 8, 10, 60
Riudavetz, P. 18
Roca Rotja (Soller) 96
Román, C. 20
Román y Calvet, J. 19
Rosselló Bordoy, G. 8, 10, 19, 22, 28, 29, 32, 34, 36, 40, 42, 47, 60, 88, 128, 134
Rosselló Coll, G. 10, 20

S'Albaraliet (Campaner) 109
S'Almudaina (Alayor) 91
Sa Begura (Sant Llorenç) 67
Sa Caballeria (Mercadal) 82
Sa Canova (Ariany), cave 24, 28, 36, 38, 42
Sa Canova de Morell (Artá) 55, 58
Sa Carrotja (Manacor) 132
Sa casa nova de Pina (Algaida) 58
Sa Comerma de Sa Garita (Torre den Gaumés Alayor) 88
Sa Cometa dels Morts cave (Lluch), 30, 31, 38, 42, 99
Sa Cova (Artá), 109, 125
Sa Font de sa Teula, cave, (Alganyarens, Ciudadela) 43, 44
Sa Madona (Santanyí) 109
Sa Mata (Mijorn gran) 38
Sa Mola (Felanitx) 32, 42, 67, 108
Sa Plana D'Albarca (Escorca) 58
Sa Pleta (Mandia) 109
Sa Punta (Son Carió), Felanitx 60
Sa Talaya (Lluchmayor) 58
Sa Tanca (Alcudia) 32, 34, 42
Sa Torre redona (Palma) 109
Sa Torreta (Mahón) 18, 82, 84
Sa Vall (Santanyí) 37, 38
St Hippolytus 132
St Isidore 133
St Paul 132
San Antonio bay (Ibiza) 15, 119, 124, 131
San Jordi (Palma) 36
San Luis (Minorca) 95
Sanpere y Miquel, S. 18
Sant Agustí vell (Mercadal) 82, 84
Santanyí 95
Sant Salvador (Felanitx) 13
Sant Vicens de Cala en Porter (Alayor) 72
Santa Agueda (Ferrerias) 122
Santa Ana (Ciudadela) 90
Santa Mónica (Mercadal) 74
Santa Ponsa (Calviá) 91, 108
Sardinia 11, 17, 23, 24, 28, 53, 54, 79, 86, 111, 112, 115, 133
scarab seals 120, 121
schnabelkanne 96
Schulten, A. 20, 92
Scipio 115
Seguí Rodriguez, J. 18
Senisera 127
Serra Belabre, M. L. 8, 9, 19, 70, 72, 73, 74, 76
Ses Arenes de dalt (Ciudadela) 44
Ses Paisses (Artá) 19, 46, 47, 52, 53, 54, 106
Ses Salines (Mallorca) 116
Ses Talaies (Campos) 32
Severus 132
S'Heretat (Capdepera) 58
S'Hostal (Ciudadela) 42
Sicily 11, 23, 24, 43, 92, 95, 107, 112, 113, 115
Silenus 122
S'Illot (Sant Llorenç des Cardessar) 19, 50, 59
Sineu 95

Sirtes culture 112
sling 93, 94, 98, 104
Soller 12, 24, 28, 31
Solleric (Lluchmayor) 31, 38, 79
Son Agusti Vell (San Cristobal) 55, 74
Son Antelm, cave (Lluchmayor) 31, 34
Son Baulo de Dalt (Sta. Margarita) 88
Son Bauçá (Establiments, Palma) 36
Son Bou (Alayor) 89, 91, 132
Son Carlá (Son Catlar) (Ciudadela) 70, 71, 80, 82, 91
Son Carrió 96
Son Coll Nou (Algaida) 55
Son Corró (Campanet) 95, 107
Son Cresta (Lluchmayor) 109
Son Danús (Santanyí) 67, 109
Son Favar (Capdepera) 95
Son Jaumell (Capdepera) 33, 37, 38
Son Juliá (Lluchmayor) 18, 46, 61, 109
Son Lluch (Son Servera) 55, 59
Son Maimó, cave (Petra) 108
Son Mari (Sta. Margarita) 38, 96, 108
Son Marroig (Deyá) cave 31, 36, 42
Son Matge, cave 31
Son Mayor (Felanitx) 60
Son Merce de Baix (Ferrerias) 75, 78, 80
Son Mulet (Lluchmayor) 38, 42
Son Oms (Palma) 36, 58, 61
Son Peretó (Manacor) 132, 133
Son Puig, cave, (Valldemosa) 38
Son Real (Can Picafort, Sta. Margarita) 8, 19, 59, 61, 66, 67, 108
Son Sastre (Inca) 58
Son Serra (Felanitx) 109
Son Serralta (Puigpunyent) 98
Son Siurana de dalt (Alcudia) 55
Son Sunyer (Palma) 32, 33, 34, 38, 42
Son Sureda (Manacor) 33
Son Taxaquet (Lluchmayor) 107
Son Toni Amer (Sant Llorenç) 29, 32, 33, 38, 42
Son Torrella (Coma de) cave (Escorca) 31, 36, 42
Son Valent (Capdepera) 79
Son Vaquer (Manacor) 109
Sona Casana (Alayor) 73
Stephanus Byzantinus 92
Strabo 92, 93, 98, 104
Suetonius 128

Tacitus 128
Talaia Joana (Ses Salines) 50, 103
Talamanca (Ibiza) 119
Talati de Dalt (Mahón) 69, 72, 80, 82, 84
Tanit 118, 122
Tarradell, M. 10, 64, 110
Tartessos 54, 92, 94, 95, 115
terra sigillata 61, 120, 129
Timaeus 93, 94, 104, 115
tin 40
Tolós, V. 10, 70, 75
Toraixer de l'Amo en Pete (Villa Carlos) 80
Torelló (Mahón) 19, 70, 84, 95
Tornaltí (Mahón) 74
Torralba d'En Salort (Alayor) 73, 80, 82, 84
Torralbet (Alayor) 75, 78
Torre del Ram (Ciudadela) 88
Torre den Gaumés (Alayor) 69, 70, 72, 80, 82
Torre den Lozano (Ciudadela) 74
Torre Llafuda (Ciudadela) 70, 82, 90
Torre Lisá Vell (Alayor) 75, 78, 82
Torre Nova (Mercadal) 74
Torre Trencada (Ciudadela) 82
Torreta Saura (Ciudadela) 89
Tossals Verts, cave, (Escorca) 31, 38
Trepucó (Mahón) 18, 70, 82, 84
Triquadra, 117, 128
Trispolet (Artá) 29, 30, 37
Tucis 127
Tyre 114

Valencia 92, 98, 119
Valentinian III 133
Valldemosa 12
Vargas Ponce, J. 17
Veny, P. C. 10, 20, 29, 31, 32, 36, 40, 42
V-perforated buttons 38, 61
Verneau, R. 18, 43
Vernissa, cave, (Sta. Margarita) 28, 30, 38
Vilarets (Llenaire, Pollensa) 55
Vitruvius 102
Vives Escudero, A. 18, 20, 72, 84, 96
Vuillier, G. 18

Waldren, W. 10, 19, 25, 26, 31
Watelin, L. C. 18
weapons 105
weaving 100
wedding 93
women's ornaments 98
wells 100
Wernsdorff, J. Ch. 17
wine 98
wood coffins 108
Woods, Daniel 10, 19, 64

Xoirades 93

Zama 94